IN
PURSUIT
OF
ORPHAN
EXCELLENCE

D0169821

IN
PURSUIT
OF
ORPHAN
EXCELLENCE

My Kids, Your Kids, Our Kids

PHILIP DARKE
KEITH MCFARLAND

Published by Credo House Publishers,
a division of Credo Communications, LLC, Grand Rapids, Michigan.
www.credohousepublishers.com

ISBN: 978-1-625860-09-5

Cover design by LUCAS Art & Design
Interior design by Sharon VanLoozenoord

Printed in the United States of America

Good intentions alone are flat-out insufficient. The Christian must cheer every effort to care for orphans deep in both knowledge and wisdom. *In Pursuit of Orphan Excellence* pushes hard toward this goal, spurring us all to serious study and reflection on what it means to love vulnerable children wisely and well. Yes, there's plenty to debate in this book. That's one part of its great value. We must continue to challenge and refine each other as we pursue the very best for each child we serve.

JEDD MEDEFIND
President, Christian Alliance for Orphans,
and author of *Becoming Home*

The God of the Bible is the God of the underdog. Scripture makes it unmistakably clear that his heart is uniquely focused on those who lack the advantage of loving earthly parents. *In Pursuit of Orphan Excellence* challenges each of us to sync our hearts with God's by refusing to settle for sincerity alone, and daring to give our best to those who need it most.

PHIL TUTTLE
President, Walk Thru the Bible

Let's be honest. We all want to demonstrate compassion and seek justice. But if we care about these things, care about people, care about orphans, and care about the gospel, we must have the courage to ask *how* we go about these things. This book is a courageous gift to the wider church and I'm grateful to the various authors for having the courage to examine themselves and call us to a more thoughtful, prayerful, and dignified way of engaging in orphan care.

EUGENE CHO
Pastor @ Quest Church // Visionary @ One Day's Wages,
and author of *Overrated: Are We More in Love with the Idea
of Changing the World Than Actually Changing the World?*

My life is full, ministry is growing, my mind is busier than ever, yet now, after reading this book, I'm somehow more gloriously ruined for what is certainly at the core of the Father's heart. If you care for the kids in this world who come from unfair backgrounds and had no choice in the matter, then reading *In Pursuit of Orphan Excellence* will increase your compassion and understanding of how we can love them well and bring them real hope.

VICTOR MARX
Founder and President of
All Things Possible Ministries, and author of
The Victor Marx Story: With God All Things are Possible

This book is an important conversation starter about rethinking the best practices of orphan care. When even the most well-intentioned expressions of love and help can unknowingly cause damage to orphaned children, the Christian community needs this dialogue now more than ever. *In Pursuit of Orphan Excellence* sheds light on the dangers and challenges and provides a framework for transforming orphan care practices to be more comprehensive and effective.

MARK FOREMAN
Lead Pastor, North Coast Calvary Chapel,
and author of *Wholly Jesus*

Darke and McFarland have brought together some important voices in the orphan care movement. This collaborative effort will bring a fresh clarity to the way we approach orphan care, and more importantly, to the way we practice it.

KEVIN PALAU
President, Luis Palau Association

It has been said that one way to determine the health of a nation is to take notice of the way it treats its orphans. Darke and McFarland offer us a full court press against the usual ways to think about what we call an "orphanage." This demands not simply fair treatment of the orphan, but excellent treatment. One of the strengths of this book is that it offers the voices of global experts in the field of orphan care. And with their nine-pronged best practices approach, the authors present biblically-based methods for caring for the "orphans in their distress" by addressing the many variables that are involved in the formation of a healthy adult. This book is a major contribution to the field and offers a blueprint for carefully thinking through how to respond to the many parentless children in our world. Praise God that it was written.

REV. RON NYDAM
PhD, Professor of Pastoral Care,
Calvin Theological Seminary,
and author of *Adoptees Come of Age*

In Pursuit of Orphan Excellence will touch your heart and move your soul. With this book, Darke and McFarland show how far we have to go to serve orphans as if they were our own children and provide practical advice on how to do just that. This book is a must read for any of us who long someday to hear, "Well done my good and faithful servant."

JEFF SANDEFER
co-author of *A Field Guide for the Hero's Journey*,
and co-founder of the Acton School
of Business and Acton Academy

I am excited about this new resource, *In Pursuit of Orphan Excellence*, and I am honored to have played a small role in its development. I love how this book uses several voices to touch on so many different areas of orphan care. You will find it practical for your ministry and a great resource from which to draw ideas when seeking best practices in caring for orphans. Work through it as a team in your church and let it guide your discussions as your ministry to orphaned and vulnerable children grows and expands.

JOHNNY CARR
Vice President of Strategic Partnerships,
Help One Now, and author of *Orphan Justice*

In Pursuit of Orphan Excellence is a well-researched, thoughtful, and careful handling of a complex issue that includes insight from some of the orphan care community's top leaders and thinkers. This outstanding collaboration leaves the reader with rich resources for best practices in orphan care learned from many years of practical experience.

SCOTT VAIR
President and CEO, World Orphans

As the Father to the fatherless and Defender of the defenseless, God expects the body of Christ to join him in that work by caring for orphans around the globe. *In Pursuit of Orphan Excellence* gets at the essential issues and best practices to consider as we do the work of orphan care. Read it, grow from their challenges, and care for orphans to the glory of Christ!

RICK MORTON
author of *KnowOrphans* and co-author of *Orphanology*

In Pursuit of Orphan Excellence is an important and timely addition to current conversations within and around the Church regarding orphan care. I am encouraged by this collaborative effort and the call to work together as companions toward a common goal—improved care and better lives for orphaned and vulnerable children. The book helps us examine how to move away from traditional institutional care to more holistic family models and addresses our call as Christians to help bring redemption to the fatherless. The authors are not afraid to ask, "How can we do better?" or point out the failings in the current systems, as they seek best practices for orphan care. I hope this book fosters change in our paradigms regarding orphan care and opens our eyes and hearts to redeeming brokenness around us.

TROY LIVESAY
Director, Heartline Ministries, Port au Prince, Haiti

Praise God for *In Pursuit of Orphan Excellence*! McFarland and Darke have taken timeless biblical truths and shaped them into a coherent philosophy of ministry for orphan care. Whether you are an advocate or practitioner, you'll be encouraged by the authors' thorough treatment of this vital area of ministry.

DAREN BECK
Director, ACTION Cambodia

This book is a voice for the voiceless, and a banner of justice for the orphan. I pray it stirs you to action.

JOHN SOWERS
President, The Mentoring Project,
and author of *Fatherless Generation*

For those in the midst of orphan care and those praying about jumping in . . . please read this book. It's like an orphan care time machine that will save you ten years of heartache and misguided hopes. Thank you Phil and Keith!

MARK STUART
Executive Director and co-founder, Hands & Feet Project

In Pursuit of Orphan Excellence is a wonderfully comprehensive review of both the great need for orphan care and the answer to that need. The authors have captured both the emotional and rational aspects of orphan care in this stirring account that will inspire all who are called to the abandoned and unwanted. This book is for the curious first-time viewer as well as the seasoned practitioner of orphan care.

REV. SCOTT ROLEY
author of *Hard Bargain: A Beautiful Place to Live*,
and *God's Neighborhood: A Hopeful Journey
in Racial Reconciliation and Community Renewal*

It is wonderful to finally have a book on Christian ministry to orphans written by those with actual experience in working with orphans and with a true biblical framework of the gospel and compassion. As an advocate for ministry to orphans, street, and underprivileged children for forty years, it has always puzzled me why there were not more Christian Family Communities to care for and raise the millions of orphans in our world. *In Pursuit of Orphan Excellence* is an excellent, practical, and biblical fulfillment of James 1:27. Praise God for this book, which will be a great encouragement and stimulus to God's people, the church internationally.

DOUG NICHOLS
Global Missions Advocate/Mobilizer serving internationally
with Commission To Every Nation (CTEN), and International
Director Emeritus of Action International Ministries

In Pursuit of Orphan Excellence begins a desperately needed conversation within the Evangelical church. While the church's efforts to bring the fatherless into adoptive families are commendable, an unintended consequence has been a failure to focus on how to improve orphan care communities. The authors' work here goes a long way toward addressing that failure, helping the church understand how this type of care is often necessary and how to most effectively engage in it.

DANIEL BENNETT
pastor and author of *A Passion for the Fatherless*

As Christians, the role that we are entrusted with in caring for, protecting, and raising orphans in a way that is consistent with Scripture and in *their best long-term interest* is an overwhelming task that can't be taken lightly. Authors Darke and McFarland know this to be true, and their well-written book, *In Pursuit of Orphan Excellence*, demonstrates why it is so critically important to "love each child as God loves them . . . with perfection." While challenging and guiding us along the path to excellence, this book also reminds us of our "true north" calling which is what all lovers of orphans long to see, "former orphans walking in freedom and fullness in Christ, creating families and impacting generations."

DIANE LYNN ELLIOT
Stateside Operations Administrator for Oasis for Orphans
in southwest Kenya, and author of *The Global Orphan Crisis*

This book is a rare gift of grace. To orphans. To readers. To all who in their deepest heart know we all are orphans needing the grace of first-rate inclusion. This excellent book is matched only by the authors' excellent work around the world.

KEVIN ADAMS
Senior Pastor, Granite Springs Church,
and author of *150: Finding Your Story in the Psalms*

In Pursuit of Orphan Excellence is refreshingly collaborative and very hopeful for all who care about orphans. It is both accessible and challenging, rooted in Scripture and experience from people practicing in the field. Whether reading as a group or individual, taking time to ingest and reflect on the contents will impact your heart, your mind, your soul, and your actions.

DUNCAN MCFADZEAN
Investment Banker, Edinburgh, Scotland

Dedicated to all of the people
who have been, are, and will be
tirelessly working to love
orphaned and vulnerable children
around the world as God loves them.

☼

CONTENTS

FOREWORD

We have all been orphans, for all of us have been alienated from our heavenly Father. You see, God created humans to have an intimate relationship with Him, but the fall of Adam and Eve severed this relationship and we all became orphans, at least in a spiritual sense. This separation from our Father has eternal consequences, but it also has consequences in the here and now. Because we are wired to have a relationship with our Father, the severing of this relationship undermines our very personhood, creating a vast range of psychological, social, and physical problems.

We were created for something else.

We were created for something more.

But there is good news! If you are a Christian, then you are no longer an orphan, for you have been adopted. Indeed, adoption is at the very heart of the gospel:

> But when the fullness of time had come, God sent forth his Son, born of woman, born under the law, to redeem those who were under the law, so that we might receive adoption as sons. And because you are sons, God has sent the Spirit of his Son into our hearts, crying, "Abba! Father!" So you are no longer a slave, but a son, and if a son, then an heir through God. (Gal. 4:4-7)

This adoption has eternal consequences, but it also has consequences in the here and now. As we are restored to an intimate relationship with our heavenly Father, we start to experience healing from the psychological, social, and physical trauma that stems from the time we spent as orphans. Indeed, as we bask in the security of His unconditional love, we start to experience restoration of our entire beings.

Furthermore, as adopted children we are being renewed in the image of our heavenly Father. In other words, over time we become "chips off the old block" and start to exhibit many of our Father's qualities. In particular, we start to care about the things that our Father cares about;

His affections become our affections. And as we know from firsthand experience, our Father loves orphans! He is a "Father to the fatherless," (Psalm 68:5) and so we find ourselves loving orphans as well. Indeed, a passion for orphans is inevitable for "chips off the old block": "Religion that is pure and undefiled before God, the Father, is this: to visit orphans and widows in their affliction, and to keep oneself unstained from the world." (James 1:27)

Clearly, it would be ideal if all orphans could be adopted into a loving family, the institution that God has ordained for the nurturing of children. Unfortunately, at present, most of the exploding number of orphans worldwide will not be adopted for many reasons. Thus, while Christians must continue to promote the ideal of adoption, we must also passionately seek to help the millions of orphans who will not be adopted.

Providing such help is easier said than done, for good intentions are not enough. It is entirely possible to hurt orphans in the very process of trying to help them. Indeed, while I am far from being an expert on orphans, I regularly hear about all sorts of problems with orphan care:

* Neglect and abuse of orphans in both institutional and foster care
* The stigma attached to growing up in an orphanage
* Parents who place kids in orphanages because it's a cheap way to raise them
* Pastors who run fake orphanages in order to get money from donors
* The culture of dependency that orphanages sometimes create in the orphans
* Orphanages that engage in human trafficking
* Agencies that exploit orphans by using their pictures and stories to raise money

The gospel compels us to do better than this.

Our Father compels us to do better than this.

In the book, *When Helping Hurts: How to Alleviate Poverty Without Hurting the Poor . . . and Yourself*, Steve Corbett and I challenge churches and individuals to seek genuine and lasting impact for poor people rather than hurting them through dependency-creating approaches. For many, the book shifted their paradigm about the fundamental nature of poverty and moved them to practical strategies for alleviating poverty with excellence. *In Pursuit of Orphan Excellence* seeks to accomplish a similar paradigm shift in the context of orphan care and orphan care communities—to radically affect the way people think about what "excellence" looks like in orphan care and to explore ways in which they can implement such excellence in our world.

It is absolutely imperative that we find the best ways to help orphans without hurting them. And that is exactly what the individuals and organizations involved with this book are working to do. This book invites you to join them on this mission. Drawing upon the insights of both researchers and practitioners, *In Pursuit of Orphan Excellence* seeks to stimulate an ongoing conversation about the best practices in orphan care, asking: What works? What doesn't work? What can be improved?

Will you enter the conversation? Will you join the mission?

This book is not the final word; it's not meant to be. Rather, what follows is intended to spur the entire Christian community to further research and intentional dialogue about the very best strategies for truly helping those children whom our Father loves so deeply. May our Father find us, His adopted children, faithful in this incredibly important endeavor.

DR. BRIAN FIKKERT

Coauthor of *When Helping Hurts: How to Alleviate Poverty Without Hurting the Poor . . . and Yourself*

Founder of the Chalmers Center at Covenant College

INTRODUCTION

Have you ever felt like your well-intentioned love for others hasn't resulted in the good you intended? That it might have actually hurt the person you intended to help?

I know that I have. Probably because some of the work I have done around the world likely has, in fact, hurt the people I intended to help more than it actually helped them.

Like when I held the beautiful, two-year-old orphaned[1] girl in her home in Honduras just a few weeks after she was placed with her new family. I learned later that what she likely *really* needed was for me to leave her alone so that she and her new parents could bond and attach to and with each other.

Or when I simply served food at the shelter without connecting with the people whom I was "serving." As I have since discovered, what the people likely *really* needed was for me to take time to share a meal with them and get to know them. That little bit of interaction could have made room for storytelling and hospitality, combatted my "God complex" (i.e., "saving" the people by "serving" them), and enabled me to "do life" with them in all our brokenness.[2]

Fortunately, I'm pretty sure that my actions, which were done out of love, didn't do any permanent damage to the little girl or the people in the shelter.

Unfortunately for millions[3] of orphaned and vulnerable children[4] around the world, however, much of the well-intentioned work that churches, organizations, and individuals collectively have been doing over the past several decades through institutional orphanages and other orphan care likely has actually been hurting the children's ability to develop and thrive in this world. And some of the "help" that we've been providing can actually cause permanent damage to the children under our care. This book explores how we can work together to identify "help that hurts" and avoid such unintended consequences.

In their 2008 book, *When Helping Hurts: How to Alleviate Poverty Without Hurting the Poor . . . and Yourself*, Brian Fikkert and Steve

Corbett make a strong case that we might actually be hurting the people that we are trying to help (as well as ourselves) with our financial and in-kind aid around the globe. For instance, they opine that some short-term mission teams, which seek to "serve others" with great intentions, could be more valuable if they stay home and send a check to the ministry they seek to serve. And that even the check itself could hurt the recipient if it isn't given in a proper manner.

Fikkert and Corbett do that through biblical study, anecdotes, and evidence of what constitutes poverty in the developing world. After establishing what poverty is, they show how much of our work around the world, especially relief work, often exacerbates the poverty, and conclude with a very wise discussion of how we can help without hurting. Much of that conversation focuses on how we need more developmental work (i.e., asset-based community development). That is, we need to empower the people we are working with to thrive in their respective communities rather than simply provide the people with material things (i.e., providing relief) with survival as the goal. We need to deal with the foundational issues underlying our world's problems, not simply put "Band-Aids" over the symptoms.

This book leapfrogs off of the general principles set forth in *When Helping Hurts* and applies them to the specific area of orphanages and orphan care communities. For the purposes of this book, "orphanages" or "institutions" refer to an institutional orphan care setting where the orphaned children have no family and/or other permanent parental figures caring for them and typically are housed in a dormitory-style setting. "Orphan care communities," on the other hand, refer to communities caring for orphans that place orphaned children from institutions or other nonfamily settings into homes or villages with permanent caregivers. Typically, there are multiple family homes or huts in the community (i.e., a cluster of homes), but not always.

In the following pages, you will dive right into a conversation discussing how we can work together to develop a framework that will facilitate the transformation of institutional orphanages and orphan care communities from places that often inadvertently provide "help that is hurting" into places where the "help" actually helps the children develop into stable family members, community leaders, and disciples of Christ.

Before getting into that conversation, however, it is important to point out that some people have objected to this book's premise because they believe orphan care communities simply cannot provide excellent care and should not be permitted to exist anywhere. While I appreciate and agree with the heart behind that position—i.e., every child needs a permanent, legal family to love him or her and most orphan care communities cannot provide such a high level of care for every child—the "immediately close all orphanages" position lacks a grounding in the harsh and unfortunate reality that we live in a very broken world and not every orphan will have relatives or an adoptive family to love him or her in the foreseeable future. I fully agree that orphan care communities are imperfect measures that pale in comparison to permanent, legal families, and that we need to work continually toward providing such families for every single orphan. However, I also recognize that orphan care communities are necessary at this time as a stopgap measure until we wisely and properly implement the ideal solutions (which very well might not be in our lifetimes).

As Jedd Medefind, President of Christian Alliance for Orphans, states in the "Christian Alliance for Orphans' White Paper: On Understanding Orphan Statistics":

> God intended the family as the essential environment for children. We believe the ideal outcome for every orphan is to know the love and nurture of a permanent family.
>
> Our world's brokenness at times makes this goal unattainable. Thus, alternate forms of care are sometimes necessary. This reality calls us to affirm two seemingly opposing truths at the same time.
>
> First, that amidst the deeply painful and complex situations facing orphans around the globe, there are times when care outside of a permanent family may be the best that can be attained. This can be especially true in countries in which war, disease or other factors have done great harm to the fabric of society. . . .
>
> Second, that the need for triage measures should not obscure the ideal or diminish our pursuit of [the ideal solution].[5]

In Pursuit of Orphan Excellence lives in our common reality, seeking an answer to this question: "While holding onto the permanent, legal family as ideal and constantly working toward that ideal, how can we develop orphan care communities with as much excellence and best practice as possible?"

Together, we will deeply examine this question, starting with why everyone in the world, Christian and non-Christian alike, should care to the core about loving and caring for orphans well. Once we establish "why" everyone should care deeply about orphans, we will examine a framework of "what" constitutes excellent, best-practice orphan care in situations where kinship care, legal adoption, or reunification with biological family is not possible, feasible, or likely to occur. Finally, we will take a look at how you and everyone else in the world can advocate for orphans around the world . . . and in your own backyard.

What exactly are we pursuing in this book?

In preparation for our exploration into what best-practice and excellence-driven orphan care communities look like, I'd like to take a step back and clarify what this book is and what this book is not.

This book *is*:

* A skeleton framework of foundational components to excellent, best-practice orphan care communities, and real-life stories reflecting the various prongs of the framework.

* An indictment of the apathy toward orphaned children and at-risk communities in societies, governments, and the church, and the oppression of orphaned and at-risk children (e.g., human trafficking, drug trade, etc.) resulting from the current paradigm under which they are viewed as a waste of resources and second-rate humans who are given, at best, scraps off of our proverbial tables. We seek to cause a paradigm shift that helps us view the orphaned and vulnerable children in the same way you view your own children and we view our children—as investments who can be gospel-driven[6] leaders and anything God created them to be.

* A thought provoker and conversation starter seeking to frame a thoughtful, deep conversation amongst orphan care providers, church leaders, orphan care advocates, and any other human being who cares about how we together can transform institutional orphanages from places that often unintentionally hurt children into places that bring

children into families and demand excellence, best practices, and comprehensive care for the orphaned and at-risk children for whom they are created.

* A tool to equip church leaders, potential donors/ministry partners, and other concerned individuals to make informed decisions about partnering with an orphanage or orphan care community.

* A tool to equip church leaders and concerned individuals to make informed decisions about whether to start an orphanage or orphan care community (hopefully dissuade them from starting a new orphanage) and how to do so with excellence if they ultimately decide to start one.

* An attempt to begin redefining "orphanages" so that they eventually become "orphan care communities" synonymous with families and developmental, comprehensive, excellent care, *not* relief-minded institutional care.

* An effort to unify everyone involved in orphan care (i.e., adoption, kinship care, reunification with biological families, foster care, and orphanages) to ensure that we all can agree on key definitions and strategies. That we collaborate so we don't compete with each other, continually reinvent the wheel, and waste valuable resources. That we together can figure out how to shift the tragic prevailing paradigm surrounding orphan care. We can't begin to even make a dent into the global orphan crisis unless we all collaborate and work together to determine how we can best love orphaned and at-risk children in every part of the globe, today and for generations to come.

With that in mind, there are several things that this book *is not*:

* It is *not* advocating for orphan care communities as a final or long-term solution to the orphan crisis, or an ideal replacement to *healthy* reunification with a biological family, adoption, kinship care, or foster care. We fully agree that the solution we collectively are working toward is a

healthy, legal, and permanent family for every child in the world.

✳ It is *not* a 12-step (or any number of step) formula to creating or an exhaustive survey of everything that is needed to create a perfect orphan care model that will work for every culture, community, and individual vulnerable child in the world.

✳ It is *not* an answer key to all of the questions that you have ever had about how to execute orphan care or an orphanage "the right way."

✳ It is *not* a condemnation of existing orphanages or their directors, most of whom are well-intentioned and driven by an immense love for the children under their care.

✳ It is *not* advocating for institutionalization of orphans in orphanages or any other setting that lacks a committed family to love the children in a manner that is as permanent as possible under the particular situation's realities.

"A Threefold Cord Is Not Quickly Broken" (Eccl. 4:12)

I am extremely excited about the broad range of organizations and individuals that have contributed to the creation of this book. In writing this book together, we have taken one large step toward loving every orphaned child with excellence. We have actively agreed to collaborate to determine how to best care for orphaned and vulnerable children when the ideal solution of a healthy, permanent, and legal family is not available to them.

Collaboration allows us to work side by side, as companions and teammates, toward real solutions with people smarter than us in various fields. We complement each other's respective weaknesses with each other's respective strengths. Others are strong where we are weak and we all become stronger by working together. We will accomplish much more by pooling our resources and working together as a team, especially when the team includes people as great as the ones we've assembled on this project.

In the next couple hundred pages, you get to read stories and valuable insights about loving orphaned children with excellence from leaders of respected orphan care organizations and experts in fields affecting the lives of orphans. After engaging with the nuggets of wisdom, we hope that you join our conversation, become part of our team, collaborate with us, and advocate with excellence for beautiful children around the world who currently have no advocate in their lives.

We all need to be companions, not competitors, in this fight to address the plight of orphaned children. We need more projects like this one and collective action applying the principles set forth in projects like this one. As Eugene Peterson once said to a group of ministry leaders:

> We can sure use companions. Companions accompany. We don't tell one another how to do it. We accompany one another in this Jesus way in the company of God's people. . . . Companions eat bread together. Share life, share stories, live generously with one another. Refuse to be competitors. The moment we look on a companion as a competitor, we are no longer a companion. A competitor is a failed companion.[7]

We can and should challenge each other to constantly be better and sharpen each other to be the best we can be. But we cannot compete with and tear each other down if we ever hope to reach our common goal of loving every orphan in the world with excellence, as God loves them.

Ultimately, all of us working on this project hope that the analysis, expertise, and stories shared in the following pages will frame and further the conversation already started by many of the authors and our orphan care colleagues and address what we believe is a neglected component of the orphan care conversation: *How can we love with excellence the tens of millions of orphaned and vulnerable children in our world who have lost their parents, have no relatives to love them well, and likely will not be adopted?*

Then, after we establish what excellent care looks like, we hope and pray that you and everyone else reading this book will put the principles into action.

In Pursuit of a Dream

A few years ago, I visited an institutional orphanage outside of Lima, Peru. The institution housed many children, with what seemed like one hundred children living in each of the huge dorm rooms. Some of the dorm rooms had only mattresses on the floor. Rotating house "mothers" were the children's caregivers. An animal farm and hordes of flies contributed to the property's unsanitary conditions. And the kids' education was training in the textile industry that just so happened to be the business run by the orphanage's owner.

The priest hosting me that day, let's call him Santiago, who himself runs a different, family-model orphan care community in the area, told me this story:

> A few months before the visit, Santiago attended an event at the orphanage that included many wealthy people from Lima and other surrounding cities. During the event, a major donor, let's call her Martha, was gushing about how amazing the orphanage was and how great the "mothers" were caring for and raising the children. As she went on and on praising the institution, Santiago's frustrations grew and grew because he knew that the orphanage's level of care was lacking in so many different ways.
>
> So when Martha finished her praise and looked to Santiago for his thoughts on the orphanage, Santiago asked her this simple question:

"I guess you wouldn't mind if your own kids were growing up here, would you?"

After recovering from the initial shock of the question, Martha composed herself and responded, "Well of course not . . . but my kids aren't orphans."

Unfortunately, Martha's view of orphaned and other vulnerable children as, at best, second-class humans is not uncommon in our world. It's not the exception—it's the rule. In fact, the typical view of orphans around the world doesn't even rise to "second-class" humans. Most people are completely apathetic to the orphan's plight. Most people never even think about orphans in any way, let alone how they might be able to help them. And when people do actually think about orphans, the majority sees them as an "underclass" (i.e., below the lowest of the low class or the "untouchables") who are a waste of resources and can never amount to anything productive in society. In most eyes, orphaned children certainly are not seen as God sees them or as we see our own kids—as unique children with special skills and talents to be nurtured and developed in furtherance of their unique purposes on Earth.

This tragic reality results in one of the major barriers we have in our quest for bringing excellence and best practices to orphan care in general and orphanages in particular. The prevailing view is that orphans are not our children—they aren't "our own"—so why should they get anything more than leftovers?

Tens of millions of orphaned and vulnerable children live among us around the world.[1] In recent years, these precious children have been, among many other tragic things, gunned down by the police (who were supposed to be protecting them) in the streets of Sao Paulo, Brazil, forced into prostitution and the drug trade around the globe, and forced to kill family members and act as soldiers by lunatics in Africa. The "fatherless" are often completely cast onto the streets and left to fend for themselves. They are given no opportunity to develop their unique, God-given sets of skills and talents. Instead, they are oppressed and abused, directly (e.g., through human trafficking, physical harm, mental abuse) and indirectly (e.g, through neglect and apathy), every day of their lives.

The "lucky" orphans under this prevailing paradigm live their lives in institutional orphanages where they usually get a very low level of care because many of the institutions have the minimal goal of helping the children survive until they age out of the system around the age of eighteen.

Under this mind-set, to the extent they get any care and love at all, it's usually under the "something is better than nothing" approach where they only get our leftovers.

So What?

The overwhelming numbers and apparent geographical distance between you and the "problem" begs the question of why you should do anything to change this prevailing paradigm surrounding orphan care.

* ❊ Why should you spend any time loving orphans?

* ❊ What do they have to do with you and your life?

* ❊ Why should you waste any of your precious time helping kids who you likely will never see?

* ❊ Assuming that you can find reasons to care about them, why should you give them anything more than what you have remaining (time, money, other resources) after taking care of your own family and friends?

* ❊ Anything you give them is better than what they would have had in your absence, right?

After all, as the woman in Peru alluded to, they're not your kids.

Since you're reading this book, you probably care at least a little bit about orphans and vulnerable children, and this discussion may be getting under your skin a little bit. Nonetheless, you still need to think through these questions:

* ❊ Why should you care?

* ❊ Is it important to care for the orphans and at-risk children and invest in their lives with comprehensive, excellent care based on best practices, as if they are our own children? Why?

* ❊ And if we actually do decide to deeply care about the children, is it possible for us to agree on what practices constitute "excellence" and "best practices" in orphan care?

*   Can we agree on how to implement such practices in the
real world, particularly when the world is made up of so
many different cultures, people groups, and legal systems?

After reading this book, you will not just be able to answer these questions. You will be able to intelligently advocate for excellence and best
practices in orphan care communities in the face of apathy and the prevailing lower standards of care.

Where Do We Go from Here?

Orphan care providers around the world are collaborating and working
hard to ensure that every child can enjoy a healthy, legal, and permanent family.

Working hard to prevent social orphans (i.e., children who are
driven out of their homes and into orphanages or onto the streets due
to poverty and other negative factors) from ever becoming orphaned
by helping their parent or parents keep their children in their homes
through education, microfinance, financial and other assistance, and by
working to alleviate the negative factors causing the abandonment (e.g.,
extreme poverty, drug use, disease, etc.).

Working hard to rehabilitate parents and reunify and integrate social orphans back into their homes in a healthy manner.

Working hard to equip orphans' relatives to incorporate the children into their families and homes.

Working hard to enable more adoptions of orphans.

All of these options along the spectrum of orphan care are critical
and necessary components to any holistic solution to the orphan crisis.
However, this book does not explore these issues in detail because many
great books and resources already exist on poverty alleviation, disease
prevention, adoption, and foster care.

Rather, as discussed in the Introduction, this book frames a conversation surrounding a framework for excellence-driven orphan care
communities—a conversation that has been neglected for too long. The
unfortunate reality today is that orphan care communities are necessary
to care for, among others, orphaned children who will not be adopted due
to governmental laws and regulations preventing their adoption, human
trafficking concerns, and other realities keeping them from being ad-

opted by families in many countries. They are also necessary to love and care for vulnerable children who: (i) have been relinquished by parents who, for whatever reason, are unable or unwilling to re-integrate the children into their home in a healthy manner; (ii) have no willing extended family to provide adequate care for them; and (iii) are not adopted.[2]

Everyone collaborating on this project hopes the conversation will engage orphan care providers, orphan care advocates, church leaders and congregants, and any other justice-driven individuals to help develop a best-practice framework for communities of care that will love with excellence the tens of millions of orphaned and vulnerable/at-risk children who, for whatever reason, will not be adopted, placed with relatives, or re-unified with their biological families in the foreseeable future. We hope the discussion will inform churches and donors thinking about partnering with or starting an orphanage about what components are essential in any excellent orphan care community.

In the end, we expect that everyone engaged in the conversation will discover that this best-practice and excellence driven approach looks a lot like the love and care that *every single* other child in the world needs and deserves. That it looks a lot like the love we seek to give our own children.

With that in mind, the framework tracks the universal, common threads of best practices for orphan care communities that cross cultural, societal, and other boundaries. It results from extensive research, collaboration between and among dozens of excellent orphan care providers, including those contributing to this book, several years of personal experience with Providence World's incubator model orphan care community in Honduras, La Providencia, and visits to many other orphan care communities and orphanages around the world. Making up the framework are the following nine essential prongs: (i) family; (ii) community integration; (iii) education; (iv) nutrition; (v) medical/dental care; (vi) psychosocial care; (vii) national leadership; (viii) self-sustainability; and (ix) spiritual formation. Each of the prongs, which will be discussed in detail, must be strategically implemented with utmost quality into any orphan care community that strives to fully develop its children to their God-given potential.

Ultimately, in discussing the framework and sharing firsthand stories of excellence-driven work all around the world, I hope this book incites a civil, "living" conversation in the church and society at-large about: (a) the necessity of the family-based community framework in the *current* orphan care landscape; (b) universal definitions of each of the framework's prongs and other key terms in the orphan care conversation (including the words "orphanage" and "orphan")[3]; (c) how each of its prongs can play out in the real world with different cultures and communities; (d) how we can continue working together toward creating a world where every orphan will be united with a permanent, loving family; and (e) how each church and individual is called to be a part of this goal.

To encourage and facilitate such conversation, we are launching an on-line forum (ThinkOrphan.com) in conjunction with the publication of this book about the best-practice framework for orphan care communities introduced in chapters 4–12. We invite your thoughts and feedback on the framework, our definitions in Appendix B, additional stories of real-world excellence in action, and any other input on the subject matter of the book.

Striving for Unity

Through healthy conversation, I hope we can stop the blanket conclusions about orphanages plaguing our world today, particularly the belief that all orphanages are poor-quality institutions without families or opportunities for attachment and development. Yes, most orphanages in the world are institutions lacking in family bonding and other necessary things for a child's development. Yes, most orphanages are doing nothing more than providing relief and raising the orphans to create more orphans in their adult years. Yes, most orphanages have major problems and often do more harm than good in the children's lives. Yes, orphanages and orphan care communities are not an "end game."

But that doesn't mean that all orphanages are all bad, or that there isn't a place for family-based orphan care communities in the current orphan care continuum. Nor does it mean that the institutional orphanages, most of which are run by well-intentioned people who truly love the children, cannot transition into family-model care communities that provide excellent, best practice–driven care for children who would have nothing or extremely poor care in the communities' absence.

Rather than alienating our colleagues in well-intentioned institutional orphanages around the world (and the churches supporting or starting them) by condemning their efforts, my coauthors and I hope that everyone can use the framework raised in this book to challenge them to recognize and understand the issues institutions cause in children's lives. Then, upon understanding the long-term developmental issues caused by institutional care, the passionate orphanage directors, churches, and individual supporters can begin changing institutional orphanages into communities where stable families and excellence in education, medicine, community, and nutrition are nonnegotiable things.

When that starts happening, we can begin to re-define "orphanages" as places that, among other things, (a) place orphans into stable, even permanent families with mothers *and* fathers, (b) provide children with top-level education, medical care, and nutrition, and (c) integrate the families into the surrounding community. As orphans are placed into families and loved, nurtured, educated, and encouraged to serve others, they will develop their identity and God-given skills, talents, and gifts on their way to becoming gospel-driven, societal leaders.

But such a world is not possible if we don't first get rid of our preconceptions and biases against orphanages on the whole, which cause us to reject out of hand anything that even smells like an orphanage. Or, on the flip-side, to think that orphanages are "good enough" and are all we need to care for orphans.

The landscape of orphan care is broad, and we need all forms of it to even begin to address the massive crisis we're facing, particularly since the vast majority of the world's orphans likely will not be adopted in the foreseeable future. At this time in history, kinship care, adoptions, foster care, reunification with families, *and* best-practice-driven orphan care communities rooted in local churches are all critical and essential components of orphan care.

As a result, it is critical and essential for us to work together to determine how we can effectuate each component with utmost excellence. We need to engage any and all people who are passionate about loving orphans well. We cannot alienate any passionate orphan care provider, church, or orphan advocate. We need to break down our walls of arrogance, remember that we are all on the same team working to address the orphan crisis, and start working together to determine how we can best fight against the crisis using every piece of ammunition in our arsenal. And in so doing, we have to ensure that we never settle for mediocrity, or less, in orphan care. That we always demand excellence as a baseline for all forms of orphan care.

This book is a step in the pursuit of that dream.

So let's get started by taking a look at why every single person in the world should care deeply about loving orphans well.

Going ☼ Deeper

1. What, if anything, is wrong with Martha's statement in the story at the beginning of this chapter, "Well of course not . . . but my kids aren't orphans?" If someone made a video of your life, would it show that you agree or disagree with Martha's statement?

2. Take some time to answer the questions in the "So What?" section of this chapter.

3. What are the positives and negatives about each "solution" on the spectrum of orphan care?

4. How can you advocate for best practices in orphan care and simultaneously disagree with the position that we should shut down all institutional orphanages?

WHY SHOULD ANYONE CARE
ABOUT THE PLIGHT OF ORPHANED
AND AT-RISK CHILDREN?

Imagine that you just returned from visiting an orphan care community or have recently adopted an orphan. Upon your return from the trip or finalization of your adoption, you tell everyone about your experiences and share your passion for orphans with them. You tell them about the plight of orphaned children and specific ways they can get involved from home and through mission trips. You expect them to be captured with a love for the children as you have been, and for them to want to act to love some of the world's millions of orphaned children in some real way.

Instead, when you're done pouring out your heart, you can hear a pin drop in the room. Or, at best, you get a polite response that sounds something like this: "That's awesome. I love that God put that on your heart. But that's just not my thing." Or, "I am so happy for you. That sounds like a great trip." Or, "I'd love to help but I have so many other things on my plate right now." Or, "I'd love to help but don't have any extra money to help out right now." Or, . . . , well you get the point.

Some people may hear your stories and see your passion, and still say, "So what? These are sad stories and these kids definitely need help to make it in society. But why should I care? I mean, they're not my kids. It's somebody else's problem, right?"

That's just it . . . it's not someone else's problem. We are all affected by orphans and are all called to love orphans in some real way.

With that in mind, how should you respond to your friends and family members who just don't get it, don't care about the orphan's plight, have no idea what to do, or think that it is "someone else's" job to help orphans?

Or, if *you* are that "friend" or "family member," how should you change your thinking?

Beyond caring, how should you respond to this legitimate question: why in the world should anyone actually invest any of his or her limited time into figuring out how to love orphaned children with excellence and best practices?

The reality is that if we didn't look for these children, we likely would never see them—and even if we looked for them and saw them, they would have little, if any, direct impact on our lives.

So why should we care? Why should anyone adopt or be a foster parent? Why should anyone advocate for orphans in any manner? Why should we love those who virtually everyone else has chosen not to love and often are very difficult to love?

The Christian Response

For Christians, the answer is clear. God's heart cries out for orphans.

Don't believe me? Take a look at just a couple of the many Bible passages that unequivocally convey God's heart for orphans:

* ✳ Psalm 10:17–18: "O, LORD, you hear the desire of the afflicted; you will strengthen their heart; you will incline your ear to do justice to the fatherless and the oppressed, so that man who is of the earth may strike terror no more."

* ✳ Psalm 68:5–6: "Father of the fatherless and protector of widows is God in his holy habitation. God settles the solitary in a home; he leads out the prisoners to prosperity."

And the Bible doesn't stop there. Scripture doesn't just talk about God's love for the orphan. It implores all Christians to love orphans (and widows, the sick, the poor, and the oppressed) as God loves them. Don't take my word for it—take a look at these verses:

* James 1:27: "Religion that is pure and undefiled before God, the Father, is this: to visit orphans and widows in their affliction, and to keep oneself unstained from the world."

* Isaiah 1:16–17: "Wash yourselves; make yourselves clean; remove the evil of your deeds from before my eyes; cease to do evil, learn to do good; seek justice, correct oppression; bring justice to the fatherless, plead the widow's cause."

* Isaiah 58: 6–7: "Is not this the fast that I choose: to loose the bonds of wickedness, to undo the straps of the yoke, to let the oppressed go free, and to break every yoke? Is it not to share your bread with the hungry and bring the homeless poor into your house; when you see the naked, to cover him, and not to hide yourself from your own flesh?"

* Proverbs 31:8-9: "Open your mouth for the mute, for the rights of all who are destitute. Open your mouth, judge righteously, defend the rights of the poor and needy."

Read together, these passages show us that if we truly are Christians, we necessarily will love orphaned children in their affliction. As Tim Keller, pastor of Redeemer Presbyterian Church in New York City, said, "A deep social conscience, and a life poured out in service to others, especially the poor [including the orphan], is the inevitable sign of real faith, and justice is the grand symptom of a real relationship with God."[1] Importantly, Scripture doesn't just call Christians to love the "traditional" double orphan (i.e., a child with no living mother or father)—it specifically refers to the "fatherless" throughout its pages. Why is this? Among other things, in that day, and oftentimes today, children without fathers had little to no voice in society, lacked identity, and had nobody to advocate for them. For all intents and purposes from society's view, their reality was (and is) one without parents. Therefore, it is the Christian's role to advocate for that child and all children like that child.

Not convinced yet? Consider this. James 1:27 mandates that Christians visit widows and orphans in their affliction. The "visit" referred to in the verse isn't just some ordinary hang out with a friend. Another place this Greek word for "visit" is used in the Bible is in Luke 1:68, when Zechariah prophesied about God showing up on Earth through Jesus Christ. So, while the "visit" will look different for every person in the world, we know that it is a serious and high call. If we take our call seriously, we don't have an option as to whether we care deeply about orphans.

Yes, it's that clear in Scripture.

Yes, it's that simple.

If you're a Christian, you will love orphans and widows in their distress. And you will love them deeply. The only question is what your involvement in the orphans' plight will look like.

SO MUCH MORE THAN A GUILT TRIP

I hope that you don't interpret this discussion as a guilt trip because it is so much more than that. It is a battle cry that hopefully will spur you on to fully understand how loving orphaned children and other at-risk communities is an integral part of your role as an agent of renewal and as an image bearer of Christ. Not because you *have to* as a Christian, but because you *get to* participate in it as a child of God. Understanding that concept, however, requires a deeper understanding of several necessary premises.

You need to know and accept that you are much worse than you think (i.e., a completely depraved sinner), yet more loved by God than you can ever imagine or comprehend. Directly related to this, you need to remember that your justification is based solely on grace, by faith alone, through Christ alone based on his atoning sacrifice, and not at all based on your own works or other merit.[2] Out of gratitude and an overflowing of joy founded in Christ's sacrifice for you, as part of the sanctification process, and as an agent of renewal as an image bearer of God, you will yearn to do works that please God and are consistent with the heart and character of God. This worldview shift demanded by the resurrection of Jesus will spur you on to transform the world as God's image bearer of justice, forgiveness, and shalom.

You also need to internalize the fact that God is passionate about justice and making things right in this world. Gary Haugen, in his book, *Just Courage*, reminds us just how simple God's passion for justice is: "When it comes to injustice (i.e., the abuse of power by taking from others what God has given them), God's position is straightforward. God hates it and wants it to stop. That's what the Bible teaches."[3] Tim Keller adds: "Christianity . . . teaches that God hates the suffering and oppression of this material world so much, he was willing to get involved in it and to fight against it. Properly understood, Christianity is by no means the opiate of the people. It's more like the smelling salts."[4]

The Bible also teaches that you are created in the image of God. So, imitating God's passion for justice and doing justice are essential parts of your Christian lives as you seek to follow in Christ's footsteps and imitate His kingdom mission. In *Just Courage*, Haugen continues:

> You may say, "Well, that's great that God wants to rescue the oppressed. But what is his actual plan for doing it?" Again, the answer to this question is clear in God's Word, and yet the answer is also surprising. It turns out that we are the plan. . . . God desires to shine light into the dark places of injustice, and he does that through us. For those who take the Bible seriously there can be no doubt that God has given to us the work of justice in the world. Justice is not optional for Christians. It is central to God's heart and thus critical to our relationship with God.[5]

Again, however, if you stopped here, you would only be talking about loving orphans and doing justice in response to guilt, duty, and/or obligation. This is definitely not what God wants or what the orphans want. And such actions very likely would not result in genuine, authentic, and lasting relationships with anyone. Instead, they likely would result in burnout, minimal relief work, self-righteousness, and unbiblical motives (e.g., a "God-complex" or serving from an air of superiority).[6] As Keller states in *The Prodigal God*:

> All change comes from deepening your understanding of the salvation of Christ and living out the changes that understanding creates in your heart. Faith in the gospel restructures our motivations, our self-understanding, our identity, and our view of the world. Behavioral compliance to rules without heart-change will be superficial and fleeting.[7]

Jedd Medefind, in a recent interview with *Relevant* magazine, reminds us that duty, guilt, or idealism won't motivate us to love orphans for the long term either.

I'm animated by the way loving orphans can transform the Church. . . . As we rise to meet the need of the orphan, God meets our profound need to escape flabby, self-centered Christianity and slowly see our character changed to reflect Jesus. The truth is, if you go into this work motivated solely by duty, guilt or even idealism, you'll eventually run dry. The vastness of the problems will always outstrip your enthusiasm to solve them. We must be nourished by a profound sense of grace—God's great love for us, as well as for each orphan—if we hope to continue to serve even when the need is so big and dark and tangled.[8]

So if you're feeling the least bit guilty right now, stop it! God doesn't want you to feel guilty or to serve in response to guilt. Serving based on guilt does not honor God and it strips the givers and recipients of the joy that God wants them to experience in the giving and receiving. As C. S. Lewis put it this way:,

A perfect man would never act from a sense of duty; he'd always want the right thing more than the wrong one. Duty is only a substitute for love (of God and of other people) like a crutch which is a substitute for a leg. Most of us need the crutch at times; but of course it is idiotic to use the crutch when our own legs (our own loves, tastes, habits etc.) can do the journey on their own.[9]

Easier said than done? Maybe.

How can you avoid the guilt and work with orphans and at-risk communities like God wants you to? For starters, as I alluded to above, you need to have a deep understanding of your identity in Christ as a sinner saved by grace and an image bearer of God. As Paul tells us in Ephesians 2:10, "we are [Christ's] workmanship, created in Christ Jesus for good works, which God prepared beforehand, that we should walk in them."[10] The Greek term for "good works" used by Paul is "Ergon," which denotes a purposeful work and a social or ethical task.[11] Under that definition, this verse empowers Christians to perform specifically God-ordained works that have a specific purpose for the renewal of the world and the furtherance of God's kingdom.

Here's the rub: if you truly believe that you are a sinner saved by grace and understand the truth of the gospel, the only response to the injustices in the plight of the fatherless that will make any sense to you will be to deny yourself and follow Christ's example by having compassion on others, especially the poor, oppressed, orphans, widows, and others who cannot protect or advocate for themselves. One step further—if you truly understand that you are created for good, purposeful works and are a co-laborer with Christ to "make all things new"—you will constantly be seeking out opportunities to use your skills and talents to fulfill purposes that are consistent with the heart and character of God. It will not be a question of *if* you work with the orphans, poor, and oppressed, but *how* you can work with them to bring about shalom in our broken world.

When you fully understand your role as a child of God, you will be passionate about what God is passionate about! And one thing is certain: God is extremely passionate about justice for the orphan, poor, and oppressed.

So how can you energize and spur on your Christian friends who are apathetic to the plight of the orphan?

By establishing that Christians *get to* "do justice" and co-labor with Christ to bring renewal to the world and that loving orphans is integral to any such justice and renewal.

What about the Rest of the World? The Universal Response

Notwithstanding the clear message in Scripture imploring us to love orphans well, many in the world still sing the familiar refrain: "So what?"

Both Christians and non-Christians likely still will not be moved to love orphaned and at-risk children after hearing that the Bible clearly calls them to do so and the work likely will bring them much joy. How should we respond to this likely scenario?

At the base level, remind them that loving orphans simply is the right thing to do, regardless of your religious beliefs. The "Declaration Toward a Global Ethic," which has been accepted by all 143 of the world's major religions (and sounds a lot like the Golden Rule), makes this clear, stating, "We must treat others as we wish others to treat us."[12] Under this principle, the question is how would you want others to treat you if you were an orphan? Or, maybe a little closer to home, how would you want your children treated if something were to happen to you and your spouse?

After such a reminder, many will still say, "Even if it might be the 'right thing to do,' I'm too busy to do all of the things on my own to-do list. How could I possibly care about, let alone love kids who aren't part of my family and have absolutely no impact on my life?"

When we're honest with ourselves, there is at least a little bit of this response in each of us. If there is one constant in our world today, it's that we're too busy and we pack our lives with too many things. We're all preoccupied with ourselves and our families (not always a bad thing), so pleas to our conscience that try to guilt us into doing things rarely work, especially when they have no direct impact on our lives and there is nothing tangible in it for us. And if the guilt trips do work, they typically only result in one-time or short-term "service projects" to alleviate the guilty feelings.

In light of this reality, how can you successfully convince people that loving orphans is something that they want to do when God's Word and the Golden Rule don't move them to act?

Other than telling them personal stories about how working with orphans and other vulnerable children has personally brought you incredible joy and fulfillment (which is very effective and encouraged), you can inform them about the ways that orphans who aren't loved well directly and indirectly impact our lives in very negative ways. In so doing, you can meet them where they are and let them know how loving orphans well can make their world, local and global, a safer, better place to live, for them and everyone else around them.

More specifically, you need to tell them about the real, concrete social reasons why it is important to love orphans well. Loving orphans well actually reduces many social ills that exist in our communities today *because* orphans are *not* loved well as a rule.

Neglecting orphans or simply providing orphans our leftovers is directly correlated to higher incidences of crime, unemployment, homelessness, human trafficking, and suicide. By way of example, a case study on Russian orphanages, which is indicative of results from other institutional orphanages around the world, and statistics on the effects of fatherlessness on American children show how poor orphan care has a causal relationship with higher incidences of social ills.

The Russian case study followed approximately fifteen thousand Russian orphans who left institutional orphanages when they aged out of the system at sixteen to eighteen years old. The study found that within just a few years after aging out of the orphanages, about five thousand of the fifteen thousand children were unemployed, about six thousand were homeless, around three thousand had committed crime, and approximately fifteen hundred committed suicide.[13] In so doing, it confirmed the tragic consequences and social ills typically resulting from orphan care that lacks proper familial attachment, education, nutrition, and community integration.

Fatherless homes paint a similar picture. Today, 42% of the homes in America are fatherless, up from only 5% in the 1960s.[14] During that same time, many societal problems have also increased exponentially. While we all know that other factors contribute to the increase, we can't ignore the major role that fatherlessness and our corresponding apathy toward the absence of men in our children's lives have played in the increase in social ills over the past several decades. Today in America, children from fatherless homes account for:

* 63 percent of youth suicides

* 71 percent of pregnant teens

* 90 percent of all homeless and runaway children

* 70 percent of juveniles in state-operated institutions

* 85 percent of all youth who exhibit behavior disorders

* 80 percent of rapists motivated with displaced anger

* 71 percent of all high school dropouts

* 75 percent of all adolescents in chemical abuse centers

* 85 percent of all youths in prison[15] Additionally, children from fatherless homes are nearly three times as likely to be struggling in school or to have repeated a grade. They are five times more likely to be poor, thirty-three times more likely to be seriously abused (requiring medical attention), and seventy-three times more likely to be killed.[16]

These problems shouldn't come as a big surprise. Just think about all the movies, TV shows, and other media you've watched or listened to recently. How much of the media portrays kids or adults who are messed up because they didn't have a father to love them well?[17]

Ultimately, all of these societal problems impact our lives, directly and indirectly. They impact the safety and security of our world. They break down shalom in our relationships and communities. They impact our financial health, individually and corporately, as governments must fund projects to address the homelessness, crime, human trafficking, and other social issues.

And these societal problems can be severely reduced simply by *not* neglecting orphans and vulnerable children, but by loving the children as God loves them.

Consider Your Options

During a recent tour of the Folsom prison, a medium security prison near my home, I saw firsthand the tragic effects and consequences of fatherlessness, and a truth became very real to me. If we don't love the fatherless well in their early years, the likelihood that they will end up in a prison just like Folsom increases exponentially.

No matter where they live in the world, if children don't receive love and encouragement from a family, they will seek that love and encouragement elsewhere. If they don't receive a proper "education" in school, at home, and at church, they likely will receive a less-than-proper "education" elsewhere. Unfortunately, in our world, that "elsewhere" too often takes the form of gangs, terrorist cells, and other negative influences.

As a result, every child that is neglected in his or her childhood is much more likely to commit crime, enter into prostitution, get involved in drug use, and participate in many other things that cause problems in society. In the United States, if a neglected orphaned child deemed "not worthy" of our hard-earned money to provide excellence-driven care ends up in prison, he or she will cost society over $35,000 per year for incarceration costs.

If you take a close look at these issues, you can't avoid this fact: Orphan care will cost you time and money whether or not you ever care about or love, or even think about orphaned and vulnerable children. Either you will pay with your time and money in positive ways during the children's early years to encourage them and develop them into societal leaders, or you will pay in other ways when they reach adulthood and cause problems in our society.

I, for one, much prefer capturing the children in their early childhood, loving them well with excellent, comprehensive care, giving them identity and hope, and developing them into gospel-driven, societal leaders. Sure beats the near-certain alternate fate awaiting orphans, our communities, and our world in the absence of such care.

Going ☀ Deeper

1. In your own words, write a three-sentence description of the "Christian Response" to why you should care about and love orphaned and vulnerable children. Do the same for the "Universal Response."

2. How do you believe you are called to "visit" orphaned and vulnerable children "in their affliction"?

3. To the extent that you are heeding the call to visit orphans in their affliction, are you doing so because you "get to" or because you "have to"?

4. What do you think causes the statistics resulting from the Russian orphanage study and fatherlessness in America? What can you do bring change to those statistics?

Chapter
_____
3

WHY EXCELLENCE
FOR THE FATHERLESS?

One thing becomes clear after looking at the sobering reality resulting from fatherless homes and a collective apathy toward the orphan crisis. There are some real problems surrounding orphans and vulnerable children that we need to address together or we won't be able to make even a dent in the problem. Edmund Burke, an 18th century Irish philosopher, once said, "all that is necessary for the triumph of evil is that good men to do nothing." These words definitely apply to the world of orphan care.

Fortunately, there is good news in the face of this current reality. Together we can address and reduce all of these problems by doing something that is simultaneously simple and very complex: care for orphans with excellence and best practices.

The rest of this book focuses on the framework for providing such care. Before we get into what excellence and best practices in orphan care communities look like, however, we need to answer two questions that are directly related.

    ✳   What is the problem and why do we need to do anything to change it? If we can't establish a problem that needs to be fixed, there is no reason to read any further.

* Why should we demand excellence and best practices for these children?

If you're anything like I used to be, you might be saying to yourself something like this right about now: "OK, I get it—I should help orphans. But what's wrong with the institutional orphanages existing today? Why do orphanages need to do anything more than fill the children's basic needs? Why do orphanages need best practices, excellence, and comprehensive care, including families and top-quality education? And why doesn't filling orphans' basic needs constitute best practices and excellence in orphan care? Something is 'more excellent' than nothing, right?"

What's Wrong with the Status Quo?

What's wrong with the current state of orphan care in our world? Let me begin answering that very important question with a blog post I wrote about my recent visit to an orphanage in San Pedro Sula, Honduras:

> *Last Thursday, I, along with a team from all over the USA, Douglas, Mizael, and Henry, experienced something that we all likely will never forget. We visited an orphanage in San Pedro Sula from where four of our Providence Children came. The experience was even more eye-opening than I thought it would be and it confirmed that there is a huge need to improve orphan care in Honduras, which is what we are working on through the La Providencia model.*
>
> *The experience also confirmed to me that something is not always better than nothing, particularly when the "something" is terrible, yet gives the illusion that something positive is being done for the kids. Here are some snippets of the issues we saw:*
>
> * *The bedrooms had holes in the ceiling because the kids were trying to "escape" (word used by the orphanage worker).*
> * *The inside courtyard windows had bars on them because the kids were trying to get out.*
> * *There were 143 kids in a 120 capacity building.*
> * *The budget was $3,000/month, 80% of which went to payroll; so they only used $600/month to care for 143 kids. That is about $3.50/month per kid.*

✳︎ *The "nursery" had about 25 cribs in two small rooms with many cribs holding two children who were severely malnourished and lacking in love.*

✳︎ *There were also special needs children in the nursery. One awful situation had a 10- or 11-year-old child just sitting in a crib, Indian-style, staring into space.*

Most of these kids aren't living—they are simply there. It broke my heart, but also confirmed the importance of what God is doing at La Providencia to improve orphan care and change the paradigm of orphan care around the world. Hopefully we can together see the day when places like this orphanage cease to exist. I truly believe that the situation in San Pedro is not better than nothing because it gives the illusion to the world that something is being done to care for the orphans in Honduras—in reality, these kids are simply in a prison (surrounded by a two-story high wall and guard tower) trying to escape.

Most of these kids are not being cared for at all—this is not the fault of the loving and well-intentioned workers. It results from the lack of resources and a society that, on the whole, simply doesn't care about orphans, treating them as sub-human. While they appear to have school, food, and "helpers," they are lacking almost everything they really need—families, touch, a real education, medical care, and real hope. They are kept from the world, behind the walls. It is tragic and hard to see.[1]

Admittedly, that blog post described one poor-quality, government-run, institutional orphanage that is worse than some of the other institutions that I have seen over the years. I'm sure that many of you reading this book are questioning my conclusions because you have visited orphanages that appear to love the children very well and deeply, or have met children who grew up in orphanages who are thriving in society today. While there are definitely "success stories" in the realm of institutional orphanages, both with respect to orphanages and to the adults they produce (i.e., orphans who are productive members of society and community leaders after aging out of the system), such stories unfortunately are the exception to the rule in our world today.

Or maybe you question my conclusions because you agree with the "something is better than nothing" approach to caring for orphans and vulnerable children, where mediocrity or less equals "excellence" for "those children." Similarly, while there are specific relief situations (e.g., natural disaster response) that require rapid response and simply providing for the children's basic needs may be the best we can do, such situations are uncommon and should remain exceptions, not the rule.

Contrary to the pro-institution and "something is better than nothing" arguments, many studies, research, and experience have shown that, consistent with my blog's conclusions, institutional orphanages often exacerbate the orphan crisis.[2] Despite many well-intentioned providers, the prevailing paradigm (i.e., the harsh reality) in our world today views orphans and vulnerable children as second-rate humans who somehow don't need and deserve the same level of love and care as children in stable families and/or socioeconomic classes. Under this false premise, institutional orphanages often have unintentionally worsened the orphan crisis by failing to provide the children what they really need and thus causing the orphans themselves to create more orphans when they have children of their own.

This reality has caused many of the directors of institutional orphanages who I have researched and with whom I've talked to seek ways to somehow transition to a family model of orphan care. They have seen the shortfalls and experienced the negative consequences inherent in any system that neglects family and other best practices, and they want to stop raising "broken" children.

What do institutions fail to provide? They too often fail to provide the children with social and spiritual development, which are necessary to give the children identity and hope, and develop them into gospel-driven leaders. Institutions also typically lack high-quality education, health care, nutrition, and healthy relationships with the surrounding community. And institutions fail to provide the children with permanent, real family.

Yes, institutions typically give the children their basic material needs to get them through each day. But they deny the children the things they really need to develop their individual and community identity, and fill their deep familial, social, spiritual, and psychological needs. And since those needs go unfilled and they don't develop their "new" identity, the children are unable to overcome the stigma of being an "orphan," which too often results in them experiencing overwhelming feelings of shame, inferiority, powerlessness, humiliation, fear, hopelessness, depression, social isolation, and voicelessness. Ultimately, because orphans lack these critical things in adulthood and have no model of a stable family to guide and shape them, when they grow up and have their own children, many of their children will likely become orphaned or vulnerable children themselves.

And the cycle will continue on . . . until we do something to stop it.

Reversing the Cycle

Stopping and reversing that tragic cycle is exactly what this book seeks to do by inspiring, encouraging, and equipping everyone caring for orphaned and vulnerable children in any capacity to love them in a comprehensive, excellence-driven manner. To love the children in a way that provides them every opportunity to develop their unique skills and talents, and use those talents to glorify and honor God through their future families, vocations, and relationships. The framework examined in the following chapters provides the means to accomplishing our audacious goal.

In the pages that follow, you will read stories and insights from people around the world with experience and expertise in various fields related to orphan care who are pursuing excellence and best practices in their care for orphans and vulnerable children. Together, as a unified front examining the nine-pronged framework, we hope to provide guidance and direction for orphan care providers, church leaders, and all other orphan care advocates around the world as to how to love such children as God loves them.

"As God loves them."

Apart from the fact that less-than-excellent care will likely result in exacerbation of the orphan crisis, this clause demands we love orphans with nothing short of excellence. As discussed above, God's heart cries out for the orphan and He is Father to the fatherless (Ps. 68:5–6). God loves with perfection and thus loves orphans with perfection. Assuming we are disciples of Christ, we are to seek to be reflections of God and His glory in everything we do.

As a result, we are to seek to love orphans with perfection. Since we can't do anything perfectly, however, we have to settle for what we can do—love orphans with as much excellence and as close to perfection as possible. To pursue anything less than excellence would be to misrepresent God to the orphans and the world. As Moses tells us in Exodus 22:22-24 (go ahead—read it), there are serious consequences for missing the mark with how we love orphans.

Keith McFarland, my coauthor, recently wrote something to me that captures this point:

> *God's pursuit of Himself (His Glory) is a pursuit of what is truly Most Excellent.*
>
> *God's Glory in the face of Jesus Christ is the revealing of what is Most Excellent.*
>
> *To follow Christ is to pursue with one's life that which is Most Excellent.*
>
> *To care for orphans with excellence is to reflect through love and grace that which is Most Excellent.*

I believe these are truths, based on Scripture, which we can and should live by. Whether through family, education, nutrition, medical care, spiritual formation, or any other aspect of an orphan's or vulnerable child's life, we are called as Christ-followers to reflect the excellence of God and the beauty of the gospel in all we do.

A common response to this call to utmost excellence in orphan care is to feel overwhelmed by the sheer volume of orphans in the world and then do nothing or, at best, less-than-excellent orphan care. That response simply needs to stop!

Instead, we need to respond to the vast number of orphans by doing what I've often heard Andy Stanley implore us to do. We all need to "do for one what we wish we could do for all." Each of us needs to love one or a small number of orphans with utmost excellence, in a manner that we wish we could do for all. If we all do just that, do our part to love "a few" extremely well, together we will be able to love the world's orphans with the excellence that God desires for His children.

A Few Clarifications and Caveats

Throughout the book, I've implicitly stressed the importance of a gospel-centered approach to orphan care. Here, I'm going to explicitly make that claim. If biblical excellence and truths are not the center and driving force behind our orphan care, everything will be skewed, out of balance, incomplete, and broken.

While care based and/or centered on other things might produce "leaders" or "success stories," it would more likely produce wounded and lost children, and even more likely would *not* produce Christ-followers and disciple makers who pursue kingdom-building purposes, worship God, and seek to glorify and honor Him. In the absence of a gospel-centered approach, the children more likely would pursue and worship the things of this world on which their care is based, and often seek to glorify themselves.

For example, if filling the material needs of the children is the center and driving force of the care, that likely will result in a "something is better than nothing" mentality where the care provider is satisfied simply because the children "have it better than if they were on the streets." Under this approach, to appease current donors and capture new ones, deception, exploitation of the children, and "show" is encouraged and far too common. Sometimes, the children are even taught to use their "orphanness" to solicit gain from others.

One story from my travels to a village in a developing country illustrates how this unfortunate reality often plays out in our world. When I arrived in the center of the village, the children mobbed my vehicle, screaming, "White Man," in their native tongue. Almost immediately, my host sat me down on a bench and invited me to watch a "presentation" they had prepared "for me." As I sat in front of three rows of select children from the community, I watched those children speak a few phrases in English, which they clearly had practiced for occasions like this. After sharing the phrases, several children were shuffled out of the line and an even more select group of children sang a song to me. Before leaving, I was given a tour of the one-room "orphanage" that housed many children on the floor. Within a few days, I received a request for donations from the director of the "orphanage."

Because much of an orphan care organization's funding depends on the "need," the children's poverty level is too often, intentionally and unintentionally, maintained and reinforced to help with fundraising. The children often are undereducated (because top-quality education is expensive and tough to provide) and given bare-bones medical attention, nutrition, and other care. All of these things collectively cause the orphans to have skewed cultural and personal identities, and reinforces their perceived status as second-class citizens.

Or, if education of the child is worshiped as "the answer" and the caregiver makes education central through the belief that it is the "means of future success," then school takes priority over all things and teachers have more influence over the children than parents and other primary caregivers. Home life revolves around school and homework, and devotionals, household chores, cooking, laundry often go undone or are done by someone else. Work ethic falls by the wayside. Grades and class placement becomes the determinant of value in the short term, and level of education becomes the determinant of value in the long term. This "false center" also results in skewed and broken family values, personal identity, and cultural identity.

With a gospel-centered approach to orphan care, however, we begin with the premise that we are all lost and sinful children who are adopted into God's family. Upon our adoption, we take on full identity as His children and, among other incredible things, we become vessels of His grace and co-laborers with Christ to redeem all things. As His vessels, we value *all* children infinitely and treat them with deep love and care. When we really believe this and let it transform us through the renewal of our mind (Rom. 12:2), every aspect of our care for orphans (reflected in the framework) become strategic parts of equipping children to live out their lives for kingdom-building purposes in their cultural context, according to their unique gifts and calling. With this "true center" guiding our care, the children whom we love will very likely have secure personal and cultural identities founded in biblical truths.

Just the Beginning

We pray that the words on the pages of this book are just the beginning of a conversation and collaborative action that will work to shift the paradigm in the world surrounding orphans from one where they are seen as an underclass to one where they are seen as children of God with unique gifts and talents. We also pray that this conversation will result in a world where it is normal for orphaned and vulnerable children to become gospel-driven leaders because they have loving family and friends to invest in their lives in real ways.

As we enter into this conversation of the best-practice framework, we must remember that none of the framework's prongs work in isolation. To the contrary, excellence in one prong depends on excellence in other prongs, as they work together and overlap in many ways. For example, best practice in education requires healthy family relationships and involvement, healthy mind (Psychosocial Care) and body (Medical/Dental and Nutrition), active involvement by and relationships with the surrounding community (Community Integration), and solid biblical foundations (Spiritual Formation). Healthy minds (Psychosocial care) flourish with healthy bodies (Medical/Dental care) and hearts (Spiritual Formation), and so on. While we will mention where many of these overlaps occur and briefly discuss how the prongs work together, the various authors will focus on their respective aspect of the framework and will trust that you will read the other chapters to gain a deeper understanding of the other prongs and how they flow together.

With this in mind, let's begin our conversation about excellence with something that any best-practice orphan care community, without exception, must have—Family.

Going ☀ Deeper

1. Answer the two questions posed at the beginning of this chapter: "What is the problem with orphanages and why do we need to do anything to change them?" and "Why should we demand excellence and best practices for orphaned and vulnerable children?"

2. Think of some times and situations in your life where something isn't better than nothing? When is something not better than nothing in connection with care for orphaned and vulnerable children?

3. What is the "orphan stigma" and how does it affect the lives of orphaned and vulnerable children?

4. Explain in your own words the three different approaches to orphan care discussed in the section of this chapter titled "A Few Clarifications and Caveats".

Family Matters
(Family)

"Father to the fatherless, defender of widows—this is God, whose dwelling is holy. God places the lonely in families."—Psalms 68:5-6 (NLT)

"The most important thing that faith-based organizations can do is to help ensure that every child has a family that is able to provide the nurturing and care that every child needs."—Faith-to-Action Initiative

Based on Psalm 68 and many other passages like it, as well as a preponderance of research showing that institutions fail to provide orphans with the attachment and other love and care they need, any orphan care community striving for excellence and best practice must somehow place the children into homes where they can flourish, love, and be loved in a family. We need to figure out a way to get orphans out of institutions and into homes where they are integrated members of families.

While most orphan care providers wholeheartedly agree with this conclusion, it does not take too many conversations to discover that the conversation surrounding orphan care lacks a common definition of what comprises a "family" and what represents a best-practice approach to creating families for orphans who will not be adopted due to laws or other realities. Many in the orphan care movement also don't agree on how we can get there.

As we seek to create a best-practice framework for orphan care communities with family as a critical and essential component, we need to reconcile these differences in uses of the term, "family." We need to make sure that we're on the same page with regard to a clear and comprehensive definition of what "family" actually is so that we can ensure that we're not talking past each other while collaborating to develop the best-practice framework.

To help us reach a mutual understanding of what "family" means and what excellence in family looks like, I asked my coauthor, Keith McFarland, to share some wisdom and insights on this important topic. I asked Keith to write this chapter because, as the head of New Hope Uganda's Institute of Childcare and Family, he has been researching, teaching, and writing on family for over ten years, and he has taught me a lot on the subject since I met him a couple years ago. He also brings the unique perspective and wisdom of one who lives and works hands-on in the context of an orphan care community and who desires above all things to see fatherless children find healing in Christ in the context of family. He lives what he teaches and I know you'll learn much from him.

Family

(Keith McFarland)

God made family. It is a reflection of who he is. It is a place where God is to be revealed and enjoyed. It is the longing of every heart. It is sacred.

The fall made orphans. It tore family apart. Brother killing brother. It is a reflection of sin and brokenness found in the hearts and lives of children around the world. Family is marred.

But that is not the end of the story . . . or the beginning.

The eternal story of the eternal God is one of family. It is the story of the eternal Trinity—Father, Son, and Holy Spirit—who existed forever in a glorious unity breaking into history through the creation of the world. As Dan Cruver said, "Family is the Story behind the story of creation and of God's gracious mission in the world to expand his family by billions of children through his work of adoption."[1] God's family is both the beginning and the end of the story.

At this chapter in the story we are surrounded by the voices of over

153 million orphans[2] crying out because family has been broken. Yet this is the exact place God has ordained His people to be. Why? Because God redeems family. God delights to make family a place where He is both revealed and enjoyed. He loves to see the redeemed, temporary, earthly family reflect the eternal, heavenly family. God delights to see fatherless children become fatherless no more.[3] Family is at the center of this holy delight.

God alone can transform a global orphan crisis into an orphan opportunity. As the title of the chapter makes clear, we believe that family is the model that God has given us for most effectively caring for orphans. We cry out with David that the Father of the fatherless settles the lonely in family.[4] Family is the foundation for all best practices in orphan care.

As this chapter will spell out, God has placed families in His church and around the world to be His vessels for impacting orphans and communities globally for the gospel and the glory of God. He has also strategically placed His church around the world to be impacted by the orphans around us and to know Him better through them. Through this chapter we will take a journey together that will lead us to a deeper and desperately needed discussion ranging from the heart of an orphan to family and orphan care models.

CORE ISSUES

On the surface, the most pressing issues facing orphans seem to be those related to immediate needs: food, clothing, shelter, and education. We often model orphan care around meeting these needs. But these are not the greatest need. While these needs are crucial and must be addressed with excellence, meeting external needs alone is insufficient to bring about genuine change in the heart of a wounded child. It is this place of the wounded heart that is often the most overlooked and misunderstood. If any child is to truly benefit from our efforts of care (even when done with excellence) we must first understand and enter into the place of the heart of an orphan. Even when placed into family, an orphan is quite able to remain an orphan at heart.

To understand an orphan's heart, we must enter into real lives. To do this I will introduce you to three of my friends: Paul, Godfrey, and Danielle.

Three different lives.

Three different stories.

One common orphan heart.

They are connected in different ways to the Kasana Children's Center, an orphan care community of New Hope Uganda with an emphasis on family and fatherhood. Paul is a double-orphan who grew up as one of the first "sons" of New Hope, where he found new family and his own unique place in it. Godfrey grew up fatherless and came to work at New Hope as a staff member. Danielle grew up in India with both of her parents but as a *spiritual orphan* who came to Uganda to attend the New Hope Institute of Childcare and Family, a twenty-week discipleship training course for men and women desiring to work effectively among the fatherless or in ministry.

GETTING TO KNOW THE HEART OF AN ORPHAN

I first heard Paul's story in 2002 when my wife and I attended the New Hope Institute of Childcare and Family.[5] As he revealed his story and his heart, I was captivated. So many difficult interactions I had with fatherless children over the years suddenly made sense. I could now understand more fully Jesus' statement that all behavior flows from the heart. But what surprised me most as I listened to Paul speak about the heart of an orphan was that I found my own heart being powerfully revealed and moved as well.

Here is Paul's story in his own words.

War ravaged my country, Uganda, in the mid-1980s, leaving thousands of children homeless and fatherless. My family was one of many families who survived by hiding in "the bush." We ate from what could be found growing around us and we slept anywhere bullets could not be heard. When the war ended, my family returned home, but within a short time my father died. While we were still grieving his death, my mother got sick and then died. We were stunned. We had no one. The friends and neighbors who came to the burial to bring "comfort" took anything they could find: clothes, plates, and even cooking pots. We were helpless to do anything and suddenly lacked everything. We lost everything.

For the first time in my life, I felt truly helpless and scared. During the war I at least had my parents, but now a deep loneliness came into my heart. Even when surrounded by others, including my brothers and sister, I just felt like I did not belong to anyone. I existed as an outcast, a nobody. Rejection by friends and the community left me feeling greatly betrayed. Hopelessness marked my sense of the present and the future. I felt worthless. At my core I had completely lost my identity, no longer bearing my father's name but taking on the name mulekwa, which means orphan. The joy that I had known as a boy was turned into extreme sadness. This sadness would constantly jerk me back to reality even when I found myself laughing or around others who were having a good time.

Mistrust guided my dealings with people. I felt like I could count on no one and would only be abandoned, betrayed, or let down by them. Even when people approached me with love or good intention, I found myself hiding my true self from them. I would only open up what I thought would help me get something from them. This hiding kept all relationships on a superficial level. You could never really know me. Manipulation and deceit were keys to getting what I wanted from people. Fear became the defining mark of my life—fear of man, fear of rejection, fear of failure, and fear of death. All of these things led to a deep sense of independence where I only did things "my way," refusing to be accountable to anyone. I would simply push away anyone who might get in the way of accomplishing what I wanted or who in some way did not meet up to my expectations.

The day-to-day survival mentality that was birthed in me led to a deep-seated greed. I always wanted more, more, and more; I was never content with what I had. I developed a poverty mind-set that told me that I never had enough, even when living in plenty. Even if I was promised many meals to follow, I would eat each meal as if it was the last I might have for a long time. I always felt like I was striving: striving for acceptance, striving for approval, striving for success, striving for love. Escape became a way of life and I sought it at all costs.

THE ORPHAN AND THE HUMAN HEART

Did you hear how Paul described his wounded heart? Abandonment, loneliness, rejection, hopelessness, worthlessness, loss of identity, sadness, mistrust, hiding, superficiality, manipulation, deceit, fear, insecurity, poverty, greed, anger, independence, striving, and escape. These words describe the orphan heart. They also describe the human heart.[6] Though I grew up with both of my parents, I realized that I had lived much of my life as a spiritual orphan, acting out of my own sinfulness and wounding. I needed the same healing that Paul did, a healing that is only found in God.

Take some time to think about how these aspects of the orphan heart have been working out in the lives of orphans or fatherless children in your world. How have they been working out in your own heart and life? If you are involved in orphan care, think through how your current practices are serving to either confront or strengthen these tendencies. Take time to read through the full descriptions of the orphan heart in Appendix C.

FAMILY AND IDENTITY

Who is your father?

If you are an African child this is one of the first questions you might be asked upon meeting someone. It is a question that tormented my friend Godfrey throughout his childhood because he never knew the identity of his father. *I don't have a father* was the answer that rang in his heart. It seemed as if he was a no one. Yet for Godfrey, his fatherlessness led to the deeper and harder question:

Who am I?

Though he grew up with his mother, like Paul he felt alone at all times. These questions led to the practical question:

Where do I belong?

Though he had siblings, he wandered through school feeling like he was out of place with all people and he felt at home nowhere. Life was simply for whatever he could get out of it.

What is my purpose?

Godfrey had none. He simply existed.

These three questions: *Who am I?*, *Where do I belong?*, and *What is my purpose?* are central questions to the life of every individual on the face of the earth, whether you have lost both of your parents, one parent, or neither parent. Who we are is grounded in the place of family. The past, present, and future all are held together in the story of *our* family. We are a part of something bigger than ourselves. Family speaks to the core of our identity. **The loss of family and specifically the loss of fatherhood leads to a loss of identity, belonging, and purpose. The loss of identity in the life of a child is the foundational place of the wounding of an orphan's heart.** Without a clear sense of identity, belonging and purpose will never be found. What is the answer? The gospel and . . . (can you guess?) . . . family.

CHRISTIAN ORPHANS

Paul sat in the middle of the church, surrounded by people but feeling utterly alone. On the outside, Paul seemed like a success story in the making. When Paul came to the Kasana Children's Center, he was saved out of a destitute situation. He had shelter, food, and education, but it was not enough. He performed well in school, going on for further studies while specializing in agriculture. His outgoing personality put others at ease and his adaptability allowed him to befriend people from different cultures and tribes. He heard the gospel message and believed. He liked relating to Jesus, but he was unsure when it came to God the Father. Deep inside there was one problem, a massive glaring problem no one else knew about. Paul still felt utterly broken. At the center of the brokenness was the one thing that constantly haunted him: he would *always* be an orphan.

As Christians we know that the only hope for the sinful and wounded heart, the orphan heart, for the broken family, is the gospel of Jesus Christ. The gospel is the foundation for everything and the hope for the redemption of all things.[7] There are many Christians around the world like Paul, who attend church but still feel broken and remain orphaned at heart. We must apply the gospel to this context if we want to lead orphans into healing and freedom in Christ.

THE GREATER HEAVENLY FAMILY

The gospel is huge. It is wonderfully simple and infinitely mysterious. God's story is the story of the Lamb slain from before the foundation of the world, the eternal plan of God to adopt sons and daughters *into* His family.[8] It is the unveiling of the three-in-one, the Spirit-filled Son of God who unveils and makes known the awesome and glorious Father God,[9] and then who lays down His life to bring us back into relationship with Him.

While many seem content to dwell in God's presence having attained the status of angels (holy servants), God has given us so much more—*the privilege of sonship.*

In his classic book *Knowing God*, J. I. Packer wrote that justification (forgiveness of sin and declaration of righteousness) is the primary or fundamental blessing of the gospel. Justification is the ground that all of the incredible promises of Scripture are built upon. Packer then goes on to reveal what he deems as the highest blessing of the gospel: our adoption into God's family.[10] Packer states: "If you want to judge how well a person understands Christianity, find out how much he makes of the thought of being God's child, and having God as his Father. . . . Our understanding of Christianity cannot be better than our grasp of adoption."[11]

Leading men, women, and children into relationship with the *Abba, Father*[12] is the great goal of missions, orphan care, and orphan care communities throughout the world. It is a calling given to sons and daughters who are justified and brought into the great family of God.[13] As God's children from every tongue, tribe, language, and nation, we take on a new identity as adopted brothers and sisters drawn together to worship Jesus the Lamb of God. These glorious truths led John Piper to make this incredible statement: *Adoption is greater than the universe.*[14] Earthly family is temporary. God's family is forever.

WHAT ARE WE REFLECTING?

God's story of adoption into family is the ultimate story that must forever remain as the compass to direct us as we think through the issues relating to orphans and orphan care. It is also the first step in bringing healing to the orphan heart. Adoption into God's family is the place where true identity is grounded, where lasting purpose is found, and where genuine belonging is secured. Earthly family is called to reflect this greater reality and to point the hearts of children to it through faith in Christ.

When we look at the current state of orphan care around the world we need to step back and ask ourselves: *What are we most clearly mirroring in how we care for orphans?* Is it the heavenly family reflected in redeemed earthly family or is it the fallen, broken, fatherless world that we live in?

INSTITUTIONAL ORPHANAGE CARE

When it comes to institutional orphanage care, where true parents are absent and no genuine family exists, there is little doubt that we are failing to reflect God's family or God's purposes for earthly family. Institutions, lacking true mothers and fathers, are simply unable to provide orphans with the love, attachment, and care that they desperately need.[15] The orphan heart remains untouched and children are left enslaved to their own broken orphan hearts.

The negative long-term impact on the hearts and lives of children growing up in orphanage-style institutions is astounding and well documented.[16] Because of the lack of attachment with a consistent primary caregiver, studies involving institutionalized children have shown that long-term institutionalization decreases a child's IQ by as much as twenty points (from an average to a cognitively disabled level).[17] And "currently institutionalized infants showed reductions in the brain's electrical activity (EEG) compared with never institutionalized children."[18] While studies have revealed the direct negative impact growing up in an orphanage-style institution has on children and their brain development, studies have also shown the impact that family can have as a reversal of that trend. Studies followed previously institutionalized children who were placed in high quality foster homes before the age of twenty to twenty-four months, and their EEG activity at the age of eight began to resemble the same levels of never institutionalized children.[19] There is simply no replacement for family.

Johnny Carr stated it well when he said, "Institutional care is, at best, a poor model for long-term orphan care, and at worst, quite harmful to children's development."[20] The overwhelming need of over 150 million orphans around the world often has no other answer, especially where God's people are few in number. Desperate situations driven by need often seem to have no *better* answer. But as Christians we must view institutional orphanage-style care *at best* as a short-term solution that can try to meet immediate physical and spiritual needs, while having the potential for devastating consequences in children's lives in the long run.

The question comes: if orphanage-style institutions are not the long-term solution for orphans, what is? God's answer is family. What, then, is considered *best practice* when it comes to bringing family into the lives of orphans? Are single-parent homes enough? Does this constitute excellence in orphan care?

MOTHERS ARE *NOT* ENOUGH

In 1999, as a twenty-two-year-old, I traveled by train and bus around East Africa researching various ministries to orphans and fatherless children. While orphanages were present in each country, I was very happy to see some ministries using more of a "family" model. Yet as I looked closely, I began wondering to myself, *Where are the fathers?* I could not find *any.* In my heart I was thankful that the children had mothers caring for them, but mothers are only half of the equation. Today the gaping hole of fatherhood continues to stand out in orphan care and orphan care communities with devastating impact. But the lack of fatherhood is not just an issue in orphan care; it is a global pandemic.

David Blankenhorn's book *Fatherless America* calls fatherlessness our most urgent social problem.[21] John Sowers, in his book *Fatherless Generation*, points out that 33% of youth in America—over 25 million children—are fatherless and suffering from a deep father hunger.[22] It is clear from statistics and normal life observation that at the center of broken family is broken fatherhood.

Barack Obama brought out the impact of our current state of fatherlessness in his 2008 Father's Day speech when he said:

> If we are honest with ourselves, we'll admit that too many fathers are also missing . . . missing from too many lives and too many homes. They have abandoned their responsibilities. They're acting like boys instead of men. And the foundations of our families have suffered because of it. You and I know this is true everywhere. . . . We know the statistics—that children who grow up without a father are five times more likely to live in poverty and commit crime. They're nine times more likely to drop out of schools; twenty times more likely to end up in prison. They are more likely to have behavioral problems, or run away from home, or become teen parents because the father wasn't in the home. The foundations of our community and our country are weaker because of this.[23]

We are a wounded generation, wounded from broken family and broken fatherhood. Wounded and passing on the wound. When it comes to orphan care, the situation is no different—wounded people working with wounded children. And if you have ever worked in orphan care, you know the result. Mothers are a necessary part of meeting the needs of children, but not at the expense or neglect of fatherhood. Fatherlessness produces fatherlessness.

FATHERHOOD AND DAUGHTERS

Over the years, I have encountered quite a few individuals that have conceded that while boys desperately need fathers, girls on the other hand most desperately need mothers. Applied to an orphan context this means that while some are not comfortable raising boys in mother-only families, they have no problem with orphaned girls being raised by mothers. Kevin Leman's book *What a Difference a Daddy Makes* paints a very different picture. He argues:

* A woman's relationship with her father more than any other relationship is going to affect her relationship with all other males in her life. . . . Research clearly demonstrates that a father sets up a daughter for success.[24]

* Rutgers sociologist David Popenoe, author of *Life Without Father*, wrote, "I know of few other bodies of evidence (in social science) that lean so much in one direction as does the evidence about family structure." . . . That evidence shows that a father's relationship to his daughter is one of the key determinants in a woman's ability to enjoy a successful life and marriage.[25]

We cannot claim that we are providing healthy family structures in the lives of children where either the mother or the father is missing. Sadly, Christian organizations are often mirroring the fatherless world we live in by raising fatherless children without mothers *and* fathers who then grow up to create more fatherless children. The logical question is: *How can we bring the Fatherhood of God to children when we do not have fathers?*

In Uganda, where the need is overwhelming, one Christian ministry has "fathers" who volunteer from the local church and who come in weekly or monthly to spend time with specific children to whom they are committed. This ministry is attempting to address the staggering need for fatherhood, yet this valiant attempt unfortunately mirrors and reinforces the fallen culture common in Uganda and the world, where fathers come in and out of children's lives, leaving them to be raised by others.

In this context of "fatherless orphan care," the level of "excellence" being displayed is at odds with the level of "excellence" displayed in the

Scriptures. We are settling for much less than excellence and what is *best* for the children.

We cannot fight against fatherlessness with fatherless homes.

This simply will not work.

Something must change.

EARTHLY FATHERS AND THE HEAVENLY FATHER

In his letter to the Ephesians, Paul reminds us that it is from God the Father that every family in heaven and on earth is named.[26] The literal word for family is *fatherhood*, the one through whom the family is named. The implication is that every father derives his name from *the* Father, revealing an incredible link between God's fatherhood and earthly fatherhood. Earthly fatherhood will always fall short. However, because of the work of Christ, redeemed earthly fatherhood is also the most powerful means for coming to know the only Perfect Father and for healing the orphan heart.

Let me give you a few examples.

Godfrey

When Godfrey came to New Hope Uganda, he was twenty-five and married with one child. After just a few short weeks, he saw godly fatherhood being lived out for the first time in his life. He saw families thriving instead of simply surviving.

After hearing his new friend, Paul, speak about the heart of an orphan, Godfrey realized that he, too, was still living as an orphan. He opened his heart to receive God the Father's love for him and for the first time basked in the incredible gift of sonship. He sought out godly fatherhood and discovered his true identity in Christ. He now knows who his Father is, where he belongs, and what his purpose is in life. He is secure in God and in God's family. Not only are he and his wife helping to care for fatherless children as support staff at New Hope, but they have committed their lives to building healthy families as a means of orphan care and orphan prevention.

Danielle

Danielle grew up in India. She had a dad in name but not in reality. She became a follower of Jesus and shortly thereafter began pursuing training for working with orphans. She was drawn to New Hope because of its vision for *bringing the Fatherhood of God to the fatherless* (Ps. 68:5–6). She had vision for caring for orphans, but did she need God as Father?

Danielle sat on my porch explaining how God the Father seemed distant to her. She spoke about being let down over and over again, never able to *earn* God's approval. As she explained the distant relationship she had with her own earthly father and her inability to earn *his* approval, things began to make sense. Her view of God was being driven by her view and experience of earthly fatherhood.

The week prior to our meeting, Danielle had written a prayer that summed up the desperate place in her heart. She wrote:

I feel so broken. I just cannot get past my experiences of my earthly father. . . . How can anyone say that physical affection of touch from a father is not required for my complete healing? That's the problem God. You are a heavenly father and right now I am an earthly daughter. Just believing your love and acceptance of me by faith is not enough for me, I need to experience physical fatherhood as much as spiritual fatherhood.

As we sat talking, it became clear that she needed something else. I asked her two simple questions. *Has your father ever hugged you?* She said that he had not.

Have you ever been hugged by a man in a pure and loving way? She had not.

With my wife next to me, I showed her how and gave her the first fatherly hug she had ever had.

She wept.

We all wept.

At that moment, she understood God's grace and His Fatherhood became real to her.

Everything changed.

Paul

After I became a Christian, I heard about the Father's love for me, but I had no context to understand it. I was in a ministry that believed the only tangible way to bring God's Fatherhood to the fatherless was through providing physical fatherhood. But whenever a father would try to pursue me, I would hide my heart and resist the relationship. I knew that God the Father was real, but he seemed distant.

Finally, after relentless pursuit where I was being loved unconditionally and consistently from physical fathers, I finally yielded and opened my heart to receive physical fatherhood. I knew it was what my heart yearned for. It was then that my heart also opened up to God as my Father. It was through God's Fatherhood being tangibly brought through earthly fatherhood that I began to find healing and freedom from my orphan heart.

Paul wrote a song to express his newfound identity as God's son. In the second verse he wrote: "Once I was fatherless, but now I've got a family, a beautiful family, with God as my Father. Look at that wondrous love! Look at that wondrous love!"[27]

In the mystery of God, He has chosen to make His Fatherhood known on earth through redeemed earthly fathers.

THE REDEEMING POWER OF FAMILY

"Man made orphanages for children, but God made the family for children."[28]

Broken family reveals our *need* for a Savior. Redeemed family reveals the *provision* of the Savior. It is in the place of redeemed family where God binds up the brokenhearted and causes grace to become living and tangible. It is here where redeemed manhood and womanhood are envisioned, displayed, and passed down. It is here where the gospel is lived out as a display of our glorious adoption into God's family through fatherless children being brought into family.

It is here, in redeemed family, where formerly fatherless children are set free to bask in God's Fatherhood and find security in their identities as sons and daughters of God. And it is in this place of redeemed family that the orphan heart is lovingly confronted and set free to rest in the Father's love as a part of *His* greater family.

How is your family, ministry, or orphan care community displaying, or failing to display, the glorious truths of adoption into family? How are they emphasizing the importance of fatherhood? What steps would God have you take to better reflect His excellence in family lived out in the lives of orphans?

FAMILY AND BEST PRACTICE

So what makes up a family? If our goal is to bring fatherless children into family, what should that family look like? If we look at the broken world we live in, we can see expressions of numerous definitions for family.

If we look at the biblical vision of family, however, it is clear. The foundation is a man and a woman joined together in a covenanted, monogamous relationship resulting in physical and spiritual offspring. There is also a wider understanding of family in the Bible that, much like the African understanding of family, embraces relatives and extended family as almost on the same level as what we in the West call the nuclear family. This is a crucial distinction to understand when we consider models of orphan care.

As we look toward a best-practice framework for any orphan care community, we must agree with what God has said and what the research has confirmed (and we have affirmed): the ideal and best practice for orphan care includes a healthy family with a mother <u>and</u> a father who are *both* committed to the children's lives. This should be from the moment they enter the home, at as early an age as possible, until beyond graduation from high school and university.

Best-practice fatherhood will seek to reflect the heavenly Father in every way. In his book *Father Hunger: Why God Calls Men to Love and Lead Their Families*, Douglas Wilson unveils a vision of fatherhood that embodies this best practice.

> What are fathers called to? Fathers give. Fathers protect. Fathers bestow. Fathers yearn and long for the good of their children. Fathers delight. Fathers sacrifice. Fathers are jovial and open-handed. Fathers create abundance, and if lean times come they take the leanest portion themselves and create a sense of gratitude and abundance for the rest. . . . They must also include among their gifts things like self-control and discipline and a work ethic, but they are *giving* these things, not taking something else away just for the sake of taking. Fathers are not looking for excuses to say no. Their default mode is not *no*.[29]

Genuine love in family is seen through fathers and mothers living lives of repentance, servanthood, discipline, mercy, and humility. Without *this* kind of love, it will not be possible to live out the expectation of caring for orphans as a reflection of the true Father's love.

How do we apply this understanding to the spectrum of orphan care today?

SINGLE-PARENT HOMES

In situations where one parent has died, keeping children with their blood parent should be our top priority. The biblical calling to care for and defend the fatherless and the widow apply in this context, as single parents need support in a number of areas. Applying the principles of heart adoption (discussed later) and the need for the community of the local church are crucial for caring for these children with excellence.

Where a parent cannot provide the care needed, alternative forms of care are acceptable, though consistent evaluation and work with the birth parent should be ongoing. There are many excellent ministries that focus on caring for single-orphans and their biological parent.

ADOPTION AND ORPHAN CARE

In situations where both parents have died, the first and most powerful means of reflecting the gospel in orphan care and bringing healing to the orphan heart is to completely adopt a child *into* a family.[30] This was most powerfully displayed when God the Father sent His son Jesus into the world and entrusted Him to an adoptive earthly father named Joseph. Joseph was not the ideal father, but he was chosen to raise his "son" Jesus in a manner that pointed Him to His true Father—God.[31]

EXTENDED FAMILY AND ORPHAN CARE

In Africa, and other places around the world, someone might say, "My father has died," when by a Western definition of the relationship it was their uncle. Cousins are referred to as brothers or sisters and aunts are mothers. There is also a much greater expectation to care for extended relatives and treat them as if they are your own. Adoption in this context often is not recognized because the "blood" relationship already implies commitment, care, and provision. This can be a healthy thing for children, especially where relatives are able to truly care for children as their own.[32] In these situations, children are able to grow up secure in their identities in the context of the bigger family. Some orphan ministries work in this area by seeking to provide support and training for families caring for extended family.[33]

However, keeping children with relatives is not always best and can be devastating, especially where abusive practices, favoritism, involvement with witchcraft, cults, other false religions, or any number of harmful cultural practices are at work. In Haiti, as in many other countries, it is all too common to find relatives bringing extended family into their homes to be a *restavec* (household worker or slave). In these situations adoption and orphan care communities that seek best practices are more fitting alternatives.

ORPHAN CARE COMMUNITIES

In our world today, orphan care communities play an important and vital role when it comes to applying family to caring for orphans. In orphan care communities, churches and organizations seek to provide family for fatherless and vulnerable children where relatives are unable to care properly for the children (for one of many possible reasons), where the need is greater than available healthy families, or where families are unable to adopt children for one reason or another.

Excellence for these orphan care communities has at its center the goal of finding parents (husband and wife) who are willing to care for needy children as if they are their own, treating them as their own, loving them as their own, and committing to them as their own. This includes a commitment to the children as a calling of God through the lifetime of each child.

Fathers and mothers then model and demonstrate healthy family while providing care, love, and stability for the children. Parents model work and roles within the home, and children grow up with a clear sense of what it means to someday become a man or a woman, a husband or a wife, a father or a mother. The committed pursuit of intentional heart relationships leads to bonding and attachment in the context of safety and established trust. The gospel is proclaimed and the values of the kingdom of God are both taught and caught. Gospel-driven Christ followers and leaders are the result.

New Hope Uganda and La Providencia are two great examples of orphan care communities that seek to bring family into the lives of fatherless children. New Hope Uganda is a ministry with two different orphan care communities that both seek to blend the biblical understanding of adoption *into* family with the African concept of extended family. La Providencia is a ministry of Providence in Honduras that pursues best-practice care through creating families that are essentially a hybrid of adoption and foster care.

New Hope Uganda

New Hope Uganda seeks to live out a holistic vision of "bringing the Fatherhood of God to the fatherless" through impacting the fatherless through family, education, church, community, healthcare, work, and self-sufficiency.[34] New Hope began in the late '80s in response to the bloody civil war that devastated central Uganda leaving thousands of children orphaned or fatherless. Lacking any church presence in the area, but with a clear call to care for the fatherless, the leaders of New Hope began bringing in the neediest children, children like Paul.

Initially, the children lived in dorm-style block houses with a single parent of the same sex. This was only a "stop-gap" measure until parents could be found. Because of the conviction that family is key to God's purposes in the lives of orphans, and fatherhood and motherhood are paramount in that purpose, family groups were soon established led by Ugandan parents. In a non-Western, "village style," the parents live in a block house that is surrounded by four boys and girls huts. A central *banda* is used for worship, devotions, study, and eating, while an outdoor kitchen and latrine serves the family as a whole.

Each family group farms between three and five acres of land, both to supplement the family income and to teach the value of work in the context of an agricultural community. Families grow maize (corn), beans, peanuts, cassava (tapioca), sweet potatoes, bananas, and other various fruits and vegetables. Family parents work alongside the children in the fields and in other income generating projects like keeping pigs or chickens. The children also share in the chores of cooking and washing.

There are currently seven family groups on the Kasana site. The goal for families is to have no more than between twelve and sixteen children, though numbers often tend to push above the goal. This is an area that is constantly being addressed in order to offer the best care to the children.

The primary (elementary) and secondary (high school) schools serve over two-hundred and fifty mainly fatherless children from the villages around Kasana. Caring for these children in the context of their biological families, relatives, and local communities is a strategic part of New Hope's ministry and community integration.

The Kobwin site focuses on children recovered from Kony and the war in the north.[35] The ministry currently has two families, while working with twenty fatherless children from the community who attend primary school on site or other local schools where our children attend.

All family parents and support staff attached to various families are required to attend the New Hope Institute of Childcare and Family. In the Institute, parents and staff receive twenty weeks of solid biblical training that is committed to preparing vessels for the Father's service out of hearts, lives, and marriages that have been set free to bring the Father's love to the fatherless. Ministries from around Uganda and other nations send their leaders and staff to attend the Institute in order to learn from the successes and mistakes of New Hope Uganda in the context of an orphan care community seeking best practices while not hiding the need for growth and improvement.

On-site pastors and elders, as well as trained counselors, provide care for the family parents, staff, and children, while offering constant training in areas of personal growth, discipleship, relationships, orphan care, and caring for the heart.

La Providencia

La Providencia serves as another example of what an orphan care community seeking best practices looks like. Because of certain legal restraints and other barriers preventing adoption, La Providencia creates families that are essentially a hybrid of adoption and foster care. Each family home is led by a Honduran, Christian married couple who commit to raise eight children as their own ranging from birth to five years old throughout their educational lives, with a lifetime commitment to love and care for the children. They refer to the relationship between the parents and the children as "spiritual adoption," under which the parents provide their children a permanent family despite the fact that the children are not adoptable under Honduran law. The children come from institutional state-run orphanages throughout Hondurus, and in so doing go from orphanhood to a family.

One great example of this is the story of Carmen and Elizabeth.[36] Before the government placed Elizabeth and Carmen under the care of

La Providencia, they were orphans living in the state-run institutional orphanage in San Pedro Sula (described in chapter 3 of this book). When they arrived at La Providencia, they were eighteen months old and could not walk. They were "behind" in just about every way. They interacted very little with others due to malnourishment and because of the lack of necessary love and care received from the institution. The lack of quality health care had left Carmen with skin problems that were not being treated. The girls were both in bad shape.

Today, about four years later, Carmen and Elizabeth's story could not be more different. Not only are they happy, healthy, free of skin problems, and running around like any typical little girls would, they are also outgoing and very funny.

What is the main reason for this massive transformation?

They became a part of the La Providencia community, going from mere numbers in an institution to loved daughters and sisters in a family. Their parents have fully committed their lives to the girls and their siblings, raising them in their home with the same proper touch and encouragement that they give to their two biological children. They have bonded as a family which has freed the girls to form healthy relationships with friends at church and in the community. They have come to know the love of Jesus because they have experienced the love of a father and mother at La Providencia.[37]

HEART ADOPTION

The La Providencia model of "spiritual adoption" is a necessary component of best practice in orphan care. Both inside and outside of orphan care communities, this sort of "heart adoption" is a decision to be absolutely committed to a child who you are called to love and care for in ways appropriate to the relationship. This is considered a lifelong relationship that will continue to grow deeper as the years go by. It can also be applied by individual families who are unable to adopt specific children or bring them directly *into* their family. In the West, it is common to hear the term *mentorship* used in this context. Many solid organizations are promoting finding mentors for fatherless children.[38]

With solid mentorship as a foundation, lasting impact will be the result of a committed relationship that spans the life of a child. This indeed is *true* mentorship, what the Bible often refers to as spiritual fatherhood.[39]

When I was younger, I did not feel comfortable being a "father," as that implied authority and discipline, as well as instruction and time. I liked being a "brother" or "mentor," someone to have fun with who could speak older-sibling wisdom at the right time. I came to realize that what the children I was working with needed most was more than a big brother. Their most desperate need was for a father. When in my own heart I was able to take on the calling to be a spiritual father, a deepening of the relationship and genuine change in their hearts began to take place. Today, I am privileged to count four other children (among others), who have not been officially adopted into my family, as true sons and daughters.

ORPHAN CARE AND THE LOCAL CHURCH

A final powerful means of bringing orphans into family is through the community of the local church. It is in the local church where the adoptive family of God demonstrates adoptive family, where grounded identity-in-God is on display, and where the greater family of God is able to provide care and support for one another. It is here in the local church where the gospel is both proclaimed and demonstrated, providing the compass to keep local orphan care grounded and accountable. Orphan care communities and families all desperately need the local church to walk alongside them in their specific calling of caring for orphans.

WORKING TOWARD CHANGE

In light of what this chapter has brought out, there is room for growth, change and improvement in each ministry or family seeking to care for orphans with excellence. Each of us must think deeply on these truths with a long-term view of God's calling for orphan care as it relates to family. Having worked with New Hope Uganda for over ten years, I am very aware of the strengths and weaknesses of the ministry. But I have watched humble leadership wrestle with God over the weaknesses and bring change in light of God's best. The ministry is thinking fifty years down the road, working to strengthen the churches in the villages through its Pastoral Training Institute geared toward village pastors, offering a biblical and agricultural education. It is New Hope's desire to see healthy churches established where families can grow with a heart for adoption, orphan care, and orphan prevention.

We have also witnessed the kingdom of God bring change in culture in good and positive ways. For example, when the Kasana Children's Center was established, it was rare to find a man carrying or playing with a child. Today it is becoming more common to find fathers interacting with their children in positive and healthy ways.

When the ministry first began receiving abandoned babies, a genuine heart for adoption settled on the community. Suddenly, a culture that had no word for or understanding of adoption began taking babies into homes and receiving them into *family* with full rights of biological children (a first for Uganda!).

PAUL'S STORY CONCLUDED (OR JUST BEGINNING)

Paul is a living example of the power of family in an orphan care community. He demonstrates what lovers of orphans long to see: former orphans walking in freedom and fullness in Christ, creating families and impacting generations. He is a pastor, church planter, agricultural specialist, and coleader of New Hope's Pastoral Training Institute. His heart is to see pastors grounded in the Word of God and in their marriages and families. They can then effectively shepherd their churches, which can then impact their communities through orphan prevention, adoption, and orphan care. Paul is living out family with his wife, their three biological and two adopted children, and countless spiritual sons and daughters.

OUR CALL: REVERSING THE TREND

We live in a world where family-based orphan care is still in the minority. There is a desperate need for change. And each one of us is a part of that change. Wherever you are in the spectrum of orphan care, there is a need for advocacy and a calling for excellence in the family model and strategic implementation of the principles set forth in this chapter. Ultimately, getting orphans to heaven is NOT the great goal of orphan care, nor is simply meeting physical needs.[40] *The great goal of orphan care and orphan care communities is to bring fatherless children into relationship with their true Father, GOD, and into the beautiful gift of redeemed family!* God's family is the beginning and the end of the story, but in between He has given us the privilege of seeing His family extended to the millions of orphans and fatherless children around us. May we see the current trends reversed as the fatherless find family and become fatherless no-more.

Going ☀ Deeper

1. How does God's family model what family should look like on Earth? What does "family" mean to you?

2. Take some time to review the Descriptions of an Orphan Heart in Appendix C and think about which aspects describe the state of your heart.

3. What do Paul's, Godfrey's, and Danielle's stories tell us about an orphaned child's need for family?

4. In terms of family, write in three sentences what constitutes best practice and excellence in an orphan care community.

5. Why are mothers not enough? Why are fathers not enough?

6. Answer for yourself the three questions that Godfrey asked himself many years ago: "Who am I?" "Where do I belong?" and "What is my purpose?"

Chapter
5

It Takes a Village
(Community Integration)

"To care for an orphan in a personal, long-term way is rarely easy. . . . The complexity of each child's need and the wounds of their past can make it a difficult, sacrificial journey to foster or adopt or mentor. This is not a road God means for us to walk as just one individual or family. God means for us to live out His call to care for the orphan in the context of Christian community. Having good, compassionate motives isn't enough. We continually need to pair zeal with knowledge, and love with skill and insight."—Tyler Charles

"Authentic relationships with those in need have a way of correcting the we-will-rescue-you mind-set and replacing it with mutual admiration and respect."—Robert D. Lupton

One's identity is intimately connected with his community. Every person thus needs to be involved and integrated with his community, local and global, if he is going to thrive and be a gospel-driven leader in society. Orphaned and vulnerable children are no exception to this rule. It is community integration, the process of being made equals in society, which frees each of us to flourish as contributing members of society.

Consequently, we cannot create orphanages or orphan care communities that isolate the children from their local communities to *protect* them or for any other reason. If we fail to connect and integrate orphaned and vulnerable children with their local community or otherwise create a subculture where they aren't involved with or don't feel a part of their local community, we will reinforce their orphan mentality (i.e., stigma of being a "second-class" citizen) and set them up for failure later in life.

Instead, any best-practice orphan care community must raise the children in a manner that fosters a vision for and ownership of their community. The children need to understand the good and bad of their local and global communities, and they need to fully understand how they can engage, serve, and be served by their communities. Simultaneously, the orphan care community, at the organizational level, needs to be deeply involved and integrated with its local and global communities through healthy relationships with churches, organizations, and individuals in its backyard and around the world.

I've asked Kate Borders, with her expertise and years of experience in leadership at World Orphans (worldorphans.org), to guide us through how orphan care communities can seek best practice and excellence in community integration by developing the much-needed relationships between their children and caregivers, on the one hand, and their surrounding communities, on the other hand.[1] World Orphans works to equip churches around the world to engage with local orphaned and vulnerable children and families to determine the best way for those specific children to receive the love and care of a family and be integrated into their community. I chose Kate to partner with me on this chapter because of the experience World Orphans has working through local communities around the world. I've learned a lot from World Orphans' work. I hope that you do too.

Community Integration
(Kate Borders)

Meseret and her son, Milon, are both HIV positive. The death of their husband and father has left them alone. Alone in a dilapidated rental home made of sticks and mud in Addis Ababa, Ethiopia. Alone with very little food and even less medical care. Alone with no real education for Milon. Alone with the stigma of being "that widow" and "that orphan kid" in a world that doesn't think too highly of such titles and provides little opportunity for "them." Alone with little hope of escaping any of those harsh realities.

Would this widow and single orphan substantially benefit if they were involved with and incorporated into their local community? Of course!

Would anyone in his right mind argue that Meseret and Milon don't need to be integrated into their local community to give them a chance to survive, let alone thrive, in society?

But what about in the following hypothetical situation, which is not all that hypothetical?

An affluent church, in the United States or in the orphans' home country, actively works to care for orphans in the developing world. Its congregants' hearts break for children who do not have a family and this moves them to action.

Armed with good intentions and many resources, financial and otherwise, the church builds an orphan care community in a remote location outside of town, away from any local community, to make safety less of a concern. All of the orphans are even placed into family homes with committed parents. The leaders and staff are nationals from that country and they build a private chapel for their children and staff. The facilities are clean, are culturally appropriate, and meet any standards of excellence in all respects. The church makes sure the operations are consistently fully funded to provide on-site, cutting-edge nutrition, medical care, and education solely for the orphan care community's children and caregivers so that they don't have to be tainted by the world outside of their walls. All of their physical needs are met.

Do these children, parents, and other caregivers, like Meseret and Milon, need to be integrated into their local community to give them a chance to survive and thrive in society?

Does this hypothetical orphan care community need more to reach the level of excellence and best practice we are seeking in this book?

In a word . . . Yes!

A remote, isolated, safe, and secure location—being away from the crime and other negative influences—may, on the surface, seem like a major positive for any orphan care community. But caution is needed. Though many orphanages around the world are completely isolated from their local communities in the name of *protecting* the children, isolation is actually *not* a good thing.

Even if many physical, educational, and even some spiritual and emotional needs are met (which often they are not), the children are completely cut off from any greater local community. And isolation from local community is a major problem for any human being, even if all other needs are met with excellence.

That is why any best-practice framework for orphan care communities requires that the families (i.e., children *and* parents) share life with and identify with key community leaders. And they need to be otherwise fully integrated into their local community, through churches, after-school programming, service, activities, events, and other relationship-building opportunities. Without community integration, the children and their parents miss opportunities to build valuable relationships with those around them, work out their cultural identity, assimilate within their communities, and serve others. If isolation deprives the children of these opportunities, they likely will not have deep relationships and will lack a framework for how to actually live within their greater community and society when they graduate from school and leave the orphan care community. The lack of community integration could be devastating to their prospects for functioning as healthy members of society who are able to care for themselves and give back to the community.

Community integration isn't only necessary when you need material things. Community integration is necessary for everyone in every situation, including everyone in every orphan care community. Without it, orphaned and vulnerable children (and everyone else) are unable to develop their identities and self-respect, which come from knowing they have much to offer others around them, in the context of community. Without community integration, the children are far less likely to become gospel-driven leaders in their respective communities.

As we move forward, we must recognize that God created all people, including orphaned children, to serve others with the gifts and talents He gave them, and that He created everyone to do that in community with each other.[2] That is why we absolutely need to give the children opportunities to develop and use their gifts and talents in community with others. They, like every one of us, need to serve others *and* be served by others. Without involvement in and integration into a community, including deep involvement in and with local churches, children cannot fulfill that important, God-given purpose to love and serve others.

REAL LIFE IN COMMUNITY

So what does this community integration look like in real life? What are the overarching concepts that will help orphan care providers work toward and ensure community integration?

It all starts with relationship.

It ends with relationship.

And it involves relationship at all points in between.

Spiritually speaking, each person starts life with the same relationship to God. We are orphans in need of rescue, and Christ accomplished that rescue through His life, death, and resurrection. In John 14:18, Jesus said, "I will not leave you as orphans, I will come to you." And through the relationship between God the Father, God the Son, and God the Spirit, we see that He is a relational God.

Romans 12 and 1 Corinthians 12 give us the illustration of a body. Just as the parts of our physical body cannot function apart from one another, so we as people were not designed to function apart from relationship and community. Everyone, including orphaned children, needs to live in relationships that involve both giving and receiving.

In the context of community, children learn the value of reciprocal relationship. Being cared for as well as caring for others. Being served and serving. Learning from others and being able to teach. Being discipled in order to disciple. When orphan care providers are convinced of the value of the children in their care, and they address their children's need for relationship and community integration, all of these things begin to happen.

For example, take a look at Luis, a young boy thriving in a family model orphan care community. Because of his consistent academic growth and spiritual leadership, Luis has the opportunity to lead devotions for his classmates at the local Christian school he attends. Also, he gets to serve the community through involvement with the local church along with other children in his orphan care community. The children serve alongside adult church members during Saturday outreach events and participate in Sunday morning worship services. They play in their local community with other children from their school and church, and they build deep relationships with each other as they live life together.

Luis could be in a great family home and receive well-rounded meals, proper medical care, and an excellent education in his orphan care community, but his life would have a glaring hole if he didn't have these and other valuable relationships with individuals and families in his surrounding community. Without the relationships, he and the other children in the orphan care community would not be given the opportunity to overcome the pain, isolation, and other negative feelings that result from the stigma of being an "orphan" in a harsh world.

When children in orphan care communities are integrated into their community, they experience the value of being in trusting relationships where they are safe and receive care, and where they are able to serve and exercise their God-given gifts and talents for the betterment of themselves and their community. Simple relationships with other children at school, church, and other places in the local community go a long way to combat the stigma of being an orphan and enable the children to develop their identities as children of God in the context of their communities.

KEEPING CHILDREN IN THEIR FAMILIES

While it is not the focus of this book, we need to address this important aspect of community integration: identifying and helping to care for single orphans in danger of abandonment and children in danger of becoming double orphans. Orphan care communities can and should be active participants in this process by working with others to encourage and help to strengthen existing families in their local communities.

One aspect of excellence in this area of community integration is that orphan care communities absolutely should not take in children from families in their local community simply because the parents believe that their children would have a better life in the orphan care community than in their home. But the orphan care community's responsibility does not consist of simply refusing to accept the children from their families. The community, along with other individuals and ministries in the surrounding area, should commit to help the parents or other caregivers properly care for their children so that the families can stay together in their homes and thrive in life. This could take the form of providing education through a school, proper nutrition through a feeding program, medical care through a clinic, or many other things.

Being in relationship with church leaders around the world, World Orphans has seen how healthy relationships with and involvement with a community can strengthen families and keep children in a family in their homes, even in times of crisis. For instance, immediately following Haiti's devastating earthquake in 2010, World Orphans began their OVC (Orphan and Vulnerable Child) Program in Haiti. Before doing anything else, the WO OVC team spent time meeting with church pastors and leaders to find out how they were caring for newly orphaned children. The backdrop to these conversations was the news reports of surging orphanages and the realization that many of the children living in orphanages prior to the earthquake were actually social or poverty orphans, having living parents or family members.

What World Orphans learned from the local churches is an example of community integration at work. Most of the new orphans had been taken in and were being cared for by someone—a grandparent, surviving mother or father, sibling, other relative, neighbor, or friend. But sadly, many of the surviving friends and family were saying they would not be able to continue caring for the additional children. In response to that need, the local churches were working, as best they were able, to help these children and families stay together. The churches were helping with food and clothing, and they hoped to be able to help provide access to education and medical care. Their objective was to enable the children in their community to remain with a family in their homes and provide care for them in a way that was supportive, encouraging, and sustaining, rather than see the children abandoned at orphanages. And, if the children's caregivers were to die or otherwise become unable to care for the children, the church hoped to have people in place to love the children through their grief and help to plan for and to provide for their care going forward.

When community integration starts by recognizing and caring for children who are in danger of becoming orphans, the possibility of families staying together longer and children being spared suffering if and when they are orphaned becomes a reality. This is not something that happens by accident. The church, group, or organization committed to best practices in orphan care has to be proactive in identifying at-risk children. Then they need to help provide timely, excellent, and appropriate care and resources to the extent they are equipped to do so.

Importantly, orphan care communities are not immune from this responsibility. This is something that every excellence-driven orphan care community can and should be doing in its local community.

LOCAL COMMUNITY INTEGRATION IN ACTION

For an orphan care community, integration with the *local* community can take many different forms, shapes, and sizes. As we take a look at a few examples of such work, recognize that there are myriad other ways that an orphan care community can integrate its children into the local community and otherwise be deeply and intimately involved in its community.

One way an orphan care community can immerse in and develop relationships with families in the local community is through after-school programs and community centers. The orphan care community can either run these programs itself or, preferably, partner with another church or ministry with expertise in this area. An example of these programs and centers is found in the Child Development Centers (CDCs) in Managua, Nicaragua. These centers, run by the local church, provide a safe place for the children to stay while their parents are working. They also provide a place for the children to grow, as the children are fed, taught basic academics, and truths of the Bible, such as God's love for them and their hope in Christ, while they are there.

The CDCs and other such centers and programs have the ability to make a profound impact on their community. Struggling parents have a safe and nurturing environment for their children to be during their long hours of work, which helps the parents to avoid feelings of desperation that otherwise might cause them to abandon their children at an orphanage. Also, when the orphan care community works with a local church or other organization to run the centers, the community's children, families, and staff can participate in the programs and establish meaningful relationships with others in the local community in the process. The children can also serve in the centers, which helps them to develop their skills and talents, and understand their identity in Christ.

La Providencia,[3] a family model orphan care community in Honduras, provides another example of what community integration can look like in practice through its deep involvement in its local community. La Providencia's families and staff are fully integrated into their surrounding Aguas del Padre and Socorro communities through partnerships with several community churches and organizations, and through relationships with other families in the area. While La Providencia's director is the pastor of one of its partner churches in Aguas del Padre, the community's families and staff are involved in several different churches, allowing them to have a broad reach and impact in the surrounding area.

The local community likewise is integrated into La Providencia by having children from the surrounding communities and from all income levels attend its school, Academia La Providencia. Having children from the different socioeconomic levels attend the school simultaneously accomplishes a couple things. It provides a great education for the children in the community, many of whom would have no or poor quality education otherwise. And it helps the children living in the family homes at La Providencia and other vulnerable children in the community to overcome their "orphan" stigma by enabling them to develop deep friendships with children from all socioeconomic levels in their area at an early age. This hopefully will result in less discrimination and elitism amongst these children as they grow up together.

La Providencia also hosts community and church programs and cultural and community events in its community center building. The families and staff also work with local churches to complete various projects in the local community, such as well projects, Vacation Bible Schools, and soccer clinics. Through this local community integration, La Providencia is taking steps to build up the local community and its people, and simultaneously hone its children's understanding of their identities in the context of their community and develop them into gospel-driven leaders.

Another example of excellence-driven local community integration is a local church ministry in Nairobi, Kenya, caring for orphaned children on church property. This ministry includes the children in the church's ministries, including outreach in the greater community, so they experience the truth that there is value in what they have to offer others. For instance, the church has a Saturday feeding program where they offer food, fun, and biblical teaching for other vulnerable children. The children in the ministry invite children from the community to come to the program and are involved in facilitating the event. As the children talk with, play with, pray for, and share life with other children in their community, they learn the value of community and see firsthand the gifts God has given them to serve others.

In addition to serving and spending time with other children from the community, the children spend time with families from the church, which allows both the children and church families to serve and encourage each other in various ways. The family members help the children with schoolwork and vocational training. Or it could be as simple as a family inviting one or more of the children to attend informal family gatherings. Continually looking for opportunities for all the children to spend time (outside of Sunday morning and formal church events) with families from the church and others from the local community will promote community integration.

Ultimately, every orphan care community seeking best practice and excellence must determine ways to integrate its children, families, and staff into the local community, and vice versa, so that the children can fully develop their skills and talents, and their identities.

ENGAGING THE GLOBAL COMMUNITY WITH EXCELLENCE

Excellence-driven orphan care communities should also work to effectively develop relationships with their global community through partnerships with churches, organizations, and individuals around the world. The most common way to accomplish this goal is through healthy short-term mission teams and interns from other countries. We need to take caution, however. While trips and interns can go a long way to integrate the children, staff, and families of an orphan care community to their global community in healthy, productive, and life-giving ways, they also can be destructive to the very communities and children they are attempting to serve if they aren't executed properly.

There are entire books dedicated to excellence in short-term missions, including *When Helping Hurts* and *Toxic Charity*, and I encourage you to read them. In the paragraphs that follow, I'm not going to rehash the concepts set forth in those books; rather, I hope to examine how orphan care communities can host and churches can conduct short-term trips in a manner that results in both sides working *with* each other in ways that encourage and give life to each other.

Excellence in partnership between an orphan care community and a global partner, and best practice in any short-term trip begins with a deep relationship based on mutual admiration and respect. Part and parcel with that relationship is that every team or intern must have an in-country, local contact who is in charge of the trip—that is, the team or intern defers to his or her wisdom and leadership. This is important to protect against the team unintentionally or intentionally working to take over the project or otherwise do things to damage the orphan care community and/or its children.

A deep, healthy relationship between a church and an orphan care community will also result in both sides of the relationship continually working together to determine how the team's members, individually and collectively, can serve the community, and how the community can serve the team's members and its church. It will be a dynamic and symbiotic relationship. At La Providencia in Honduras, they have accomplished this by creating long-term relationships with churches throughout the United States and hosting a Summit with team leaders a few months before their trips to discuss and determine how the teams and La Providencia community can serve *each other.*

Remember Meseret and Milon from the beginning of the chapter? The rest of their story further conveys the incredible potential for deep relationships between local and global churches, and families. When we left them, they appeared to be alone with little hope. Because of global community integration, that couldn't be further from the truth. They are not alone and have plenty of hope, including the true hope in Christ.

They are part of the Repi Kale Heywet Church's home-based orphan care program,[4] through which they receive physical, emotional, and spiritual support from the local church. Repi Church partners with World Orphans and the Journey Church of Everett, Washington.[5] Through a visit to the home and developing relationships, the churches were able to determine that Meseret's house needed major repairs. It would have been easy for the American team members to think they could fix the problem and save them. It would have been easy to fall into the mind-set that money was the answer. Journey Church did neither. Instead, they saw not just the need for physical materials and manual labor, but an opportunity for a child to stay with his mother, his family.

As the US church and Ethiopian churches worked together, they birthed a solution to keep this child with his mother and integrated with his local community. Repi Church began sending its own leaders and members to work on this home, to donate their time and their labor to improve the lives of this widow and orphan in their community.

The side-by-side work of these two churches allowed each to see what they may not have seen individually. Repi Church highlighted the possibility of the landlord taking advantage of the family by increasing rent upon increase of the value of the improved shelter—a conflict the Journey team may not have foreseen. Utilizing this knowledge, the church negoti-ated a contract with the local landlord to keep rent stable and affordable for the family. When the landlord saw the Ethiopian church sacrificially give of itself to help this family, it moved him to action. He took respon-sibility for his property, and at his own expense, did many of the needed repairs. With the contribution from the landlord, Repi Church took the funds that would have been spent on home repairs and put some aside for Meseret's and Milon's future medical expenses. The church also gave some funds to Meseret so she could start a small business.

In addition to relationships between local churches and orphan care communities (or families), long-term relationships between foreigners and orphan care communities (through their leadership and typically sustained through short-term mission trips) potentially can develop two-way, life-giving relationships in which the children can see that they are valued and have value. The harm to avoid is children being excited about an outside visitor, only to again feel abandoned when that visitor leaves. But when there is context of relationship, the children can un-derstand that they and their orphan care community are in relationship with a community that is far away. When they can anticipate a visit and realize that it will be brief but that, most likely, there will be another visit, the context can allow the children to enjoy a special and life-giv-ing visit from friends without the feelings of abandonment.

Additionally, context of relationship can let the children see that their US partner can learn from them and their orphan care commu-nity. Take the example of church partnership (which can easily be ap-plied to an orphan care community). A church in the northeast United States partners with a church in Port-au-Prince, Haiti. The US church acknowledges that they struggle to reach out and care for those in need in their local community. On more than one occasion the US church has brought leaders from the Haitian church to visit them and facilitate trainings and seminars on community outreach. Haitian pastors caring for orphans in their community are actively involved in helping their US church partner learn how to care for the vulnerable in their com-munity. The US church also takes regular trips to Haiti and is develop-ing relationships with church members, families in the community, and orphans being cared for through the church. The children will hear people with whom they have built relationships talk about what they are learning from the children and from the church. Over the course of many years, the children will hear what they, their church, their culture, and their community have to teach and offer to others. Lord willing, this will be a tangible reminder of their value and worth, and identities as children of God. When relationships are built and stories are shared over the years, children will see that their lives and their community, combined with what God says about caring for others, serve to challenge and inspire their friends around the world. And the children will be given opportunities to further develop their identities as children of God with unique skills and talents that can give life to others.

There are significant potential pitfalls, however, which all churches and orphan care communities must guard against in connection with mission trips to orphan care communities. The first revolves around the potential negative affects of wealthy visitors in an economically challenged community. A team from the US (or other western country) spending time with orphaned children can be fraught with challenges a visitor may not notice. Americans visiting an orphan care community or walking around an economically poor neighborhood will likely convey the message that they are giving money to their host, which builds expectation from the community that the local host has increased resources, potentially leaving the host with challenging situations after the team leaves. The orphan care community needs to work to let others in the community know that simply is not the case.

Another likely scenario is a team singling out orphaned children in a desire to bless them with a prayer or a gift. But what they may not realize is the hurt felt by children and families who did not receive attention or a gift.

Another common problem is when teams expect to be able to visit family homes or a school in an orphan care community on-demand, with no regard for the family's privacy or the attachment and bonding needs of the children. We need to remember that the homes are not fish bowls or petting zoos, but are homes like yours and mine. And we need to treat them with the respect that we expect from others in our homes. Just imagine if someone knocked on your door when you were getting ready for dinner and they said they were there for a tour of the house, during which they would take pictures of your children and family pet.

While there are many other examples of pitfalls we could cover, the key to avoiding them as a team member is to always look out for the needs of the children and orphan care community before your own, and to look to your local host to understand the best way to engage the orphaned children and others in the community. And the key for the orphan care communities is to set and share clear and firm guidelines with the teams that help the teams understand what they can and cannot do (e.g., cannot hand out toys, candy, or gifts to the children, must work with nationals on projects, can and should share meals with staff and families, etc.), and why they can and cannot do those things.

Those of us who have the opportunity to travel and the privilege of meeting the children in person are representing the larger global orphan care community. It is incumbent upon us to be excellent representatives to the children of the community around the world who loves them and is advocating for them, even though they may never meet.

We need to love them and tell them they are valued.

We need to humble ourselves and allow ourselves to be served by them. Sometimes the most important thing we can do for a vulnerable or orphaned child is allow her to serve us so that her identity in Christ can be reinforced and she can be reminded once again that God created her to serve others with her unique skill, talents, and gifts.

And we must be intentional to always point them back to their local caregivers reinforce the love and provision of their local community, and, most importantly, point them to the hope of Christ.

CARING FOR THE CAREGIVERS

"To care for an orphan in a personal, long-term way is rarely easy. . . . This is not a road God means for us to walk as just one individual or family. God means for us to live out His call to care for the orphan in the context of Christian community."[6] If we agree that caring for an orphaned child in a personal, long-term way is rarely easy and that it is not a road God means for us to walk alone, let's think about that from the perspective of the people caring for orphaned and vulnerable children every day of their lives with everything they have.

Who is doing the day-in and day-out caring for the millions of orphaned children around the world who will not be adopted? It certainly is not the people visiting the children on short-term trips. Single parents, extended families, adoptive and foster families, and other unrelated caregivers care for the millions of orphaned children who will not be adopted.[7]

Another critical aspect of excellence in orphan care communities, and orphan care in general, is proper support, encouragement, and equipping of the people caring for the children on a daily basis. Indeed, one could argue that there is no greater impact on an orphaned child, no greater way to work toward best practices in orphan care and healthy community integration, than to train, disciple, and otherwise positively impact caregivers in orphan care communities. If a caregiver is able to provide a safe, loving, and nurturing environment where a child has the opportunity to heal, learn, grow and thrive, would we not say that goes a long way toward excellence in orphan care? If the answer is yes, than the big question is what does it look like to train, encourage, and equip caregivers so that they are healthy and thriving and able to provide an excellent environment and excellent care for the children. If in our zeal to care for children we overlook caring for the caregivers, we will have done a disservice to the children we long to serve.

So, why talk about caring for caregivers in a chapter covering community integration? Because caring for the caregiver potentially is a prime opportunity for the local and global community to be involved in orphan care by directly impacting the lives of the caregivers most intimately connected with the children. Community integration does not only have to mean orphans themselves being integrated with their local and global communities. When there is integration of the entire global orphan care community, orphaned children will benefit exponentially and on a long-term basis. This is crucial to best practices in orphan care.

So what does it look like for the global community to support, train, encourage and equip caregivers? While there are many ways it can be accomplished, World Orphans uses a conference-style model as an opportunity to encourage and equip caregivers. World Orphans gathers church leaders and orphan care providers from a community for a two- to four-day conference-style gathering. The time includes biblical worship and teaching that is geared toward encouragement as well as providing the time and space for the leaders and caregivers to be encouraged and refreshed by time with one another and in God's presence. Additionally, there is teaching and training on specific topics based on particular needs. Topics range from trauma care to safe-birth delivery to education. Topical teaching based on the needs of the community is an opportunity for the global orphan care community to be involved, specifically those from the US where educational resources are readily available. Not only is this a healthy opportunity for global community integration, but it is an opportunity for caregivers in orphan care communities to grow in their knowledge and understanding of best practices and to experience community themselves in order to better foster that among the children in their care.

As mentioned throughout this book, we would be wise to heed the counsel in *When Helping Hurts* and not blindly provide help and resources that are not beneficial to a community and/or the caregivers in the long run. That being said, within the context of relationship, we can share educational and other materials that are developmentally focused and serve to empower people to thrive in their communities. When this sharing of resources and materials is geared toward encouraging, empowering, and equipping caregivers, not only does it help them thrive within their community but also in their care of orphans.

MOVING FORWARD

Thankfully there are plenty of examples from around the world of communities responding with compassion to the needs of orphaned and abandoned children. But there are also plenty of examples of children falling through the cracks, being isolated, or left to fend for themselves. There are people willing to work hard and give sacrificially to see children cared for in families in a way that integrates them into their community, but that is not going to happen by accident.

If we want to see children loved and cared for and integrated into their communities in ways that lead to them becoming self-sustaining adults that are able to give back to their community, we have to be intentional. From the advocates working from a distance, to the community leaders facilitating programs, to the caregivers loving the children on a daily basis, we have to be proactive. Starting even before they are orphaned, when possible, we have to recognize their need to be a part of a community, receive from others, and give to and serve others. The hard work will pay off as we see the benefits of children who are integrated into their community able to heal, grow, thrive, and, in turn, serve others.

Going ☀ Deeper

1. What is community integration and why is it important for orphaned and vulnerable children? Why is it important to you?

2. What does community integration look like in your local community? How is it different from and how is it the same as the community integration described in this chapter?

3. What constitutes a healthy short-term mission team visit to an orphan care community? If you've ever visited an orphan care community, was your trip healthy? Why or why not?

MASTERS IN EDUCATION (EDUCATION)

"Around the globe, it is widely accepted that education is both a path out of poverty and the key to having a voice in the community. . . . Too many school systems around the world are under-resourced, underfunded, and understaffed. Educational success depends upon children getting the support they need within their households and within their communities, and upon schools being fully resourced."—Julie Gilbert Rosicky

"The student is not above the teacher, but everyone who is fully trained will be like their teacher."—Luke 6:40 (NIV)

With orphaned and vulnerable children, best-practice, excellence-driven education involves more than simply sending them to the "best" schools in their respective country, or developing schools that imitate those same top schools. While we know that, with extremely rare exceptions, children need education to thrive and become leaders in their society, there is much more to excellence in education than great teachers, administration, and curriculum in reading, writing, and arithmetic. There are certain educational best practices that need to be present to reach the level of excellence and best practice covered in this book.

As we provide education for our own children and children in orphan care communities, we also must always remember that education (i.e., a child's school) is a pillar of spiritual formation and one of the key opportunities for discipleship in a child's life. One implication of this truth is that teachers need to be educated, qualified, *and* have a healthy, biblical worldview. As a recent article states:

> Contrary to popular opinion, there is no such thing as amoral or value-neutral education. All education teaches and shapes morality. It is impossible to separate one's view of God, man, truth, knowledge and ethics from the educational process. Every day our children sit behind a desk, they are either being taught to know, love and obey God, or they are being taught to love and obey someone or something else that is attempting to usurp God's authority and role. . . . We must do everything in our power to place our child in an educational environment that facilitates their discipleship.[1]

Beyond spiritual formation and the school's basic structure (i.e., teachers, administration, and curriculum), an excellence-driven education for orphaned and vulnerable children involves several other components, including parental involvement, addressing special needs, and diverse learning methods.

To walk us through these and other aspects of best-practice education in orphan care communities, I've asked Andy Lehman[2] and Katharine Marrow[3] to share their collective wisdom with us because they have valuable experience working in Christian education for orphaned and vulnerable children in various cultures.[4] Since 2002, Andy has served as Vice-President of Lifesong for Orphans,[5] which works with orphaned and vulnerable children around the world through many initiatives. Three of those initiatives are excellence-driven education projects in Zambia, Honduras, and Ethiopia.

Katharine was born in England (which is why you'll see some British flavor in this chapter), and raised in a family of missionaries involved in ministries in the United Kingdom and Africa. She received an education degree from Oxford University and has followed in her family's missionary footsteps by teaching for the last thirteen years in schools in Uganda, the United Kingdom, and Honduras, where she has served for the past several years at Academia La Providencia[6] as the director of its English program. Katharine seeks to bring the love of Jesus to each child in her care through an educational experience of the highest possible quality.

Let's take a look at how Katharine and Andy work to accomplish that audacious goal through their respective ministries. Andy will write in reference to Lifesong and their work in Ethiopia and Zambia, while Katharine will write from Academia La Providencia in Honduras.

Excellence in Education
(Andy Lehman and Katharine Marrow)

Like many countries around the world, the Honduran education system has had a rocky road. Like in many developing countries, the public schools are overcrowded, and children are squeezed into small classrooms—if indeed they have classrooms. Often, children do not continue school past the sixth grade, and many such children are forced to work to help provide for their families.

Many teachers in the schools are forced to take on two or three jobs to provide for their families, resulting in compromise to their commitment to excellence in education. Strikes, due to government policies and changes—or lack thereof—also affect the children's education. Parents, many of whom did not complete school further than first grade, can view education as unimportant or simply not feasible for the family.

These issues, and many more like them, are what we (and many around the globe) are up against in our pursuit for excellence in education for orphaned and vulnerable children. So where do we go from here?

WHAT IS EXCELLENCE?

In Honduras, the pursuit of "excellence" in education often takes the form of striving *only* towards educational excellence, or competing with or trying to become like the international bilingual schools in the big cities.

Is that wrong? What is excellence in education for orphaned and vulnerable children? Is it simply emulating the best schools in the cities, in their academic, technological (e.g., laptops, iPads, etc.), and other education-related practices? Does excellence mean striving *only* towards educational excellence? Or is there something more?

The Bible offers a very different picture as to the application of excellence in various areas (bold and italics added):

* **In mission:** "Since you are eager for manifestations of the Spirit, strive **to excel** in building up the church." (1 Cor. 14:12)

* **In loving:** "And I will show you a still more **excellent** way." (1 Cor. 12:31)

* **In self-sacrifice and service:** "But as you **excel** in everything—in faith, in speech, in knowledge, in all earnestness, and in our love for you—see that you excel in this act of grace also." (2 Cor. 8:7)

* **In wisdom:** "Finally, brothers, whatever is true, whatever is honorable, whatever is just, whatever is pure, whatever is lovely, whatever is commendable—if there is any **excellence**, if there is anything worthy of praise, think about these things." (Phil. 4:8)

* **In obedience:** "I want you to insist on these things, so that those who have believed in God may be careful to devote themselves to good works. These things are **excellent** and profitable for people." (Titus 3:8)

As these verses show, excellence is much more than simply striving to *be the best* in the world, and it is not about competing with or gaining superiority over others. While we do need to strive for academic excellence and high standards—in order to give the children the tools they need to succeed and develop their skills and talents—we greatly need to change the way we think about educational excellence as a whole.

Our school, Academia La Providencia (ALP), likely will not have all the resources that wealthier, bigger schools have. But that does not hinder us in pursuing our goals and desire to reach gospel-driven excellence in everything we do because God's excellence entails much more than academic prowess and the newest, biggest, or best resources.

So what does striving for God's excellence look like in the context of education for orphaned and vulnerable children in orphan care communities?

AN EXCELLENCE-DRIVEN EXPERIMENT

A few years ago, some ordinary people happened upon something extraordinary. In Ethiopia, a country wracked with desperate poverty and a growing number of orphans, *hope* was starting to peek around the corner.

Two small, struggling villages were trying something new. Instead of building more orphanages, they were working to keep families together. Instead of accepting the cycle of poverty, they were working to break it. Instead of increasing dependence on outsiders, they were working to create paths to economic self-sufficiency.

And education played a major role in their *grand experiment*. What did they do? It was pretty simple, really.

With some assistance from Lifesong for Orphans, the people from these villages started feeding their vulnerable children twice a day, helping their families to stay together. In an area where an estimated fifty percent of the children (mainly orphaned and vulnerable children) don't attend any school at all,[7] the schools provided an excellence-driven education to the children. They also provided discipleship (i.e., spiritual formation) and mentorship for the children, equipping them to become the future gospel-driven leaders of Ethiopia. These seemingly simple things are having profound effects on the children and the communities of which they are a part.[8]

Abaye is one of the children we are impacting (and who is impacting us). He recently moved from an impoverished living situation into a family-model orphan care community and began attending one of the Lifesong schools. He shared his story with me:

> My dad died and my mother was blind, so I was given to a relative to be raised. They did not take good care of me. When I was five years old, they began to send me out to work every day, herding the cattle, donkeys, sheep, and goats.
>
> I wanted to be in school so much that I would try to herd animals near the school building. I would sit under the window of the schoolroom and listen to the teacher and children recite their lessons, and I would recite them to myself.
>
> I was so excited when I was able to live at Samuel's Home [a family-model orphan care home] and finally able to go to the Lifesong school.

Abaye typifies what this chapter is all about—providing children, who are constantly told by those around them that they have no potential, with opportunities to discover through excellence in education that they are overflowing with potential.

PURSUING EXCELLENCE IN EDUCATION

While there is no magic formula to create a perfect school and education system throughout the world, or to impact lives like Abaye's, we want to share some common threads of excellence in education that cross most, if not all, cultural bounds.

Sensitivity to Local Culture

There is always a need to balance the local culture and its educational system with standards and ideals brought from the West. There is beauty in both, and when merged properly, they can make a strong and beautiful educational experience for the children. In order to do this effectively, we need to take the time to know and understand each other on a deep cultural and personal level. This is often a slow process that demands our time and intentionality. As Lifesong-Zambia's school directors Shane and Mitzi McBride learned:

> *When moving to a foreign country with little understanding and experience in third-world education, unprepared and underqualified are certainly two feelings one can acquaint themselves with. However, over time we have learned to take things "ponono ponono," which means bit by bit in the local Bemba language.*

In Honduras, like Zambia, approaching things slowly and really getting to know the native educational system's requirements, without condemning the local system and culture, is very important. You are not trying to bring your country into theirs, to be a "Little England" or "Little America." You are in their country working to promote an excellent education. In ALP's case, we do not want to create an American or English school within Honduras; we want to create a Honduran school that encompasses the "good bits" of education from wider afield.

Remembering this concept is especially important to us out in our village. Whilst we are bilingual and encourage new standards and concepts, we still must work within the Honduran framework, whatever we may think of it. It is crucial to get to know what you are working with, to ask advice from well-established schools about the realities and realistic expectations of the education system, and not to charge in "knowing everything."

One practical way we've worked to incorporate the "best of both worlds" is through ALP's Mission, Vision and Philosophy, which was written by people from both Western and Honduran cultures. While the methodology of reaching and achieving our goals may be different, both cultures are on the same page and working together—not the Westerners dominating with their new ideas.

As we continue to know and understand each other (a process that will continue on as long as there is relationship), we can develop common educational goals and strategies that will continue moving us together toward excellence.

Spiritual Formation and Integration of Biblical Values

Any excellence-driven educational system needs to integrate biblical values and commit to discipleship and spiritual formation of the children. In countries open to Christianity, the challenge is to maximize the opportunity to bring a holistic biblical worldview into the classroom and weave it through the different subjects taught. Spiritual formation is discussed in greater detail in chapter 12, but we want to provide you with some examples of what spiritual formation might look like in practice, even in situations where the local culture is unfriendly to Christianity and the Bible.

In Ethiopia, we (Lifesong) adhere to the curriculum of the Ministry of Education, which prohibits teachers and staff from teaching Christianity in the classroom. But we also hold fast to our conviction that a solid understanding and grounding in evangelical Christian living is necessary for the student. We do this by using time outside the classroom for spiritual formation activities. At the flagpole each school morning, in addition to singing the Ethiopian national anthem, the student body hears a Bible reading, a devotional, a prayer, and practices saying their Bible memory verse for the week.

While a large percentage of our students are Muslim and Orthodox, their caregivers understand that in order to attend our schools their children must participate in these activities. Since our school has the highest standards, feeds the students two meals a day, and has high-quality facilities, their caregivers do not object to the spiritual development. Even Muslim and Orthodox parents comment on how their children have become such well-disciplined and astute scholars since being enrolled in our schools. As our students develop their identities in Christ as children of God, they simultaneously are able to share the gospel with their families when they take the Word home each evening, discuss their school activities, and practice memorizing their Bible verses.[9]

Unlike Ethiopia, Honduras is open to biblical teaching in the classroom, and ALP provides it. Within our school day at ALP, our children receive Bible classes where they grow in their identities in Christ as they discover the Bible and learn morals and values for life. I often wondered about how much the children take on board (how much they share at home), until the father of one of my students came in to talk with me. He said that his family was about to eat dinner at home when his son Jorge piped up saying that they couldn't start eating until they prayed and thanked God for the food. Jorge then led the family in saying grace.[10] So from our Bible classes and school devotions, even if the children seem like they aren't paying attention, we know they are soaking it in and passing it on. From tiny acorns great oak trees grow!

Staffing

Staffing a school with qualified, competent, and gospel-driven teachers and directors is another key component to an excellence-driven school.

Without gospel-driven staffs, Christ-centered schooling cannot go on, and long-term life change for our children will not occur. At our Lifesong-Zambia school, we partner with a training institute within Zambia that trains up teachers professionally *and* missionally. They are not only teachers—they also are disciple makers. While we know this will never solve all of the staffing issues that are common in developing countries, it certainly gives us a strong foundation and core upon which to build.

Finding and keeping highly trained, committed, Christ-following believers can be a challenge. However, because of our commitment to excellent education, we have decided to not cave in to the needs or what appears to be an urgent situation and hire someone with less than what meets our vision and goals.

Additionally, in Honduras, we have found another important thing related to staffing. Starting at the top, having a local, national principal is vital. This is important particularly where the education system is somewhat unique, like our Honduran system. It would take an outsider coming in many years to fully grasp it all and work effectively under the regulations and paperwork the government requires. Further, parents tend to trust a local leader and build relationships with them far quicker than a foreigner or outsider.[11]

Integration of Diverse Backgrounds

Excellence in education also includes providing for all areas of the children's development and growth, including their need for healthy inter-action with their peers and surrounding community. At ALP, we work to facilitate this need by seeking to integrate all demographics from the local community, including children from La Providencia's family homes and children from the surrounding community. While most of our community children are in some form of risk due to poverty, we have some children from more affluent families at our school.

We work hard to integrate our school so that our children learn to socialize with, and not discriminate against, a variety of backgrounds and social classes—learning that people and lifestyles are different yet, at the core, are the same in so many ways. It's not so much about valuing different lifestyles, but about teaching them to see and value the Imago Dei in each of their peers despite different lifestyles. This not only helps kids get along, it works to break down stigmas and class warfare from an early age.

Parental (Caregiver) Involvement and Buy-In

Another integral part of a child's education is parental (or caregiver) involvement. As stated earlier, orphaned and vulnerable children often come from backgrounds lacking educated, supported, and involved parents. When children lack educated parents, it is very difficult for them to reach the higher levels of education because their parents are unable to help them at home. To achieve their maximum potential, children need to feel that their caregivers/parents are investing in their education and are collaborating with their teachers. Without educated and involved parents, children often need more specialized teaching styles and other resources to draw out their God-given potential.

Further, because of several economic and cultural factors, parents of vulnerable children often discourage education because of any or all of the following: they fail to see its value (under the mind-set that says, "It didn't help me and my other friends in poverty"); they view it as a threat because it reveals their inadequacies to properly raise their children; they believe their children cannot complete school; or they genuinely need their children to use their time to work and earn money for the family.

As a recent article in *The Economist* puts it:

> *Surveys in many countries show that poor parents often believe that a few years of schooling have almost no benefit; education is valuable only if you finish secondary school. So if they cannot ensure that their children can complete school, they tend to keep them out of the classroom altogether. And if they can pay for only one child to complete school, they often do so by avoiding any education for the children they think are less clever.*[12]

The article went on to note that parents often misjudge their children's skills, all but ensuring the failure of the children whom the parents deem to be "less clever." Recognizing this reality, excellence-driven care for orphaned and vulnerable children should also seek to include an adult education program for the parents and caregivers of children to inform and educate them about the various subjects their children are learning, as well as the value of education itself. While it will look different in virtually every location, here are a couple ways parent involvement can take shape.

Because we recognize that many of the parents and caregivers of the children at our Lifesong-Zambia school are uneducated, and we fully understand that caregiver involvement is primary to the children's success, we coach the caregivers on how to help their children with homework, organizational skills, and time management. We host parent-teacher meetings three times a year to discuss individual needs of the students. From these meetings we take concerns and build them into workshops for parents to attend, as a way of empowering them to play a key role in their child's education.[13]

Another important aspect of parental or caregiver involvement is that they sufficiently "buy into" their child's education. The student *and* his family must both make some sacrifice to appreciate the value of what they are receiving. This starts with research into the background of each student to determine how much his or her caregiver can pay for education. At Lifesong schools, if the staff determines that the caregiver is able to pay, they require a monthly school fee from them.[14]

At ALP, most of the children receive free education[15]—with parents paying only for uniforms and to register their child each year. So how do we get the parents involved when many of them have received little schooling and may not value education? We have our parents volunteer at the school. We have a rota[16] system where mothers (a few fathers, but not many, and some grandmothers, of course) come for one day every two weeks and either cook the school lunch or clean the school. This allows them to see their children in school, see the environment, and see how their children are learning, while providing an opportunity for the parents to talk to teachers when necessary—and vice versa. It also gives the parents a feeling that they are contributing to their child's education in ways other than financially—of which the children are also very aware.

Filling Nutritional Needs

One of the principles we have learned in our Lifesong schools in Ethiopia is that a hungry student cannot learn. Hungry children are weak and unable to focus in the classroom. Their concentration is on their rumbling stomachs rather than the math lesson on the blackboard. To address this issue, we provide breakfast and lunch at school, which allows children to stay in school longer, increases attendance, and improves their attentiveness and grades. By simply providing better and more consistent nutrition, we have been able to double the amount of class time, impact, and influence on the children.[17]

Learning Methods

While examining the plethora of learning methods is beyond the scope of this short chapter, we still want to offer you some things to consider with regard to what our children's classroom and school time should include in this area.

Play

> "It is in playing, and only in playing, that the individual child or adult is able to be creative and to use the whole personality, and it is only in being creative that the individual discovers the self."—D. W. Winnicott, British paediatrician (1896–1971)

In Honduras, as in many cultures around the world, children go to school and sit "learning" at their desks all day long. The importance of learning through play is not acknowledged—in fact, it typically is viewed as a chaotic waste of time. In reality, though, play serves an important role in learning. Why is play so important at ALP and other schools like it? Many of our children just don't get to play at home, as it is not natural for Honduran mothers or other caregivers to sit and play with their children or to engage them in some kind of creative activity.

So, we help our children learn to play at school. We give them the time and the space to learn to play and to increase their creativity through play. At recess and in the classroom, appropriate play takes all forms and can be accomplished under all budgets—and let's be honest, it makes teaching far more fun!

Analytical Thinking

In Honduras, children typically are not taught to think for themselves in an analytical manner. A culture and history of didactic teaching, where the teacher speaks and the child listens and memorizes, results in a system that simply spoon-feeds students answers for exams. Whilst this approach has its benefits, alone it does not equip children to face a world in which they must make decisions for themselves. One of our challenges at La Providencia is moving away from this as the *only* tool for teaching.

One of the best ways I found to explain the need for change to other teachers is by modeling it with my own class, showing them that there are other ways in which to help the children study, ways that help me to know and assess their comprehension. Once it was seen that the children do need more than just memorization—and that the children are capable of doing so—it became easier for other teachers to jump on board with this line of thinking. It really has been a slow but great process.

Hands On

Many of our children, like many others around the world, need learning to be "hands on," or kinesthetic. Children learn in three main cognitive styles: visual, auditory, and kinesthetic. Didactic teaching only includes the auditory and visual learning whilst missing out on kinesthetic—touch. We are trying to make sure we keep up with all of these teaching and learning methods. Children who are out cutting coffee in the fields after school, who are tired from working so hard, are more likely to learn by touch than by sitting and listening.

Bilingual

At ALP, we want to give our children the very best opportunity in life, a great base and starting point in their education. In countries where multiple languages are spoken or used, a bilingual education is a priority. Whilst the national language of Honduras is Spanish, the proximity and influence of the United States upon Honduras requires proficiency in English to open doors and opportunities for the children. Local businesses also are requiring some level of English. We want our children to have the same—or better—educational opportunities. We have structured it so they have half the day in English and half the day in Spanish. We have English classrooms and Spanish classrooms so that when the children are learning English, they are surrounded by English words and phrases on the walls—and vice versa for when they are learning Spanish. This means they can be fully immersed in the environment and have their work displayed around them. They then change classrooms half way through the day. This has proved to be very successful.

Similarly, the children at our Lifesong Ethiopia schools are taught three languages (English, Amharic—the national language, and Oromo—the local tribal and state language) beginning in nursery school. Since they start at that young age, it is just a normal part of their everyday activities of going to school. And those three languages will make them very versatile citizens of Ethiopia some day. Like in much of the world, English is a growing necessity for any good job, and advanced education and foreign organizations (such as ours) require English competence.

Technology

Another important aspect of excellence-driven education is teaching the children to understand and properly use technology. At Lifesong Ethiopia, we recently launched a computer lab outfitted with laptop computers and a projector. The enthusiasm and competition for time on the computers is intense and the kids cherish every minute of it. We begin technology instruction in third grade. In addition, our teachers and staff, most of whom never had the opportunity to learn to use a computer, now have the opportunity to also learn to operate computers in after-school sessions taught by our technology instructor.

Physical Education

Sports and physical activity are also important aspects of education. And part and parcel with the athletics is learning to be good sportsmen on and off the field. In a recent city-wide football tournament, our (Lifesong Ethiopia) girls' team became the city champions. However, more than winning the cup, we were most gratified that our student body was given the "Best Sportsmanship" award.

The Arts

At ALP, we want to encourage each child as a whole, whether in academics, in athletics, or in the arts. Not all of our children excel academically or athletically, yet some have gifts and talents in music and art. The challenge in Honduras is that some of the arts are only recently being recognised as true subjects. Fortunately, music schools and bands are becoming more popular as people are embracing the importance of music and the arts in general. In our classes we try and encourage creativity, something that is not always a norm for them at home, while letting them see what they enjoy and have a gift for. Our aim for the future is to have an orchestra or band, sports teams, art clubs, and theatre groups.

Skills Training

Lastly, we must educate our children not only through books, athletics, and arts, but also through skills training. In Zambia, we accomplish this using several different locally appropriate mediums. For instance, many of our older children are learning entrepreneurial business skills through our farm and selling our products for profit. We also have older children learning to make baskets and a variety of art to sell in order to support their families.[18]

For more discussion and an ongoing conversation about learning methods, philosophies, and mediums, visit ThinkOrphan.com.

Addressing Special Needs

We also need to address the fact that many of the orphaned and vulnerable children in our schools come into the classroom with emotional, physical, and mental "baggage," such as attachment deficits and trauma.[19] It is critical for all staff to be made aware of and learn how to address these issues.[20] Often, the conduct manifests itself in learning difficulties. Other times, it simply looks like bad behaviour, such as the child who just sits in class crying for no apparent reason, or the child who is constantly shouting out to be heard or noticed.

In addressing the behaviour, teachers need to consider why the children are acting out, learn their story, and create an environment that is safe, predictable, and healing.[21] Ideally, we will fill their educational and spiritual needs, while simultaneously striving to implement plans that help them heal from their emotional and social wounds.

In a culture where special educational needs are not widely accepted, people need to be aware that many orphaned and vulnerable children do come along with attachment deficits to some degree. Positive reinforcement needs to be encouraged, and boundaries and routines need to be established from day one. Children need to know that they are accepted and will be heard. They need to be loved. Routines and reminders of what is happening next, and time checks so that there are no surprises are all important parts of good classroom management.[22]

While addressing the children's needs, we also need to remember that they are resilient. We must not be afraid to speak of high expectations in their lives if we are giving the appropriate support within the system. Often they desire to attach themselves to a label of "orphan" or "vulnerable," and this creates a victim mentality that is self-defeating. We must speak truth and expectation into their lives and help them realize their precious and true identity in Christ.

Interaction with Visitors

Like many ministries, each year brings several mission teams to La Providencia. At ALP, we have found that it is important to have some rules that we stand by when it comes to teams and visitors. ALP is not just a goldfish bowl for people to come and ooh and aah at. Our children are indeed very sweet—and yes, of course, team members want to come and look around—but we indeed are running a school. It is not proper to interrupt our (or any other) school's daily schedule on a regular basis—we have curriculums to finish!

Oftentimes, teams come wanting to do a craft or something similar with the children in the middle of the school day. If teams were continually allowed to do this, it would create chaos and instability for our children and all routine would go out the window.

With rules firmly in place, we do encourage teams to visit if they can come and help us—teachers to come in and teach the teachers, or to teach science or math lessons to demonstrate methods or experiments—helping our teachers to expand their knowledge, teaching art techniques, or teaching skills in PE. We seek teams to show us different things to help us develop and grow as a school and as teachers.[23]

When teams are well planned out, they can add great value to any school serving orphaned and vulnerable children, particularly if the school lacks adequate resources.

WHAT IT'S ALL ABOUT

In the end, it takes different, culturally appropriate iterations of these aspects of education, and a whole lot of hard work, to provide excellent education to orphaned and vulnerable children around the world. But the hard work and commitment is worth it when it results in children who are effectively developing their skills, talents, and identities as children of God who can be anything He created them to be—children like Abaye, who you met earlier in this chapter. Through his school and family, Abaye is coming to understand his uniqueness, potential, and identity. One day, when a guest playfully rubbed his hair, Abaye responded wittily, "Be careful, there's a doctor inside there."

Abaye is a very smart young man who likely would never have had the opportunity to develop his God-given gifts, talents, and abilities without the education his new school provides. Abaye is what striving for excellence looks like.

We hope that you will join Lifesong for Orphans and La Providencia in our pursuit of excellence in education of orphaned and vulnerable children, by continuing this conversation on ThinkOrphan.com and actively seeking to improve schools around the world to a level of true excellence.

Going ☼ Deeper

1. How, if at all, has your definition of educational excellence changed after reading this chapter?

2. In the particular cultural context where you're involved or have been involved with a ministry, how can your culture and the native culture be integrated to further the best-practice principles discussed in this chapter?

3. What are some practical ways that an orphan care community can increase the parent/caregiver buy-in and involvement in the children's education?

Chapter 7

YOU ARE WHAT YOU EAT
(NUTRITION)

"There can be no argument that proper nutrition and access to health care, including childhood immunizations, are necessary for the healthy physical and emotional development of all children. It is also true that adequate nutrition and basic health care is necessary for adults to be fully functional members of their household and society."—Julie Gilbert Rosicky

"'All things are lawful for me,' but not all things are helpful. . . . Do you not know that your body is a temple of the Holy Spirit within you, whom you have from God? You are not your own, for you were bought with a price. So glorify God in your body."—Paul (I Cor. 6:12, 19–20)

E very child needs proper nutrition to fully develop his or her brain and body—to thrive in society as a child and, eventually, as an adult. Unfortunately, most orphans living on the streets or in institutions are undernourished, which leads to many other physical and mental issues in their lives. About 80 percent of brain development occurs before a child turns two, and if a child is not properly nourished during that critical twenty-four-month period, his or her brain simply will not be able to develop properly. And it's impossible to *completely* make up that development with proper nutrition later in life.

To avoid these tragic consequences and to give undernourished children the best chance to develop in life, children need proper nutrition at as early an age as possible. And they need the proper nutrition to continue through their developmental years to help them (and the future generations they will impact) to break the cycle of conditions, minor and severe, related to nutritional deficiencies. In implementing a proper nutritional plan, it is important to be sensitive to local culture and foods, speak to qualified nationals about their views and expertise on nutrition, and develop a plan that looks beyond the "American" perception of nutrition while not compromising on excellence.

To give us a better idea about how to instill excellent nutrition into orphaned and vulnerable children's lives, I've asked Kristina DeMuth[1] to share some of the insights and experiences she has learned over the past few years studying and working in this field. Kristina is a registered dietitian and a candidate for her masters in public health nutrition at The University of Minnesota. Over the past few years, Kristina has spent much time working in different capacities with orphaned and vulnerable children in Haiti, seeking to bring nutritional excellence to their lives. I hope that you'll engage her words of wisdom and learn from her as I have.

Nutrition
(Kristina DeMuth)

"For I was hungry and you gave me food."—Matthew 25:35

It was my first time visiting the clinic in one of Haiti's poorest slums. I didn't know what to expect. I just knew that the Haitian nutrition educator accompanying me was about to share the same message I planned to share with the people at the clinic: "Nutrition is prevention."

When we arrived, the room was full of people with all kinds of problems and ailments: mothers and their children with anemia and/ or who were malnourished, adults (young and old) with acid reflux, hypertension, and diabetes, to name a few. During our presentation about balanced nutrition, the educator told the crowd, "Medicine can't do everything for you!" Later, he explained to me, "People believe in medicine. People need to believe in food." With regard to nutrition, there is definitely truth in that statement.

After our presentation, as we continued to spend time with the people at the clinic, discussing individual medical and nutritional needs, an overweight woman who appeared to be in her late fifties came to the clinic to pick up medications for some of her chronic ailments. We spent time talking with her about her diet and going through the things she typically eats throughout the day. Knowing I wasn't getting the full story, I probed her about her use of margarine, excessive use of oil, sugar, and a seasoning packet known as "Maggi." At this point with my work in Haiti, I knew many of the questions to ask. As she spoke, my mind filled with advertisements for sugar-sweetened beverages, corner stores full of highly processed snack foods, and street food—white rice with fried or processed meats and fried plantains, typically lacking native whole grains and produce. As I talked with this woman in a room full of people with problems stemming from poor nutrition, I found myself experiencing, firsthand, the dichotomy of a huge challenge presented by the world's nutrition epidemic—obesity and chronic disease plaguing the same communities where chronic and acute malnutrition are prominent.

THE TWO SIDES OF POOR NUTRITION

In our world today, we face a double burden of nutrition related diseases. It's not just about children starving and struggling with lack of food, and obesity is not just a problem in developed countries. In 2010, the World Health Organization (WHO) estimated that about 104 million children under age five were underweight *and* about 43 million children under age five were *over*weight.[2]

Both conditions resulting from poor nutrition, being overweight and being underweight, contribute to death, chronic diseases, long-term impairments, and high risks pregnancies or complications.[3] Furthermore, undernutrition has long-term physiological consequences that make children more susceptible to chronic health conditions and can lead to higher accumulation of fat, lower energy expenditure and fat oxidation, and insulin resistance. It also can cause inadequate brain development, difficulties in school, and behavioral problems. However, if undernutrition is caught and treated early enough (i.e., before the age of five), its detrimental effects can be prevented and possibly reversed.[4]

In addition to issues arising from undernutrition, transitioning to a more "Westernized" lifestyle (e.g., lack of physical activity and dietary shifts) also can increase a child's risk of chronic health problems.[5] On a global level, traditional meals in many countries are being displaced by the "Westernized diet"; a transition commonly referred to as the "nutrition transition." The transition is marked by an *increased* intake of refined carbohydrates, animal-sourced foods, and added sugars and fats, *and* a *decrease* in legumes, whole grains, and produce.[6] It's no wonder this happens when bottles of soda, snack foods, and juice are more readily available and cheaper in many parts of the world than water, fresh fruits, and fresh vegetables. What would you gravitate toward if you were a child (or adult) in a similar situation?

NUTRITION AND ORPHANED CHILDREN

How does this all relate to orphan care? Simple. Orphaned and vulnerable children, just like everyone else in our global community, are at-risk for both malnutrition and chronic disease resulting from poor nutrition. Underfeeding as well as overfeeding can lead to undesirable health outcomes that prevent the children from fully developing their minds and bodies *and* can eventually burden all of us due to an increased number of sick and unproductive individuals in society. In my work with orphanages that haven't previously focused on proper nutrition, I've found that the children's diets were not much different than the diet of the woman I met at the clinic—a lot of refined carbohydrates, highly processed meats, added sugars, and refined fats, and very little to no fresh fruits and vegetables. Orphaned and vulnerable children, just like other children around the world, are highly susceptible to health consequences, positive and negative, from changes in their food environment.

Further, orphaned and vulnerable children living in institutional settings without families are at increased risk for nutritional deficiencies and nutrition-related diseases, particularly when the caregivers fail to closely monitor and properly address their children's eating and growth patterns. The Spoon Foundation has identified the following as possible root causes of poor nutrition and poor growth in orphan care: inadequate prenatal care or dietary intake, not being breastfed, special health care needs, poor diet or poor quality of formula, poor hygiene, failing to screen for anemia, no anthropometric data (e.g., height, weight, arm circumference), lack of supplementation for children in need, stress from instability or lack of structure from family support, no individual care, lack of stimulation, and improper feeding practices (e.g., how much food they are fed, the position in which they are fed, and the utilities used for feeding).[7] Failing to address these issues with excellence-driven care can lead to serious lifelong consequences related to growth, development, cognitive functioning, and health, and it can even lead to death.

On my second visit to Haiti, I was able to sit alongside a Haitian doctor while he assessed children in orphanages sponsored by the organization with which I was working. I will never forget how sick the children were with basic, seemingly preventable ailments: coughs, fevers, infection, poor wound healing. As I looked through the charts of the children after the assessments, I e-mailed the sponsoring organization to ask a simple question—"What are these children eating?" I went on to write, "Medical costs can be greatly reduced with well-balanced meals. Prevention on a daily basis can greatly reduce future complications!"

I didn't have all the answers (and still don't), but I knew that we couldn't just keep checking up on these children and providing responsive, reactionary medical care. I knew we had to be proactive and work to prevent diseases and ailments by improving their daily lifestyle conditions and nutritional intake. Nutrition, when adequate and balanced, fuels the body to maintain life and thrive. Nutrients help with organ function, physical movement, mental cognitions, repair and growth of cells, immune support, metabolism, reproductive systems, and many other functions. Thus, when nutrition is compromised and overlooked as a component of health, many acute and chronic diseases, infections, and psychological growth problems result and/or are exacerbated.

Any excellence-driven orphan care community must do its best to never let that happen. So how can we be proactive and encourage optimal development of our children through proper nutrition?

NUTRITION 101

Our bodies need many things to keep them running properly, and food is our main source of fuel. So it's important to know what type of fuel we need and the composition of the fuel.

Food is made up of three macronutrients (i.e., carbohydrates, fats, and proteins), and a vast number of micronutrients (i.e., vitamins and minerals). There are fifteen minerals and fourteen vitamins that humans must obtain from their diet. Additionally, plant-based foods are rich in phytonutrients and antioxidants that help protect cells from oxidation and development of diseases like cancer, heart disease, and infections.[8]

Carbohydrates are typically the staple foods in many diets around the world and are used as a primary source of energy in the body. Whole grains (e.g., sorghum, wild rice, bulgur, oats), starchy vegetables (e.g., squash, potatoes, tubers), as well as fruits and vegetables are carbohydrates that provide a rich source of fiber, which promotes a healthy gut and works to prevent chronic diseases.[9]

Protein is comprised of amino acids, which aid in cellular function, tissue maintenance, and growth. Protein also plays a role in the structure of antibodies for enhancing immunity, as well as hemoglobin in the blood. There are more than twenty known amino acids, of which nine are considered essential because they cannot be produced by the body and must be obtained from food. All sources of protein contain varying levels of the nine amino acids. Generally, animal-sourced protein foods, soybeans, quinoa, and spinach contain a higher amount of the essential amino acids, whereas many plant-based foods are lower in one or more essential amino acids. A diet that is limited in animal-sourced foods therefore must contain legumes (i.e., beans, lentils, soy) to complement limiting sources of other amino acids generally found in a grain-rich diet. Importantly, as long as an individual consumes a variety of foods and an adequate amount of calories throughout the course of a day, one likely will obtain adequate intake of all nine essential amino acids.[10]

Fats come in several different forms based on the chemical bonds of the fat structures. The different bonds have varying properties and can either promote poor health or be health promoting, depending on the structure of the fat molecule. Fatty acids in food contribute to cholesterol production, sex-hormone synthesis, cell membrane structure, growth, energy, and aid in absorption of fat-soluble vitamins (Vitamins K, A, D, E). While research is still developing around the health implications of various fatty acid molecules, trans fat and hydrogenated oils (generally found in processed foods) should be avoided and dietary intake of saturated fat should be limited. Unsaturated fatty acids, primarily found in plant-based foods (e.g., seeds, nuts, and avocados) and fatty fish, are generally lower in saturated fat and rich in polyunsaturated and monounsaturated fatty acids and thus are the more health-promoting fats for our bodies.[11]

Further, in many developing countries and low resource areas of the world, meat is generally more expensive, and historically, the cultural cuisine has been primarily a plant-based diet (comprised of mainly plant foods like grains, legumes, fruits, vegetables). Despite popular belief, such dietary patterns can be beneficial for a child's growth and development as long as the diet is adequately designed and measures are taken to ensure proper food preparation.[12] For instance, pairing fruits and vegetables with healthy fats (e.g., avocado with carrots in a dish) can help to enhance fat-soluble vitamin intake, and pairing sources of vitamin C with plant-based iron foods (e.g., mango or oranges with a bean or whole grain dish) can enhance iron absorption.[13] On the other hand, if children only eat white rice every single day, there is a very high chance they could develop deficiencies in a variety of essential nutrients. Ultimately, diet diversity is optimal for obtaining maximum essential nutrients.

To ensure that the children properly fuel their bodies, it is essential to keep nutrition quality and purposeful meal planning in mind when developing orphan care communities. Creating menu plans and using a variety of locally sourced, unprocessed foods from within the surrounding communities will help ensure a variety of nutrients over the course of the days, weeks, and years.

ADDRESSING ACUTE AND CHRONIC NUTRITION ISSUES

During the initial stages of my nutrition work, a Haitian ministry contacted me to look into which nutritional supplements should be provided to orphaned children that would soon be moving into their orphanage. In my research, I discovered a peanut butter based food produced in Haiti that seemed to fit the bill. While the product originally was intended for use solely with infants and small children, it also was very effective in dealing with weight restoration and treating refeeding syndrome (i.e., potentially fatal shifts in fluids and electrolytes that may occur in malnourished patients when receiving food) because of its macronutrient/micronutrient makeup.[14]

Before purchasing and delivering the supplements, I performed nutritional assessments (i.e., weight, height, arm circumference) using World Health Organization (WHO) growth charts on each of the children to identify which of them were malnourished and would benefit from supplementation.[15] Using the charts and critical judgment, I identified children in need of supplements for growth, and advised the orphanage's staff to begin providing those children with the supplements. Not surprisingly, the children immediately showed signs of improvement after eating the nutrient-packed supplements.[16]

I want to pause in the story to highlight the importance of tracking and analyzing anthropometric data (height [stature for children under age two], weight, and arm and head circumference) and using proper growth charts (e.g., WHO charts) in connection with the care of orphaned and vulnerable children. Such data, in conjunction with someone qualified to interpret and apply the data, helps to identify possible macro- and micronutrient deficiencies, and cases of chronic and acute malnutrition. That information can then be used to guide supplemental nutrition programs and other necessary treatments for the nutrition-related problems.[17] In treating the nutritional deficiencies, it is important to not stop at dealing with severe cases of malnutrition. Excellence-driven orphan care communities need to pay attention to the importance of proper feeding and nutritional practices for all of their children. Failure to provide adequate nutrition, even in mild and moderate cases of malnutrition, can lead to poor growth and development and decreased immunity, which could lead to many other short- and long-term problems.

Now, back to the story. . . . As I continued working with the Haitian orphanage, I knew that we needed to do more than simply supplement the malnourished children's diet with additional nutrients—supplementation should be nothing more than a temporary, stopgap part of a long-term solution. I knew that modifying dietary intake and increasing variety in the diet was the most cost-effective and sustainable solution to achieve optimal health, development, and quality of life for the children. Thus, I knew we needed to change their diet and nutritional practices.

So, after the supplement program began, I observed and analyzed the children's diet for several consecutive days to determine what they were eating throughout the week. I discovered that the children's diet contained very little fruits, vegetables, and protein—just a lot of rice, spaghetti, cereal, juice, and a flour-based porridge for dinner. Seeing poor micronutrient intake and lack of diversity in foods consumed, I started to dive deeper into the orphanage's overall meal patterns and food preparations. I looked at the overall food budget and started to determine which items were of optimal importance and how we could reconstruct the food purchases to increase the children's micronutrient intake.

While analyzing the budget, I realized we were spending a lot of money on things like corn flakes, condensed milk, sugar and ice (used for juice), and meat. Despite spending a lot of money on the meat, none of the orphanage's fifty-six children were getting enough meat to provide them with adequate protein. Though we spent roughly $400 per month on meat, each child only ate about an ounce of meat, ten times a month. This shocked me, especially when I realized we could serve the children one egg every day for the same cost. I also knew it would help them reach a sufficient amount of protein in their diet simply by increasing their consumption of whole grains and beans, which are very inexpensive. Apart from the meat, I was disappointed to find that we were spending more per month on sugar and ice (about $250) than we were spending on fruit.

In an attempt to provide a solution to what I thought to be a simple problem, I repeatedly requested that the staff increase the amounts of fruits, vegetables, and beans in the children's diet. But they continually rejected the idea, arguing that it was too expensive. This didn't add up in my mind because whenever I purchased produce in the local market, it was incredibly *in*expensive. We appeared to be at an impasse.

Since the status quo simply didn't make sense, I decided to sit down with a few of the Haitians—specifically the feeding center director and our Haitian translator—to talk nutrition. As we were talking about what I discovered in the budget and about the importance of increasing fruit and vegetable intake, the Haitian translator stopped interpreting, looked to me, and asked, "Can I say something, Kristina?" "Of course," I said and expressly invited him into our conversation as a full participant. And I'm glad I did. As he spoke, a gold mine full of information unveiled before my very eyes. "I am sick of eating rice every day," he said. My excitement picked up as he started to tell me about different foods, names I had never heard before: pitimi (sorghum), blé (bulgur), Kasav (cassava bread). He spoke with such excitement about these foods; it was obvious to all listening that they brought him great joy. He even placed special emphasis on pitimi (sorghum), telling me how doctors were recommending people to eat it because of its high iron content. Needless to say, he provided much more than great interpreting that day.

Immediately following our conversation, I returned to my computer to do research. I learned that sorghum and bulgur were two "lost grains" in Haiti. So I asked myself, "Why were they 'lost' and why weren't we incorporating these into our children's diets?" Well, it turns out these grains were often referred to as peasant food. As I'd learned in my studies and experiences, people often desire and thus develop a taste for "Western" foods and abandon traditional, native foods and eating patterns as they move out of poverty and into wealthier classes.[18] In our instance, refined carbohydrates and animal-sourced foods (i.e., "Western" foods) were perceived as luxurious foods and preferred over plant-based foods or "goat food" as the children often called it. Unfortunately, the "status" of the food was a barrier to improving the children's actual nutritional intake, health, and development.

After my research, I knew that we had to make some changes in the children's diets, including use of the "lost" grains and other local plant-based foods. By switching the diets of the children to a properly planned, plant-based diet[19] that included moderate consumption of eggs, fish, and smaller amounts of meat or chicken, we would provide increased micronutrient intake and diet diversity for the children, *and* be more cost-effective for the ministry. Fortunately, I was able to convince the staff to make the change, and we began to uncover a number of traditional cuisines (i.e., tchaka). We also made some new "creations" with the resources we had.[20]

RESPECT YOUR ELDERS

Another thing I've experienced during my time in Haiti is that elders in the communities in which I've worked have provided vast amounts of nutritional wisdom. They have wisdom about dietary practices and local resources that will help our children attain optimal health, as well as rich native practices for how to grow, cook, and prepare food in these communities. Clearly then, any excellence-driven orphan care community should use any such sources of nutritional wisdom in their surrounding area, in conjunction with the scientific side of food, health, and nutrition. Seeking wisdom from the elders in our communities, especially the healthy ones, can provide direction and practices to help feed and provide for our children in the best way. Additionally, elders may share information about nutrient-dense foods native to the area that are not commonly utilized or well known by foreign missionaries.[21]

Great nutritional programs must also take into account the local culture, good and bad. In particular, we need to pay close attention to the local folklore and ideologies about food that may be interfering with the ability to provide proper nutrition for the children (some of which will come from the same elders who have great things to offer). One such example is that several staff members at the orphanage thought that eating protein, specifically beans, before bed caused weight gain. Working to understand the traditional cultural practices, current food phenomena, *and* addressing the scientific purposefulness of certain food groups and preparation methods can help to increase a balance between research and culture.

Learning about the food system in Haiti was almost a backward approach for me. While I could write all day about nutritional deficiencies and malnutrition amongst orphaned and vulnerable children, at the end of the day a lot of dietary intake comes back to food systems and cultural ideologies. As I spent more time in Haiti, I realized I needed to stop just "doing" nutrition-related activities, and I needed to really listen to others a whole lot more than I had before. So, that's what I did. I listened to the elders in the community, showed openness and appreciation for their knowledge and was able to learn a lot about true native practices being used amongst community members. And I didn't stop there. Women that worked at the orphanage started picking weeds and bringing me greens to eat. They told me what the greens were used for and how to prepare them. My excitement for their knowledge about the native foods encouraged them to continue using them for their own purpose. Through these and many other conversations and efforts, I learned a lot about the "hidden treasures" of foods that were widely available and being used in many of the surrounding communities. Openness to and appreciation for native foods created opportunities for us to utilize these hidden treasures to improve our children's nutrition and development.

FOOD POLITICS

The longer I stayed in Haiti, the more I learned about food politics (i.e., the political aspects of the production, control, regulation, inspection, distribution, and consumption of food) and its impact on the foods that our children consume.[22] I was introduced to this vast and complex topic as I sought to understand the battle between food aid and food sovereignty (e.g., tariffs on rice that were impacting the businesses of small farmers). As I dove into the topic, I learned more and more about how food is not just about providing nutrition and fueling our bodies—

food is also about power. Imported foods, through aid and businesses, in many developing countries are taking away the businesses of small farmers, and with the farmers go many nutritionally dense traditional cuisines.[23] Learning about the food politics affecting our local community helped me to stand my ground and demand that our orphan ministry take pride in supporting traditional, local farmers and adopt more native cuisines in the nutrition program. I strongly encourage all other orphan care communities to do the same. Knowing that some day our children will be grown, independent, and productive members of society, it is best for them to develop a taste for and knowledge of healthier food options available in their local open-air markets, from their fellow community members. Such food often is not only best for their physical, cognitive, and mental health, but the health of their communities as well.

NUTRITIONAL EDUCATION AND BEHAVIORAL CHANGE

Education

All children should be educated about the role food plays within their daily life and the detrimental effects a poor diet will have on long-term health. In our world today, we see more marketing of processed foods and sugar-sweetened beverages than ever, and more people are choosing these foods over the nutrient-dense options that promote health. Often, such decisions are made due to lack of knowledge about nutrition, and the increased marketing and availability of less desirable products.[24] Teaching children from a young age about the role food plays in maintaining health and implementing these foods into their daily dietary intake will help them to accept, appreciate, and hopefully choose these foods when they someday move out of their home. Also, involving children in the process of food preparation—growing their own fruits and vegetables and cooking meals/snacks—can help children to gain a sense of responsibility and appreciation for foods served in their orphan care community.

Division of Responsibility

Initially, when we started to introduce "new" foods and more traditional meals in the feeding center, there was push back from the children. I often refer to it as the "food wars." With fifty-six children, it was virtually impossible to cater to all of their food preferences at the meals. Together, the feeding center director and I agreed we would follow the basic principles from Ellyn Satter's "Division of Responsibility,"[25] which is a nutritional practice between the parent and the child. It is the parent's responsibility to decide what food will be served and when it will be served. Under this principle, it is assumed that the parents know what is best for their children and what they should be consuming for proper growth and development. Additionally, the child is responsible to decide if she is going to eat and how much she is going to eat. Regardless of the caregiver/child ratio in an orphan care community, it is important to establish and follow the division of responsibility because it helps the children develop their ability to independently regulate food consumption and intuitive eating, both of which are very important to develop in children.[26]

Ultimately, the division of responsibility allows the child to feel secure that there will always be food available, which may help reduce overeating and hoarding for children affected by food insecurity. The division also should encourage children to try new foods and learn about new foods because the parent is responsible for providing the items served.[27] By not allowing children to drive the menu, caregivers can work to ensure their children are getting the appropriate foods to help them grow and develop. Perhaps providing the children the ability to participate in menu planning or selecting from two menu options will further encourage their participation.

For example, throughout my time in Haiti, our children participated in preparing meals and serving food. Such participation allowed the children to learn about the food and to feel some control in the division of responsibility. One evening in particular, as I was helping the night staff prepare a black bean salsa for dinner, a few teenagers were in the kitchen watching and helping me prepare the salsa. They helped chop onions, tomatoes, and green peppers, and mixed them in with the beans. When I told them to add mango to the salsa, they all gasped in surprise that I would even suggest such a crazy thing. So, instead of catering to their preferences based on their limited experiences, I cut a mango and mixed a few slices in a small bowl of the mixture we had already created. I made them sample it and, to their surprise, they actually liked it! As a group, we decided that we would prepare two batches of salsa for the rest of the children—one with the mango and the other without. And we would make all the kids try both. Having a few teenagers already accepting the new creation made it easier for others to be willing to try it at dinner.

Through this experience, we learned that allowing the children to participate in the meal preparation helps them to develop skills to prepare meals for themselves, learn how to create new food combinations, and be more accepting of new foods/combinations that they helped to create. The children in the orphanage became so much more accepting of the "goat food" when they were able to participate in making the food (and even growing it)! And as the children simultaneously learned in classes about nutrition, they were better able to understand my rationale for the dietary changes.

Behavioral Changes

Obtaining optimal food consumption and nutrition for orphaned and vulnerable children may also require behavioral changes amongst the caregivers, kitchen staff, and the children themselves. Generally, people are driven to act in ways that make them feel like they belong. Status, community, and emotion often motivate people to act in certain ways, and sometimes the social pressure has a negative impact on the diet and nutrition. As with the "lost grains," people may choose to eat (or not eat) in a way that makes them appear to be a part of a social class and/or part of a community. Though I cannot deeply address this topic here in this chapter, excellence-driven orphan care communities must develop and implement strategies to address the negative effects of social pressure and work to promote positive behavioral change that impacts the nutritional care of their children.[28]

Food really is about more than just nutrition and health—food is also about emotions and memories, pleasure preferences, power, social class, and systems. In pursuing excellence, we need to be aware of and address this reality.

EQUIPPING TEAMS

Another area we must quickly discuss in our excellence conversation is how to properly prepare for and equip mission teams. With any mission team visiting any orphan care community come the risk that they will view the children as "poor orphan kids" and want to shower them with "treats," often unhealthy snacks and candies high in refined sugars and fats. Week after week during my time in Haiti, I'd see (and I'm sure many of you reading this have seen) well-intentioned team members bring sweets, treats, and processed foods for the children as part of their effort to provide the children with love and affection. As you probably know, there are many reasons why handing out gifts and candy is not a good idea, and nutritional reasons are definitely on that list. One problem that arises from this practice of continually bringing candy, chips, cookies, cakes, and sweetened beverages in place of fresh fruits and vegetables is that it encourages a taste preference for those foods over ones that promote good health and proper development. It should worry any American that white people in Haiti (at least from my experience) are associated with sweet foods.

What can an orphan care community do to equip teams with proper nutritional practices? For starters, it can tell them to not give the children candy or other unhealthy foods. Further, it can share with them suggestions on healthy, local options for foods that they can provide to the orphan care community. In my case, the more teams became aware of the work I was doing, they would contact me before their visit and ask for suggestions on such healthy alternatives. I'd receive e-mails asking me about local foods available that they could purchase in Haiti and share with the children. I could sense that the team members were interested in learning. They genuinely wanted to help promote local "treats" like fresh fruits that the children didn't always get to have, and I could sense that they too wanted to learn about and experience foods they'd never heard of. And as the team members began following my advice, it was nice to also see that the children were just as excited to see kenip and tamarind (two Haitian fruits) as they were to see a piece of candy.

MOVING FORWARD

Identifying and implementing all key aspects of nutrition from diet diversity to behavioral changes surrounding eating and meal preparations will continue to promote best practice in orphan care communities. By incorporating wisdom from elders, enhancing micronutrient intake by utilizing a wide variety of native, plant-based foods, and encouraging the children *and* caregivers to participate in the education, preparation, and serving of health-promoting food options, orphaned and vulnerable children under our care will obtain optimal health that will provide for their present growth needs, prevent future chronic diseases, and give them real opportunities to fully develop their minds, bodies, gifts, and talents.

Going ☀ Deeper

1. How do your personal food choices and knowledge of food and nutrition influence others' meal patterns and dietary intake?

2. Have you done research on the local foods (e.g., whole grains, legumes, whole fruits, and vegetables) in your care community? What are strategies that orphan care communities can take to use local resources rather than food donation or food aid shipped from other countries?

3. How can we best equip staff and children for changes in dietary intake? How can we promote positive changes with education, participation, and positive reinforcement?

Chapter 8

WHAT'S UP, DOC?
(MEDICAL AND DENTAL CARE)

"For vulnerable children, the need for immediate access to health care is of the highest importance. If a child has suffered abuse or neglect, medical and psychological resources must be made available to her as quickly as possible."—Julie Gilbert Rosicky

"More than half of all Africans do not have access to modern health facilities. The result is ten million annual deaths from the four most common preventable diseases: diarrhea, acute respiratory illness, malaria, and measles. In many cases, one simple shot could save a life."—Peter Greer

You'd be hard-pressed to find anyone who would argue that a child could fully develop his or her brain, body, or skills and talents without proper medical and dental care. Despite that reality, most orphaned and vulnerable children in our world today lack such care. In fact, in too many instances, their medical and dental needs are completely neglected.

Consequently, orphaned and vulnerable children typically need a lot of medical and dental attention when they arrive into a family after spending time in an institution or on the street. Often they suffer greatly because of conditions, such as clubbed feet, poor eyesight, gum disease, malaria, diarrhea, and measles, which can be easily dealt with through simple medical or dental treatments (including vaccinations).

To guide us through this important area, I've asked John F. Campbell, MD,[1] and Brent Phillips[2] to share with us their thoughts and lessons learned through many collective years of experience about how we can all pursue excellence—to stop at nothing short of the best we can give and do—when providing medical and dental care for orphaned and vulnerable children in orphan care communities and beyond.

Dr. John, a board-certified internist who has practiced internal medicine and emergency medicine for twenty-two years, has been actively involved with a mission called Asia's Hope since 2002. Through over twenty trips to Cambodia, Thailand, and northern India during that time, Dr. Campbell has established and initiated medical and dental protocol and policies in those countries, where Asia's Hope has twenty-nine family-based homes for orphaned children. Brent has been serving with Cherish Uganda, an orphan care community in Entebbe, Uganda, for the past three and a half years as the Village Pastor/COO. Cherish Uganda serves orphaned children with HIV in its community, and Brent has learned much about medical care in an orphan care community through his experiences with these children.

Get ready to learn because these two men have a lot to teach us about what excellence in medical and dental care can look like for orphaned and vulnerable children.

Medical and Dental Care
(Dr. John F. Campbell and Brent Phillips)

For you parents out there . . . remember the first time your newborn was handed to you in the delivery room? You teared up and got a little sniffly and looked in your baby's eyes lovingly as you said, "I am so blessed. I commit to raise this child in mediocrity. In fact, I seek only the best in mediocrity."

Really? I don't think so. No loving parents purpose to raise their child in a mediocre, half-baked manner. Rather, the first time they see their child, they see that baby taking on the world, becoming a famous president, missionary, lawyer, or statesman. They will spend no less than full energy and very likely considerable fiscal resources to see their child accomplish his or her dreams.

If we are to be the church as God intended it to be, we need to have the same heart for orphaned and vulnerable children—to care for them in the same way. Just as we want our own children to build the kingdom through their giftedness, have a family of their own, and live life to the fullest, we should have the same dreams and vision for the parentless among us. We have an opportunity to change the story, rewrite what the world might have already written, and be a part of changing the world through investing in those that the world has kicked to the curb.

Imagine your world without good medical and dental care. Imagine feeling pain and having no ability to stop it. Imagine feeling sick, having no idea what you are sick with, and having no options. Now . . . imagine excellent care for children who are currently living like that. What does that look like? What does it require? Is it achievable? These questions need to be asked in the context of any discussion about excellence—we'll do our best in this chapter to give practical advice on how to answer them.

Our goals are to initiate a discussion, to pool resources and experience, and to invite others to join us so that we might paint a picture of excellence in the medical and dental care of orphans. As we ponder what best practices look like and study our passions, we see that the motivation that gives birth to excellence is simply this: *we love these kids as our own.*

Before getting into the actual care, we must consider each orphaned and vulnerable child's overall makeup when he or she first enters the orphan care community. Any child finding himself in a newly orphaned situation likely will be stressed physically, emotionally, psychologically, and even spiritually.[3]

Our organizations, Asia's Hope and Cherish Uganda, have found that many recently orphaned children end up in situations where they live with extended family and are treated as unpaid servants for their relatives. In many countries of the world, orphans do not have a very bright future. They are not welcome anywhere, are considered second-class citizens, or worse, are not recognized as citizens by any country. Governmental authorities are not interested in taking care of them or have no resources, so they turn their head, hoping that if they look away the problem will disappear.

Almost universally, the children entering orphan care from such backgrounds are "hug deficient." They can absorb unlimited amounts of personal attention, eye contact, physical touch, love, and affirmation from anyone willing to provide it. Indeed, they seem to sense that they are treated as second-class citizens who do not have a family to watch out for them, and thus, they are desperate for some love, from anyone. They need touch, and they need someone to look them in the eye and tell them the truth. They need someone to start to take away the pain, ease the fear, and start the process of healing.

Can you see the brushstrokes of what the orphaned child is like? Can you begin to imagine his/her attitude and fears as he comes into orphan care? How then do we establish a health care program that cares for them with excellence? Good medical practices take children beyond survival. We too often find ourselves in the place of "making someone better" and do just that—make them better right there in the moment and only give them what they need to survive another day. That's simply not enough.

We are called to help children thrive. To go beyond the immediate need and start to look at their life beyond the blood test and the symptoms they currently are presenting. We can look at the "orphan problem" simply as a problem to address and fix, or we can go deeper and start to look at the beautiful children as our responsibility, not allowing our shortsightedness to get in the way of true healing. Pursuing excellence results in us addressing the medical issue with so much more than medicine and with goals that go far beyond stopping the pain. Every one of these children deserves the same excellence that we dream of for our own children.

To provide a picture of what such excellence might look like, this chapter unpacks the following framework that any orphan care community can use to develop its health care program:

1. Take care of the immediate.

2. Prevent the preventable.

3. Restore the restorable.

4. Establish an ongoing long-term plan for health maintenance, education, and record keeping.

5. Institute policies for critique and review, and commit to make necessary changes in your plan.

TAKE CARE OF THE IMMEDIATE

Excellence begins with *taking care of the immediate*, which is self-evident to most health care practitioners. When a child first arrives, or a group of children arrives, it is incumbent upon the provider to engage in a cursory health assessment to establish that the child is not acutely ill and not likely to be contagious. It also means making sure the child is provided a chance to get cleaned up if they are dirty and provided with clean clothes. These practices care for the child *and* protect the rest of the community from illness and infestations that are difficult to control.

When assessing the children, it is wise to address any pain first. Pain is God's gift to tell us where to begin. A child walking into your door for the first time, or one that you have been caring for over time, will always focus on the pain. If the children's pain is not properly dealt with, it will hinder all treatment going forward and the orphan care community will find little success in its ability to provide meaningful medical and dental care.

In starting to address the child's immediate needs, providers should take care with their reactions (especially in the difficult situations), as their facial expressions, body language, and words will set the tone for the child's care moving forward. Cameras should be kept in their bags and audiences away. The caregiver must do everything possible to restore the dignity that the child has lost. She is entering the orphan care community with much more at stake than her physical health and will need to know that she will be loved, accepted, and cared for as Jesus would love her.

If the child arriving in the community has any extended family with her,[4] the staff needs to obtain as much health and social information (e.g., medical history, contact numbers, family history, location of known family members, religious affiliation) about the child as possible at that time. In the moment this information often doesn't seem priority, but it may be the only chance that the orphan care community has to get it.[5]

Apart from taking care of the immediate upon arrival, the orphan care community's families/caregivers need to be prepared to be the first line of ongoing defense against sickness and injuries. To accomplish this, it is important to have an acute protocol in place. Such protocol should include a "home kit" containing basic information and supplies for house parents and staff to handle simple, nonemergent medical illness or trauma,[6] and a "crash box," containing materials needed for emergency/urgent care.[7] All of the community's caregivers and on-site staff must know the existence and whereabouts of their kits and be trained in the familiarity and use of their contents. This, of course, involves ongoing training and someone tasked to diligently ensure that the contents of the boxes are kept filled and current.

In any excellence-driven orphan care community, the bulk of the responsibility for everyday health care falls upon the parents. This is normal, appropriate, and good. Parents are likely to be first responders and therefore are going to be called upon to use this "immediate care" knowledge more frequently. Best practice demands that the parents in the family homes feel empowered with the knowledge that they can be responsible for making these choices for their family, *and* provide initial treatment and other encouragements to their children. The more they become familiar with routine and their children, and the more they are properly trained in the health care protocols and procedures, the more comfortable they will feel taking on this responsible role.

PREVENTING THE PREVENTABLE

With *preventing the preventable*, let's start with the importance of establishing immunization programs. What sense does it make to spend money on children for shelter, food, education, and other things, only to watch them die of a preventable disease? While an immunization program is important and needs to be done, implementing one is not easy. With such programs come issues and obstacles, all of which must be considered and accounted for when developing the program. These issues and obstacles include the well-defined "life" of the vaccines (i.e., the sera are only happy in certain, limited conditions), the high cost of some vaccines,[8] the difficulty of obtaining vaccines in some countries, and different government agencies may be involved with immunization recommendations that often conflict with each other.[9]

Once the program is in place, the community will need plenty of personnel if it administers the vaccinations on-site. In addition to the people actually giving the vaccines, others are needed to organize and administer the patients in the waiting area, to keep diligent and detailed records (very important),[10] to hold arms still for the injection itself, and to simply provide encouragement.[11] Remember . . . many of the children and staff in the community might have never seen an injection before.

Searching out the serums, getting the money for them, administering them to each child, and keeping good records—that is *excellence*.

Apart from immunizations, an important part of preventing the preventable for any community is to ensure that the campus's environment is safe for the children and caregivers—making sure the water supply is safe and plentiful for washing and drinking; the food supply provides proper nutrition; the food preparation and hygiene is proper; and that other things are in order relating to sanitation—hygiene, living conditions, and overall health.

For instance, in northern Thailand, hill tribe children were sleeping in bamboo structures, which were recently constructed and projected to last three to five years. Everyone was happy until poisonous spiders started migrating into the sleeping area through cracks in the floor. These poisonous spiders triggered an immediate need for a health care response because of the danger to the children.[12] The solution to ensure safe conditions for the children: Build new cement block structures impervious to poisonous spiders. Was it an opportune time to build a new building for the children? Was it the right time fiscally to build a building? Most certainly not, but *in pursuit of excellence*, it prevented additional medical issues.

An additional way to prevent sickness is to maintain good health through training. What might seem very obvious to care providers might not be so obvious to those they are treating. If preventable diseases continue to happen in a particular community, care providers cannot assume that the knowledge necessary to prevent such diseases is present. In fact, excellence requires the providers to assume that the knowledge *isn't* there and take the opportunity to train those who are well in proper hygiene and other necessary things, such as proper hand washing and safe ways to cook, clean, and prepare drinking water. Any assumption that the people know how to do such things and are just ignoring the good advice likely is inaccurate. Not always, but often.

Similarly, excellence requires that one never assume the existence of a common understanding of *basic medical health knowledge*. If the assumption is wrong, it will derail training and treatment. Thus, it is necessary for health care providers to determine that they are speaking the same concepts and vocabulary as the caregivers and children on the medical playing field.

Additionally, it is vitally important that every organization providing care for orphaned or vulnerable children anywhere in the world have and enforce a very clear, simple, and transparent Child Protection Policy. This policy needs to clearly outline limits and guidelines for staff, for youth, and for visitors of any kind, including how the community will resolve alleged infractions, and it must be consistent with any national policy guidelines. The organization also must train its staff, nationals and foreigners, on the ins and outs of the policy on an ongoing basis. In making and implementing the policy, remember that it is in place for *the children's* benefit and protection.[13]

RESTORING THE RESTORABLE

In *taking care of the immediate*, the children have been welcomed to their new home and received triage and basic health care. In *preventing the preventable*, the children have been protected from some future illnesses. Here, in *restoring the restorable*, we now take a look at residual needs of some of these children and determine how to meet these needs with excellence.

A short-term dental team came to assess and treat the children in Asia's Hope's Cambodian orphan care community. Upon arrival, they found that most of their work would be of the urgent variety—abscesses, facial infections, rotting and broken teeth.

"Who's next?" called out the dentist. A scared, uncertain twelve-year-old girl hesitantly came forward and sat down in the dental chair. As she opened her mouth, the dentist immediately knew that her two upper front teeth and two lower front teeth were in bad shape. He was mortified. He looked repeatedly in her mouth, took a deep breath, and left the room. He went into the adjacent room and wept. Why? He knew the teeth had to come out but it distressed him because he knew it would be devastating for the girl to enter her adolescent years having empty spaces instead of her four front teeth. At the time, the dentist had no idea whether restorative dental services were available in the country, but it did not seem likely. The dentist felt that he was sentencing the girl to certain psychological injury from taunting if he pulled her teeth. What to do?

Fortunately, the Asia's Hope staff assured him that because they were committed to excellence, they would ensure that the girl receive restorative surgery if he provided the much-needed dental care. With that assurance, he proceeded with the extractions he knew needed to be done. After a few months spent finding the right people and resources,[14] the Asia's Hope team was able to get their girl's restorative dental work within the year. *This is excellence—treating the child as one of our own.*

Furthermore, *restoring the restorable* is the place where specialized surgical interventions or treatments fit in. This is a great place for short-term surgical mission teams, which can provide interventions or treatments to repair cleft lips, congenital deformities, and many other conditions. Surgical repair of these handicapping or self-image injuring disabilities can do wonders for a child's mental and psychological health. Excellence is clearly served and children are clearly helped.

In this area, as with others, excellent orphan care communities are not afraid to ask for big things when they come into contact with specialists who might be able to help their children. They step into an advocacy role and ask for help for their children. Nothing speaks love like someone fighting for you. This not only creates the possibility of quality care taking place, which the community might not have been able to handle itself. It communicates love to the orphaned/vulnerable child who has rarely (or maybe never) had someone fight for them. Such a showing of love is irreplaceable. It will further build the trust that is so necessary for development in the children's lives.

Excellence in restoring the restorable is also found in simpler things. Like when you spend time with a child and notice that one eye doesn't seem to track properly when he is interacting with you. Here, you have a great opportunity to choose excellence . . . or not. If you go with the latter choice (not recommended), you'll view the lazy eye as an obstacle that is too hard to overcome. The better, excellence-driven choice? See it as an opportunity. Ask questions. Does he need glasses? And even more excellence: are there others like him? How can we provide them with glasses? Get answers. Be creative. A little passion and flexibility to collect glasses goes a long way. All you need is a twenty foot eye chart (you know, the one with the big E), someone who can interpret the eye chart (it's really *not that hard*), and let the fun begin. An expensive ophthalmologic machine is not necessary. And after the testing, when you start passing out eyeglasses, you will be able to tell by the shrieks of glee and the jabbering in a tongue you cannot understand that you have just hit the jackpot!

Sometimes we just need to do something. It is the doing that creates the change. We can often step into a difficult situation with an "all or nothing" mentality, where if we cannot do it all or if we cannot do it the way we are used to doing it, we do nothing. But this helps no one. Obviously we must use good judgment and sound practices, with as much excellence as possible in the given situation, but we have a God that often moves as we move in faith (Josh. 3). So put your feet in the water and try something. (Visit ThinkOrphan.com to read a story about how I [Brent] saved a girl from an unjust execution by simply showing up and saying something.)

When love and justice show up in a situation to restore the restorable, there can't help but be some change. It might not be visible and it might not be the outcome you desire, but gospel-driven love and justice showing up in you and through excellence-driven orphan care communities will bring about transformation, either now or later.

ESTABLISH AN ONGOING LONG-TERM PLAN

With any journey, you need to know your ultimate destination, or you will never be able to know whether you've reached your destination and you'll have no idea where you're going along the way. The journey of providing excellent medical and dental care is no exception to this rule. Best practice requires an orphan care community to establish an ongoing long-term plan to ensure that it knows where it is going and how to get there.

Over time around the world, many orphan care organizations have used short-term mission teams as their strategy to provide health care for their orphaned and vulnerable children. While they can effectively serve many purposes and definitely have their place (e.g., training),[15] short-term medical teams are not very effective for regular, ongoing health care needs and cannot be the foundation of a community's excellence-driven long-term health care plan. The problem is that the children are there 24/7, while teams are only there for short stints, two to three times a year.

Anyone who has ever been sick can conclude that medical care two or three times a year by teams who come halfway across the world is not excellence. Orphan care communities need to resist any urge to allow short-termers to do what only those who are onsite year round can do, even if it might be easier and cheaper for the organization. There is something that comes from a long-term doctor-patient relationship that can't be substituted and shouldn't be pushed aside.

To find quality health care providers, orphan care communities should network with other practitioners in their area, nationals, and missionaries, and evaluate any candidates recommended to them. Through this process, the community should be able to provide a solid base for the delivery of quality care for its children.

Any excellent long-term plan needs to establish goals and define the decision-making process for health care. It needs to provide clear direction for the community about ongoing medical care, ongoing prevention, teaching for independence in hygiene and preventable diseases, ongoing training of the staff, maintenance of the extensive medical network, and organization and maintenance of records.[16] For organizations just starting an orphan care community, these areas of long-range planning can also serve as a framework during initial start up planning.

Long-term planning also needs to explore and determine how to provide care in a fiscally prudent manner (e.g., in-house doctor, insurance, socialized medicine, self-insurance).[17] For example, by exploring the available possibilities and asking a lot of people a lot of questions, Cherish Uganda was able to secure a partnership with the leading pediatric AIDS hospital in Uganda and, through the PEPFAR[18] fund, the Cherish Uganda community receives anti-retroviral drugs (ARVs), follow-up visits, and dental clinics free of charge.

Excellence also demands establishment of a chain of command so that the community's caregivers and staff know *who* they can go to if they have questions, need to obtain medical information, and/or make medical decisions for the child. For instance, with an ill or injured orphan, the house parent first initiates appropriate local care (e.g., acetaminophen, first aid). The policy then will provide the next step(s) of intervention (e.g., contact a physician), if necessary, when that intervention is to be invoked, and who needs to be informed that it is happening.[19]

As these policies and procedures become ingrained in the minds of the staff, house parents, and children, the children will learn that they live in a family-centered environment where their parents will make sure that they get proper medical attention. This provides security for the children, the confidence that they *know* they have someone who loves them and is caring for them. *This is excellence.*

INSTITUTE POLICIES FOR CRITIQUE AND REVIEW, AND COMMIT TO MAKE NECESSARY CHANGES IN YOUR PLAN

One thing about excellence that we need to always remember is this: *Excellence is a moving target.*

Like most everything else, orphan care communities are constantly changing and in flux. Thus, best practice requires that they continually survey their policies and practices, and make any necessary changes to continue on the road to excellence. Remember from high school physics the concept of entropy (i.e., the state of disorder or chaos)? If you need a mental picture, think of a typical teenager's bedroom. If any system is left alone, that is, without any energy input, it will eventually deteriorate to maximum entropy, or maximum disorder—chaos. Therefore, with any system, work must be put into it to maintain its order.

To maintain order in an orphan care community, its plans, policies, experience, and programming should be done in a codified, organized manner. Simply examining key areas at a reasonable, periodic interval (quarterly, semiannually) will go a long way toward keeping the medical/dental care plan (and the rest of the community) in a healthy state.[20] Asking a qualified and competent person from the outside to give an objective opinion of the long-term plan, policies, and procedures also is a great idea. As humbling as this can be, they often will be able to see blind spots and other missing components. In most cases, collaboration and a team approach is better (and more fun). No excellence-driven organization attempts to operate in a vacuum and thinks it can handle everything on its own. That simply is not how the body of Christ works.

Ultimately, if you decide to really pursue excellence in anything, you need to constantly keep tabs on it and cultivate it. But if you pay attention and do your job well, you will find that your hard work will pay off and the *excellence will grow.*

SOME LESSONS LEARNED IN THE FIELD

As we near the end of this chapter, we want to share with you some things that we've learned in the field that will impact the quality and success of any orphan care community's health care plan.

Drug Quality

It pays to do investigative work about prescription medications in the community's area. There's a fair amount of difficulty with counterfeit drugs in Asia, Southeast Asia, and Africa, so one must inquire where the drugs are made. Much of Eastern Europe and Europe uses drugs made in France or Thailand. While those tend to be relatively more reliable, providers still need to be careful of drugs that look improperly labeled. In the end, trust instinct *and* investigative prowess.

Drug Compliance

When prescribing a medication or treatment program, patients often smile graciously and say, "yes, yes." Then, despite the double affirmation, they might take your prescription to the local pharmacist to counsel with him about the course of action. They often will even counsel with all their friends in village or with their family about what to do. They, not the provider, will ultimately make the decision as to whether to fill and follow the prescription or not. Particularly when the prescription comes early in the doctor-patient relationship (or the prescription comes from a doctor/nurse on a short-term team), the patient will often choose to do what a local healer recommends instead of what the doctor recommends. The doctor needs to take this with grace. The patients will watch the doctor more and if she is consistent and maintains a positive, healthy attitude over time, she eventually will earn their trust. Then, she will see things move forward.

Medical care birthed out of authentic, deep relationship will always be more effective than a mere provider/patient relationship. Obviously this can't be done with all children. But for the ones where it can, excellence demands that it be pursued diligently. And how is such a relationship started, built, and cultivated? Through love. Nothing communicates like love. How we speak, touch, and care for children will lead to more good health than any of us realize.

Interpreters

Organizations pursuing best practice in medical care invest in excellent interpreters when a language barrier exists. Accurate and effective interpretation is a special skill that requires a high level of competence in both languages being used. Great interpreters are also confident. An insecure translator often is timid in communication and doesn't ask enough questions to make sure his translation is strong.

Highly skilled and confident translators are difficult to find for normal everyday interpretation and even harder to locate when dealing with health-related issues. Indeed, most interpreters don't feel comfortable translating in the medical context because it involves such a large amount of technical, specialized language. But providers must not let these barriers stop them from finding the excellent interpreters if they are needed to help the providers really communicate with their patients.

Here is a story to show the difficulties one can encounter in the absence of a quality interpreter. During one medical clinic I (Dr. John) was part of in Cambodia, the patient spoke Khmer and the doctor spoke English. Unfortunately, we were unable to find an interpreter competent in this critical Khmer-English language exchange. As an attempted solution, we cobbled together a collaborative approach using three interpreters: a Khmer speaker, a French speaker, and an English speaker. We used a French translator because that was the common language between the Khmer and English translators. Well, here's what happened: the patient's Khmer was translated into French, and then retranslated into English for the physician. Then, the physician's response was translated to French, which was then relayed to the Khmer translator, who then spoke to the patient. Do you remember that telephone game we used to play as children? Can you imagine the distortion of the patient's and doctor's actual words, let alone their meanings, as they passed through so many translators? As you might imagine, it's hard to provide excellent care when you don't even know if you understand the patient's problem, and you don't know whether your patient understands your diagnosis and course of action.

Cooperation and Collaboration

As we've discussed throughout this book, excellence is served by a cooperative and collaborative spirit. If another organization, church, or NGO has a known need or asks for assistance, an excellence-driven orphan care community should be the first to volunteer if it is able. Conversely, if someone is providing a service that the community needs, the community should be willing to ask for this kind of help. We should all look for ways to collaborate and share resources when possible. This is a wiser use of our stewardship responsibility and resources. Don't reinvent the wheel, in a limited economy, use the services of others and offer *your service* to others. *This is excellence.*

Cross-Cultural Realities

Cultural realities change as you move around the globe. Working in a given culture, any organization working cross-culturally must define how its culture differs from the culture it is working in. It also needs to determine how the cultures are the same. Figuring out the reality and implications of those differences is critical to any organization's pursuit of excellence. As an organization, *failing to do your homework and failing to understand cultural "potholes" can frustrate or even terminate an other-*

wise productive work. Further, if you hope to make any changes in the cross-cultural community, you must first understand the people you are working with and develop trust between and amongst each other. Here are a couple ways these cross-cultural realities have played out in our respective medical contexts over the years:[21]

* Virtually all young women (and men) in Southeast Asia are chronically dehydrated to a degree. In an attempt to remedy the problem, I (Dr. John) have urged many of these women to drink more water. However, their initial fervent response is that they will not do so because, "it makes us get fat." They were not to be dissuaded until I was able to establish relationship, earn their trust, and provide them with basic teaching about their flawed understanding of water's impact on their body.

* Cherish Uganda has had similar issues, where local lore has overridden sound medical knowledge and practice. The following falsehoods are common: HIV can be cured by having sex with a virgin; or it is proper to use condoms multiple times. These falsehoods put communities at serious risk and take us backward in our fight for healthy living. But an outsider will have little success simply telling the people that their deeply held beliefs are wrong. Thus, relationship building, basic teaching, and training are must-haves in any organization, as is a good understanding of the local culture and the common misconceptions that exist there.

There are so many more things to watch for and talk about related to culture, and we encourage you to do so with us by joining our conversation about it at ThinkOrphan.com. What we can learn about other people and cultures has no end, and the pursuit of learning it, especially the feeling that results when you see a tiny smile on your friend's face as he realizes "you get it," is truly priceless.

The relevance of culture to health care is this: in providing health care in a cross-cultural setting, we are trying to work intimately with strangers of a foreign culture and get them to adopt new ways that they often consider foreign and quite strange. To accomplish this purpose, *we need their trust.* Therefore, excellence and best practice requires organizations to build deep relationships with its surrounding community members, learn the cultural precepts important in their region and country, learn the cultural dos and don'ts, and implement wisely what they learn.

When Tragedy Strikes

As we work with sick and hurting orphaned and vulnerable children, we also need to remember that our children might not get "better." There might be illnesses we can't diagnose and treat, and our children might even die. We must also remember, though, that even a child's death, in itself, does not constitute failure. No, failure only happens if we fail to love and do all we can to care for our children.

In seven years of caring for children with HIV at Cherish Uganda, my team and I (Brent) have seen many illnesses come and go. And, unfortunately, we have had one child die—Natasha. It was a Thursday and her CD4 (type of white blood cells) counts were low. The doctor asked her to come back on Monday to go on the next line of antiretroviral treatment. She never made it to Monday. That afternoon, she started complaining of a headache, so we treated her headache like we treated every other headache. But this wasn't "every other headache," and later that night she started to fall as she was walking. I found this out when I answered my phone while I was at the airport picking up a short-term team. On the phone was my son, Bo, who had taken Natasha to the hospital. In a panicked voice, he said, "Dad, you need to come right now. Natasha is not waking up." I told him I would be at the hospital as soon as possible and hung up. About sixty seconds later though, my phone rang again. And again, it was Bo.

"Dad, she died."

"What? What do you mean she died?"

"The doctor said she didn't make it."

"I'll be there as soon as I can," I replied.

Click!

I am not sure how fast I was driving, but I could not get there quick enough. The hospital was only a few miles away, but it felt like it took forever for me to get there. As I pulled into the parking lot, the only car there was ours. The back doors were open, with Bo standing there next to the open door. Natasha's mom, Auntie Margaret, was leaning on the hood of the car. As I pulled up next to the car, I could see Natasha's body laying in the backseat. Not wanting to believe Bo, I bolted out of the car, hugged Bo, and went to Natasha to find her pulse, praying the doctor had made a mistake. No mistake. There was no pulse.

Later that night Bo told me what happened that evening:

> We (Auntie Margaret and Bo) put her in the car and she seemed sick, but OK. We helped her into the backseat and she lay down to sleep on the way to the hospital. We then drove up our dirt road. As we got to the main highway and she coughed a weird cough. We pulled into the medical center parking lot and tried to wake her up and she didn't wake up. As Auntie Margaret kept trying I called you, Dad, as I ran in to get the doctor. He came out, checked for her pulse and said she didn't make it and walked back into the clinic, leaving her in the back of the car.

My heart still breaks for Bo and Auntie Margaret having to be the ones to endure those moments. One thing I constantly reminded them of is that they loved Natasha well and did their best. We later found out she died from a very fast-acting strain of Meningitis. There was nothing that could have been done. They gave her excellent health care and she still died. Sometimes it ends that way and excellence was still carried out. You can do everything "right" and the outcome still can be different than desired.

Excellence in medical and dental care doesn't mean that we'll always get it right and provide healing for everyone in our care. But it does mean that we will constantly seek to do so.

BRINGING IT HOME

So, I ask again . . . *What is excellence in medical and dental care?*

It is *not* rocket science. The provision of quality care *should be the assumption* of all health care providers. It should be a *foregone conclusion . . . "a no-brainer." Now read and listen carefully.* The difference between good, quality health care and excellent health care is love and passion. With our children, we provide the extra measure of care that defines excellence because we love our children, and we are passionate about keeping them healthy and balanced as they grow. *This is excellence.*

So, we send this message to orphan care communities around the world: Without the foundation of excellent health care, further ministry and development for children is very difficult. Try teaching a sick child in school—little to no learning will happen. Try teaching a child the things of God as they struggle with pain—they will miss much of the teaching. Try to communicate love while hoping the medical issues will go away—neither will happen. The rest of your work will hinge on how well you care for each child medically. Do all you can to help your staff, board, and donors understand this important point. It is crucial. *Excellent medical and dental care must be a primary concern and your team needs to understand and buy into this priority.*

It is easy to accept the status quo, especially when money seems scarce and good people to help seem few and far between. We live in a broken world that needs people who will join in the redemption that God is already doing. He is looking for partners, people who want to step up and love and care for those He loves and cares for. You won't be alone and, regardless of how daunting the task may seem, know and understand that God desires every child to be loved and provided for. And incredibly, He has chosen you to do that in the lives of those that are around you.

Wow! Can you see the simple grandeur? It is awesome. How about you? Will you join us in this pursuit? As we've learned together, excellence in medical and dental care of orphans is a moving target and thus requires persistence, keen observation, and passion to learn it. Don't shortchange yourself. You do know something about excellence. Be committed to putting that knowledge into practice. Come with your ideas to ThinkOrphan.com, where you not only can see much more on excellence in the areas discussed in this book, but you also can engage in real ways with what we've written about health care in this chapter. Let us sit down around the table and discuss, in an effort to define excellence in a more excellent way.

Going ☀ Deeper

1. In three sentences or less, write down what defines excellence in health care delivery to orphaned and vulnerable children in the culture(s) with which you are familiar.

2. What are the two biggest obstacles that one would face in the implementation of excellent health care, as you have defined it in question 1?

3. What concrete, practical steps would you take to overcome the obstacles listed in question 2 on your way to providing excellent health care?

Chapter 9

Beautiful Hearts and Minds
(Psychosocial Care)

*"Without close and nurturing contact from another human being,
it becomes physically impossible for youngsters to develop optimally
healthy bodies and minds."*—Karyn Purvis

Virtually all orphans and vulnerable children in institutions or on
the streets lack the necessary attachment and bonding with a committed caregiver that every child absolutely *needs before the age of two*,
and their development suffers greatly.

*Each time an infant is held, rocked, fed, and spoken to, brain growth
is stimulated. Each time a child watches colorful scenes or listens to
sounds, her brain circuitry grows and develops. As a child watches her
mother's facial expressions and sees how she interacts with others, she
learns to read the meaning behind other people's faces and behavior.
Without all this vital sensory input, a child's brain circuitry becomes
impaired. That's why children who were neglected and mistreated early
in life so often display delayed learning, social ineptness, attachment
difficulties, aversion to touch or textured foods, poor behavior in noisy
rooms, and even problems handling changes in schedule or plans. . . .
Isolation prevents the circuitry in a child's brain from developing fully,
eventually diminishing the child's ability to concentrate, control his*

emotions, think logically, and process social cues. An infant who is rarely touched or spoken to during the first weeks and months of life can suffer critical mental and behavioral impairments, even death.[1]

In order to overcome the attachment deficits from which all orphans suffer at some level due to separation from their mothers and fathers, orphans always need extra doses of consistent and intentional attachment and bonding from their mother and father, among other things, when they enter a new family. As a result, any best-practice orphan care community must train and equip the parents in how to properly attach with their children and overcome the issues developed early in life. Attachment deficits are only one of the possible psychosocial problems that orphaned and vulnerable children endure due to the harsh realities they face early in life and throughout their childhood. To provide the best possible care for children living in orphan care communities, we must begin to understand the importance of fostering holistic development and psychosocial well-being of each child.

That's why I asked Dr. Karen Hutcheson[2] to help us to understand a bit more about the psychosocial conditions common in orphans and vulnerable children, including behavioral problems, attention problems, mood disorders, lack of optimal cognitive development, and anxiety. Dr. Hutcheson has vast experience and expertise in this area, both personally and professionally. A wife and mother of four children within two years by adoption and birth, Dr. Hutcheson has a master of arts in clinical psychology and a doctorate in clinical psychology from Spalding University, where she specialized in the assessment and treatment of children, adolescents, and families. She has more than a decade of professional experience working with children and families living in underserved populations, residential treatment facilities, foster-reunification programs, and crisis stabilization units. She is experienced in clinical consultation and training in orphan care settings domestically and internationally. Karen has a great deal to teach us about psychosocial care; I hope you're ready to learn.

Psychosocial Support in Orphan Care Communities
(Dr. Karen Hutcheson)

Imagine parenting in a perfect, sinless world. Envision having an endless supply of every possible resource needed to provide care for and raise a child. Picture yourself equipped with every single shred of knowledge related to parenting, child development, attachment, and any other conceivable subject. In our daydream, the world is perfect and all things are perfect. Mommies are perfect and daddies are perfect. Babies are perfect. Toddlers, young children, and teenagers are perfect. Fatal disease never happens and parents don't die. Starvation doesn't exist and children don't die. Greed, corruption, and poverty don't exist, and tiny babies aren't left lying in row after row of unattended cribs. Marriages aren't tarnished or broken, and children don't witness violence. There is no pain, sorrow, or death. Orphans don't exist. Families are just as God intended, and children grow up in safe, stable, and nurturing homes with their loving parents. Relationships are just as God intended them to be—perfect.

Ah, but life is not a dream. We know, all too well, earthly relationships are not perfect, and parenting certainly is not perfect. Babies scream, toddlers whine, and children disobey. Caregivers neglect, abuse, and traumatize children. Disease is epidemic, war occurs, and parents die. Babies are abandoned and children become orphans.

We do not live in a perfect world—yet.

Because of the fall, sin distorted the world and impacted every aspect of human life. Sin corrupted the perfect relationship man had with God and each other. Sin wrecked our brains, debased our psyche, and subsequently corrupted every single human relationship. Sin has irreparably damaged our thoughts, emotions, and behaviors.

Children now enter into a pain-filled world. The marriage relationship between man and woman is convoluted. Subsequently, relationships between mother and child and father and child are fiercely distorted. Bonding, attachment, and familial security are not promised to a child, and not every child is raised in a safe, stable, and nurturing family.

In the face of these common realities, the glaring need for psychosocial care seems obvious. But for many caring for children around the world, they somehow don't see the need. Or, more likely, they see or feel the need and have no idea how to fill it.

Ajani's Story

Meet Ajani,[3] a young boy who lives in an orphan care community in East Africa. He was likely between the ages of four and six when he started living there. Not much is known about Ajani's past. He was severely malnourished and physically underdeveloped when the staff first met him. He is clumsy and cannot talk very well. Ajani does not like to be touched and is highly reactive to loud noises. He is unable to make eye contact with caregivers or other kids, and he often starts fights with peers. He has difficulty eating most foods and often steals food and hides it in his sleeping area. Ajani has severe nightmares and at times uncontainable bouts of aggression.

This portion of the story is similar to many orphans in orphan care communities around the world. Many of the characteristics of the heart of an orphan described in Appendix C were well rooted and commonplace in Ajani's life. Children like Ajani often find themselves rejected and isolated from children, staff, and teachers. What can be done? Before beginning to answer that question, we need to go deeper into Ajani's and each of our children's lives.

In Ajani's case, just before entering his orphan care community, people found him tethered to a tree in a remote area near a small village. He had deep lacerations and significant scarring on both of his arms and legs from being tethered. The exact details of Ajani's history are uncertain, but it is likely that he spent the majority of his days similarly tethered to a tree with very restricted movement, receiving minimal sustaining nourishment, and at best, extremely negligent care.

Like many orphans and vulnerable children, Ajani, at first glance, appears to simply be a disruptive and problematic child. If we stop there and simply look at Ajani without considering his experiences with caregivers early in life and his unique developmental history, if we refuse to see the strength that allowed him to survive the first four to six years of his life, then we miss any impairments and deep fears that bring about his problematic and unhealthy behavior. And more importantly, we miss the deeper understanding of Ajani's behaviors, and we are less likely to be able to provide the care, support, and foundation for his healing.

Ajani, along with millions of orphans around the world, is in desperate need of strategic and intentional care if he is to be brought to a place of healing where he can thrive in relationship with God and other people. That is the goal of psychosocial care.

WHAT IS PSYCHOSOCIAL CARE?

Psychosocial, psychological, psycho-anything often ends up translating to the everyday person as psychobabble. Psychological terminology and jargon can be confusing, intimidating, and even controversial. Believe me, I know. Even as an adoptive mother who is a clinical psychologist, I remember well how terrifying and often discouraging it was to read books, scholarly articles, and less than scholarly blog posts about attachment, development, and psychological well-being as my husband and I prepared to welcome our two children from Ethiopia into our home. While I understand the feelings, I also know that psychosocial care is a very accessible concept for everyone and we should not let it overwhelm us.

The term "psychosocial" refers to the close connection between psychological aspects of a child's development and the wider social experience of that child. It is grounded in the idea that multiple aspects of development impact psychosocial well-being. The focus of care and support is on the holistic experience of a child, including areas of a child's biological, emotional, spiritual, environmental, social, and psychological development.

Psychosocial support involves a continuum of care, provided by caregivers, friends, teachers, health care providers, and community members. In some situations, it includes more specific care offered by specialized psychological and social services. Psychosocial support aims to increase resiliency in children and to create an integrated developmental approach to promoting psychosocial well-being and healthy child development.

Plain and simple, psychosocial support is being the heart of God to children. It is providing genuine love and care for the holistic development of a child. Children living in orphan care communities have all experienced a life-altering loss of family, and many have experienced other types of abuse, neglect, or trauma. They hurt, and we need to help them heal and thrive by providing a safe family environment filled with consistent, nurturing care.

PSYCHOSOCIAL SUPPORT LIVED OUT

What does psychosocial support look like? It takes on many forms, many of which don't involve a professional therapist. Psychosocial support is intently listening to a little girl talk about her school day or purposefully playing a game with a young boy. It is providing comfort and genuine concern to a crying teenager. Psychosocial support is teaching an aggressive boy healthy and appropriate ways to manage his anger and sadness. It is directing a young girl to the promises of God even when many things in her life seem hopeless. Psychosocial support is providing an environment where a child can learn to trust his caregivers. This trust then provides the foundation for healthy relationships, fosters self-worth and healthy development, and cultivates an identity based in Christ.

For Christians, a fundamental objective of psychosocial support is to help create within a child a foundation firmly grounded in the amazingly wonderful grace and knowledge of Jesus Christ so that a child hears and understands she is a precious, planned, and known child of God. Our prayer as providers and helpers to children living in orphan care communities should be that every child, through his inheritance of faith, knows that he is "fearfully and wonderfully made" (Ps. 139:14). Psychosocial support focuses on establishing a child's identity in Christ—our everlasting Father, our comforter, and our Redeemer. It helps develop unique skills and talents, and encourages children to use their gifts to glorify and honor God in all relationships and every realm of life.

Psychosocial care is pouring into each and every child's heart, mind, and soul with intentional and genuine love and care so that he knows his preciousness—his value, apart from the difficulties he has likely endured. Intentional nurturing and dependable care help children learn to have healthy relationships and promote healthy development.

DO WE REALLY NEED PSYCHOSOCIAL CARE?

We live in a complex world. And we know from what we have seen throughout this book that the global issues related to orphan care are complex. The sheer number of children living without a family is mind-boggling and sometimes paralyzing. Existing systems and regulations related to providing care for children without families often create structures that seem impossible to change or improve. Cultural expectations and international differences related to raising children are vastly diverse. Lack of resources for basic needs, lack of safety, lack of family, lack of community support, lack of access to education, and a variety of other deficits, result in an environment where survival often trumps best practice. Comprehensive care for healthy child development and psychosocial well-being become an afterthought.

For many it feels like enough work simply to provide basic needs and maintain a working staff. The number of orphaned and vulnerable children is too vast. Most underdeveloped countries do not have psychologists or social workers with extensive education, training, and clinical supervision. In considering all of these factors, it is easy to become overwhelmed and give up when considering the complexities of providing psychosocial care to orphan care communities.

But we cannot give up! We cannot be satisfied by simply understanding the problem, or do nothing because we are intimidated or paralyzed by fear or sheer volume. We must never allow our feelings in the face of these harsh realities to cause us to lose sight of this important fact: Psychosocial care and support is a vital component of ongoing care and overarching healthy development for all children. Without it, children simply cannot reach their full potential.

Since you are reading this book, I suspect you agree that change and improvement are necessary and possible. Simply helping children survive, or offering even mediocre care, cannot be considered best practice or excellence. If you do indeed believe that excellence for orphaned and vulnerable children demands more than mediocrity, then excellent psychosocial care must be a priority in any excellence-driven orphan care community.

A GREATER NEED

In most developed countries, when a child lives in a safe, stable, nurturing home, he does not require psychosocial support above and beyond the care and support offered by his family, mentors, teachers, or various other positively influencing people in his life. But, the need for intentional psychosocial support is exponentially greater for children who are living or have lived without families.

Why? Because children separated from their families, both those living on the streets and those living in institutions, are more likely to be treated as insignificant and experience violence, abuse, and exploitation.[4] Children living without families in institutions are generally at a greater risk for neglect and isolation, both of which drastically impair brain development and diminish a child's ability to concentrate, regulate emotions, think logically, and process social situations.[5] There are no longer questions or maybes related to the devastating consequences of neglect and isolation in early child development. We know that isolation is more developmentally damaging to an infant than early mistreatment.[6] We also know that children living without families in orphanages are more likely to have developmental learning delays, social impairments, and coordination and motor skill problems.[7] An analysis of seventy-five different studies on almost four thousand children in nineteen different countries shows children who grow up in orphanages have a substantially lower IQ (twenty points lower) than their peers reared in foster families.[8]

Without argument, children without families have a greater need for psychosocial care. While all children can benefit from aspects of psychosocial support, such care is particularly critical for the psychosocial well-being of orphaned and vulnerable children without families.

BUILDING A SKYSCRAPER OF EXCELLENCE

Like architecture, best practice in psychosocial support in orphan care communities is a broad and complex topic. Implementing best-practice psychosocial care in orphan care communities can be compared to teaching a person with no history or knowledge of architecture construction guidelines, material requirements, and the skills for building a house—a skyscraper at that. And, the framing, shaping, and construction of this really tall building would all occur on a piece of land where the soil conditions and composition for the foundation of the building is unknown and likely unsteady at best.

Do you see the comparison? Best practice in psychosocial support in orphan care communities is an extensive topic, and it requires education, training, and skill. We could write entire books—volumes of books—related to this topic, but the range of this chapter is just too small. (But you can read many more details and ideas about excellence in psychosocial care at ThinkOrphan.com.) Excellence in psychosocial care is essentially proposing ideas for how to best raise a child in an orphan care community—a task that standing alone is incredibly complex. This is particularly true when you consider the layout of orphan care communities, where the complex psychosocial concepts have to be implemented in a setting where house parents will also be taking care of possibly eight, ten, or twelve other orphans, foster children, or children by birth. And piled on top of all of that is the fact that every orphan living in the orphan care community has at minimum experienced the traumatic loss of a caregiver and has likely experienced multiple other types of loss, abuse, neglect, or trauma.

Like many of you, I would have no idea where to start building a skyscraper. If the task were placed in front of me, I wouldn't even want to think about it. I'd pretend it didn't exist and focus my efforts on other things. I would simply say that I'm not a builder. I know nothing about architectural design or construction. Honestly, I can barely put a LEGO house together. But, if I start to understand the desperate need to build the skyscraper, if I start to understand why it is so important that I consider the nature of the soil, the environmental conditions, and the goal for the design of the building, and if I know that I am not building this skyscraper alone, then I press on. I start reading and researching. I find skilled, experienced people to help me. I start learning. And, most importantly, I trust and pray that my insufficiencies will be overwhelmingly surpassed by God's sufficiency and His solid foundation that stands firm. (2 Tim. 2:19 NIV).

In this chapter, we are not going to be able to teach or train you to build the entire skyscraper. We're really only going to scratch the surface with a hope of showing you how to start, on some level, providing excellent psychosocial care for children living in orphan care communities. In no way do I believe that I have the answers. My hope is that I can share an overview of some ideas that will frame and start a dialogue about best practices for these issues where iron can sharpen iron through collaborating, challenging ideas, and encouraging words. Let the sharpening begin!

TRAINING AND EQUIPPING CAREGIVERS

Training and education for caregivers is the starting point and most important aspect of providing best-practice psychosocial care in orphan care communities. I realize for some countries and organizations this may sound as attainable as jumping to the moon. No one wants to staff an orphan care community with undertrained staff, but in some cases, there may be no other options. Regardless of the training and knowledge level of the staff, best practice includes specific psychosocial care training focused on, among other things, healthy child development, risk factors to development, attachment, correcting behavior, and self-care.

Because we are not able to outline the specifics related to training in this short chapter, I have included details related to essential areas of training at ThinkOrphan.com. In addition, I emphatically recommend using the Trust-Based Relational Intervention® (TBRI®) materials, developed by Dr. Karyn Purvis and Dr. David Cross at the TCU Institute of Child Development. If you have not heard of this intervention or model of training, please look it up. Find a way to access this incredibly relevant, useful research based information.

In the end, I hope this book will enable caregivers and orphan care communities to create connections and an overarching online resource base that will facilitate such training by providing ways for caregivers to consult with each other, find people willing to travel and provide training, and share strategies. But we know that the majority of orphan care communities currently have no access to quality training. How can caregivers in these communities begin to offer better care *now*?

To start, caregivers must take care of themselves. Providing care to children living in orphan care communities is complex, demanding, and emotionally draining. Regular, healthy self-care strategies equip caregivers to provide the best possible care for children. Biblical faith development through worship, discipleship, and other spiritual disciplines are essential components of self-care. When we help caregivers learn to deal with stress, burnout, and other personal problems the quality of care provided to children living in orphan care settings improves.

Many caregivers have unresolved or even unaddressed issues of abuse, neglect, trauma, or loss. And, often caring for children with difficult pasts brings up these unresolved issues. Sometimes, these unresolved issues cause problems in bonding or forming a healthy relationship with a child, and subsequently caregivers are unable to provide the care a child needs. Caregivers can start to take better care of themselves by intentionally considering their caregiving style, patterns of interaction with children, and overarching attitude toward providing care to all children living in the orphan care community. Why am I reacting in this way? Why do I respond in a certain way? When caregivers engage in this type of caregiving self-assessment, they may be able to see patterns related to difficult care giving situations.

It is also vitally important for caregivers to receive outside feedback. An outside assessment is similar to a mentoring relationship for a caregiver. It provides an opportunity for a trusted, valued person to speak into a caregiver's life. This type of assessment and mentoring provides feedback that is focused on improving the caregivers' overall wellbeing, empowering and equipping caregivers to provide the best possible care for children. This mentoring relationship combined with specific caregiving feedback also creates an opportunity for training and faith development.

Children living in orphan care communities have complicated histories, many of which we will never know. In difficult situations, children learn unhealthy strategies for surviving that are displayed through disruptive behavior. Many times children with problematic behaviors are unable to effectively express their needs and as a result are misunderstood. When providing care for children living in orphan care communities, we must strive to see the needs behind problematic behaviors. In doing so, we will develop deeper levels of compassion, strengthen our bond with each child, and ultimately become better equipped to provide care and support to children.

Caregivers need to take time to intentionally listen to children and purposely speak into their lives. Caregivers can take creative opportunities to play together and talk together, while maintaining consistent and structured time together. When the caregiver-child relationship starts to strengthen due to intentional caregiving and a safe, stable, nurturing home environment, children begin to show little glimpses into their lives. Then, caregivers can meet the child right where he or she is and continue the journey of healing together.

ONE STEP CLOSER TO JESUS

To provide best care for children in orphan care communities we must be mindful of a each child's heart, mind, soul, and strength. When caregiving in orphan care communities models the sacrificial love of Christ, children learn safety and trust. We were created in the image of the triune God who existed in community before He ever created the world. We are not isolated beings; we need fellowship and relationships with others. Children need to be safe, loved, and cared for consistently.

Our goal in providing care for children is to model Christ's love and to help create a base from which each child's identity is firmly grounded in Christ Jesus. We must remember that there are no quick fixes, and merely changing behaviors will not heal deep wounds. The common grace given to us through research and experienced and well-trained clinicians is an essential component to healing traumatic loss and deep wounds. Our goal must be nothing less than healing for the whole child—and ultimate healing by grace through faith. By providing comprehensive psychosocial care, we can give children the gift of real hope, as we teach them about and direct them toward the source of everlasting hope in Jesus Christ.

NEEDS TO CONSIDER

To achieve excellence, everyone working with children in orphan care communities needs to consider, understand, and apply some basic overarching concepts related to healthy child development and psychosocial care. Here is a nonexhaustive[9] list of several of these concepts:

* Many children living in orphan care communities may appear to be a certain age physically, but in other areas of development (emotional, behavioral, social, cognitive, spiritual) they are much younger. They are playing catch-up in all of these areas of development.

* Children thrive in safe, nurturing, stable environments.

* Developing healthy attachments is the most important factor in a child's life.

* Healthy connection with caregivers helps children develop trust, heal from past wounds, and experience a deep sense of felt safety, self-worth, and empowerment.

* Where physical, mental, social, and emotional needs are met, children will learn best.

* Most children thrive in structured and expected environments.

* Children need help planning and changing routines.

* Providing good nutrition, hydration, and regular snacks helps children in all areas.

* Playing with children (including sports, drama, art, dance, and storytelling) is a great way to build communication, trust, and facilitate healing and growth.

* Children need to be taught how to have healthy relationships.

* Daily attachment rituals or bonding experiences with caregivers (eating together/reading a Bible story after breakfast/going on a walk before dinner/playing outside before lunch) encourage healthy relationships and development.

* Caregivers need to model appropriate and healthy social skills.

* Understanding what motivates a child's behavior is crucial for proper shepherding.

* Nurture, guidance, and emotional support are consistently needed.

* Attainable limits and specific expectations must be set.

* Caregivers must be aware of histories that involve sexual trauma and the risks of the children engaging in or being exposed to sexual play or sexual acting out behaviors.

* Providing developmentally appropriate, biblically based education regarding sexual development helps protect children.

As you might imagine, there is a multitude of additional information that goes with each of these bullets. Fortunately, you can get more information, stories, and materials covering all of these issues on the psychosocial care section of our collaborative website, ThinkOrphan.com.

UNDERSTANDING ATTACHMENT

Another concept we need to understand in providing psychosocial care is that every single orphaned child deals with attachment issues at some level. For some, "attachment" is an unknown concept. For others, it is a scary and misunderstood term. But it does not have to be.

Attachment, at its core, is the idea that a special bond is created between an infant and caregiver. According to contemporary understanding, attachment is formed when a specific parent or caregiver responds in an effective and timely manner to his or her baby's needs. Bonding with a caregiver begins (or does not begin) within the first moments of life and continues (or does not continue) throughout infancy and child-hood (from birth to two years of age). Early nurturing and consistent care helps an infant learn about his environment and learn to trust his caregiver. It also helps his tiny brain develop. A break in this primary caregiver relationship can lead to attachment deficits and problems.

Optimally, all children need to receive nurturing, consistent care during the first two years of life.[10] But, if it doesn't happen, the future for a child is not hopeless. The human brain was created in an amazing way. It is flexible and has the ability to change—physically, functionally, and chemically—throughout life. Children are resilient and are able to make developmental gains in a safe environment with the healing power of new, healthy relationships, particularly relationships with at-tuned caregivers who provide consistent and intentional nurture.

But it's not easy. And it takes long-term commitment. Orphan care communities with nurturing family-based home settings can be a healthy way to start mending the foundation for healthy development.[11]

UNDERSTANDING LOSS

When dealing with loss, it is essential for directors, staff, and caregivers to understand the psychosocial issues associated with the loss of a par-ent or caregiver. At minimum, those working with children in orphan care communities will see children who are sad and confused. Chil-dren will be angry. Children will hit, kick, and bite. Children will lie. Children will not listen and will have problems learning. Children will scream and run away. Children will attempt to harm staff, each other, or themselves. All of these emotions and behaviors will be at a level far more intense than what is expected from normal child development. And all of these emotions and behaviors will manifest themselves dif-ferently in different children, at different ages and stages.[12]

Understanding where a child comes from in terms of loss helps caregivers gain compassion for a child's disruptive or unhealthy behav-iors, and builds a stronger bond with the child. Staff and caregivers must be patient and willing to listen. They must be sensitive to and in control of their own emotions and actions. They must not respond with anger or harsh, physically punitive consequences. They must be sensitive to the lingering effects related to grief, loss, and abandonment. Ultimately, best practice psychosocial care in orphan care communities must address the significant and valid psychological problems and issues that many children will endure due to their difficult histories and attachment deficits.

WALKING THROUGH CRISIS

A word of caution: When providing psychosocial care, it is hard to talk with anyone about the sovereignty of God during most situations involving crisis. And I would not recommend using this strategy or tactic if you are providing counsel or even simply sitting, listening, or talking to someone during a crisis situation. All too often well-intentioned people make comments related to the sovereignty of God to those enduring situations of deep pain and suffering, and usually it is not helpful. While I most assuredly believe in the veracity of God's sovereignty, there is a time and a place for this course of dialogue and biblical truth.

Even the strongest of faith usually have some moments if not extended moments of the head-heart disconnect during a traumatic crisis. We know God is sovereign. We know He holds all things in His hands. We know all things work together for good, for those who are called according to His purpose (Rom. 8:28). Cognitively, intellectually, and faithfully we know these truths. But, in crisis, biblical truth related to the sovereignty of God often is really difficult to grasp. We feel sadness, confusion, anger, despondence, or many other emotions related to the crisis, and the head-heart disconnect occurs. We may know all of the wonderful truths of God's divine plan for our lives, but it still does not feel joyous or good. This is a normal response.

I share these bits of information because all children living in orphan care communities have experienced loss. If we as educated (and many of us well-churched adults) have difficulty wrestling with the sovereignty of God during crisis and traumatic situations, then it shouldn't surprise us when children, teenagers, and young adults living in orphan care communities are unlikely to grasp the idea that God is in control of all things during a traumatic event or memory.

I am not suggesting that any of us providing care for children in orphan care communities skirt biblical truths or provide a watered-down version of the gospel. Rather, I am imploring us to stop solely giving children, particularly children in orphanages and orphan care communities who have experienced trauma and loss, clichéd statements or a systematic shorthand. These proverbial statements are almost always outside of the capacity of a child's or even most teenagers' cognitive and faith development.

Instead, let's show love and compassion. When a child is experiencing a traumatic event or memory, if simply listening and providing a safe environment for him to grieve or talk is not sufficient (which it often is), try one of these options (feel free to make any necessary changes to provide for culturally relevant terms of endearment, concern, and care):

"I am so sorry this happened to you, sweetheart."

"I do not know why (this bad thing) happened, but I know that you did not make this happen."

"It's okay to be mad or sad."

"You are safe here."

"You are safe."

"I want you to know God loves you, and He has not left you. Even if it feels like He does not love you, I promise you He does. Even if it feels like He has left you, He has not."

"You are not alone. I am right here too. I will be with you for (give a specified amount of time)."

In so doing, you will go a long way down the path of reaching the child's heart and soul and take another step toward healing.

SPECIALIZED PSYCHOSOCIAL SUPPORT

As we have discussed, while caregivers and others in the children's lives can provide some psychosocial care and support, many children living in orphan care communities will require levels of psychosocial support above and beyond that of caregivers. Due to attachment deficits and other risk factors, children will need specific psychosocial care provided by a trained psychologist or social worker. Despite this huge need, the reality remains that access to well-trained or consistent psychological or social services is rare in most orphan care community settings. Again, however, we cannot give up because we know that excellence and best practice in psychosocial care often takes the form of trained workers, and we thus must continue pursuing that goal in our orphan care communities. If our goal is to move away from relief-minded institutional care, psychosocial support at every level of care must be considered a crucial and necessary component to providing comprehensive care.

Providing psychosocial care for sensitive issues with a child requires skill, experience, and specific training. If we try to care for those issues without proper training, we take the risk of drilling holes in a hurting child's heart and leaving him in a worse state of pain or turmoil. A well-intentioned but untrained person exploring sensitive issues such as traumatic loss, abuse, negligence, or other areas of trauma can very easily provide more hurt than help.

Some settings have a government issued "psychologist," which often consists of an undergraduate degree or possibly on rare occasion a two-year graduate degree. This is a much different and lower standard related to the educational, clinical training, and licensure process required in developed countries. Other orphan care settings have a clinician visit an institution once a month to provide services, which, as you can imagine, would be very difficult and likely ineffective for such a large number of children. Building a trusting and safe relationship is a vital component to providing psychosocial care for any individual, but it is especially important when working with children, particularly children who come from hard places. If a clinician pops by once a month and only sees a child a few times a year, then his work is virtually pointless, and the children receive incredibly substandard care.

To reach excellence and best practice, individuals providing in-depth, specialized psychosocial support in orphan care settings should be professionals who love Jesus, operate out of a biblical worldview, and have proper education and training focused in clinical child psychology or clinical social work.

The goal of specialized psychosocial care is absolutely not to "Americanize" children. All specialized psychosocial care in orphan care communities needs to be culturally sensitive and applied contextually. People in different cultural contexts perceive, understand and make sense of experiences in different ways, based on distinct norms, beliefs, and values. In this way, psychosocial care is closely linked to culture because the ways in which people experience, give meaning, and express psychological distress are tied to specific social and cultural contexts. Healing, growth, and healthy development are not defined by American culture or standards. Nor is psychosocial care.

Best-practice specialized psychosocial care is holistic, addresses all aspects of a child's development, is tailored to the age of a child, and includes caregivers. Ideally, care should occur in a stable, supportive environment with the participation of caregivers who have a solid and continuing relationship with the child. Including caregivers in specialized psychosocial care will be a vital component to strengthening the attachment bond between parent and caregiver. Caregivers and staff, with the help and training from a professional, must come alongside children living in orphan care communities and lead them into a relationship of trust and healing. It is through this process, and as a result of these renewed relationships, that a child will discover true, life-changing hope.

WHERE SHOULD AN ORPHAN CARE COMMUNITY START?

Where should an orphan care community seeking excellence in psychosocial care begin its pursuit? The community should start where it can. Maybe start by simply trying to understand the main issues related to child development, attachment, or trauma. Maybe by sending e-mails or having Skype sessions with other orphan care communities or professionals to brainstorm ideas about where its specific orphan care community can start based on its current staff, needs, funding, and resources.

Maybe the community can network and try to find someone like me who is trained and willing to travel internationally to help provide basic or specific training to staff and caregivers. Maybe the organization can write a grant or raise funds with a goal of sending a staff member to secondary school or a university to study child development, social work, or psychology. Maybe a layperson within the agency can receive basic training to provide as much care as possible and appropriate.

All of us must start somewhere and work toward the goal of a high level of psychosocial care through individuals who are trained and equipped. Hopefully this book will create a recurrent dialogue where questions like this can be asked and other orphan care communities can share ideas and approaches.

CARING WITH HOPE

There is hope for children living in orphan care communities. I like to talk about little "h" hope, and big "H" hope, especially when discussing aspects of child development. Little "h" hope is the hope of intentional, research-based interventions, holistic psychosocial support, and the healing power of healthy human relationships. The relationships are the most important part of the little "h" hope, as no program, curriculum, or workbook will ever trump the power and importance of a safe, stable, and nurturing relationship with a caregiver, a teacher, a pastor, a mentor, or any individual involved in a child's life.

The big "H" hope is ultimately the Hope we have in Jesus, our wonderful counselor, our gracious Redeemer, and the glory of God. The fall was not a surprise to God. He did not frantically brainstorm to create a plan B for mankind. Sin was at all times a part of God's plan because Jesus was at all times part of God's plan. God's sovereign plan for humanity is and always has been salvation through His perfect son Jesus Christ—our adoption into His family as heirs with Jesus, and the redemption of all things broken by the fall and sin.

As we move forward, let's work together to provide a safe, consistent, nurturing environment filled with compassion rooted in a genuine concern for each child's hurts and needs. Let's teach, train, and equip people working with orphans to provide care for their children in developmentally appropriate ways. Let's share the depth of the riches and the wisdom and the knowledge of God (Rom. 11:33). Let's be the heart of God for children living in orphan care communities.

Going ☀ Deeper

1. What specific ways can you, your ministry, church, and/or organization intentionally support or provide best-practice psychosocial care to children in orphan care communities?

2. When considering an orphan care organization with which you partner, through prayer, financial support, employment, consultation, or other ways, what obstacles or lack of resources would be or are barriers to providing best-practice psychosocial care? How can those obstacles be overcome? What specific steps can you take to help overcome the obstacles?

3. After reading this chapter, in what ways, if any, have your views changed regarding psychological or psychosocial care for children living in orphan care communities?

4. Providing care and support for caregivers of children living in orphan care settings is essential for best practice. How can you or your ministry, church, organization, or orphan care setting come alongside caregivers and help to facilitate this crucial self-care, mentoring, and Christ-centered support?

Chapter

10

CULTIVATING HOME-GROWN LEADERS (NATIONAL LEADERSHIP)

"When the vision for community improvement is championed by indigenous leadership and when that leadership has the capacity to both organize and execute community projects, sustainable progress can be realized. Supporting local leadership builds capacity. . . . Identifying and joining energies with a trusted visionary leader increases the chances of lasting impact."—Robert Lupton

"The poor, no matter how destitute, have enormous untapped capacity; find it, be inspired by it, and build upon it."—Robert Lupton

High-capacity, healthy national leadership is a critical aspect of any best-practice-driven, long-term, sustainable solution to issues in the developing world.

In orphan care communities, national leaders serve as role models and mentors to their children, and others in their surrounding community. Even without words, they demonstrate to their children and communities in real ways that leadership, and capacity for local leadership, exists even in the most impoverished communities—even in people just like them. Local leadership is also able to mentor and develop those same people in the community into future leaders of the project or leaders in their local communities in a way that foreigners simply cannot, due to gaps in cultural norms and knowledge, among other things.

The national leader, as compared to a foreigner, also creates opportunities for greater and deeper buy-in and ownership by the surrounding community in any project—buy-in and ownership that are necessary for any project to thrive over multiple generations.

This is not to say, however, that Americans and other foreigners do not have a place in global ministry. Indeed, foreigners can add much wisdom, expertise, and practical experience to an orphan care ministry, and can even effectively help to lead such a ministry. A foreigner's work just needs to be done in ways that intentionally empower the national leadership—working *with* nationals, not simply doing the work *for* them.

Whether a foreigner or a national, our collective goal should be to work together as peers, as we would with any brother or sister in our own hometown. We need to build each other up, complement each other's strengths and weaknesses, and support each other. We need to share with each other, pray with each other, mourn with each other, and rejoice with each other.

It will take a lot of time.

It will take a lot of energy.

It will be really difficult at times.

And it will be really worth it.

A great example of national leadership working with excellence in conjunction with foreigners is New Hope Uganda, a ministry that for over twenty-five years has been "bringing the Fatherhood of God to the fatherless" children of Uganda. This is why I have asked my coauthor, Keith McFarland, to write this chapter along with New Hope's cofounders and leaders, Jonnes Bakimi and Jay Dangers.[1] The unlikely partnership and lifelong friendship between these two men has resulted in a ministry that has brought hope and family to thousands of orphaned and vulnerable children. In this chapter, they impart insights from their experience in Uganda that provide food for thought (and action) about national leadership and cross-cultural relationships for orphan care communities and advocates, regardless of where they are in the world. These men have many collective years of wisdom on how to lead with excellence—soak it in as you read the pages that follow.

National Leadership
(and Cross-Cultural Relationships)
(Jonnes Bakimi, Jay Dangers, and Keith McFarland)

Emmanuel Orphan Homes has one vision: *raising up the next generation of leaders*. Virtually everything the leadership preaches and teaches revolves around this vision. *Leaders walk with confidence. Leaders talk with boldness. Leaders do well in school.* The leadership's vision is to see their children taking positions in government and other places of influence around the country. On the surface, it all sounds and looks great. Unfortunately, though, something vital is missing. It has a problem that will make fulfilling its vision very difficult, if not impossible—its own leadership does not understand, implement, and model healthy leadership to the children it is attempting to raise up into leaders. This all-too-common leadership problem results from the fact that the ministry's entire leadership structure is driven by a flawed view of what leadership is at its core.

While Emmanuel is not an actual orphan home, it typifies how foundational misunderstandings about the nature of true leadership negatively impact our ability to develop our children into gospel-driven leaders. It represents and reflects many orphan care ministries in our world today that say one thing and do another with regard to leadership.

Through this chapter, so that we can avoid similar disconnects between vision and reality, we will unpack some of the flawed leadership views and practices that plague our world today, other barriers and obstacles to healthy leadership, *and* the qualities of healthy national leadership and cross-cultural relationships in orphan care communities. Drawing from the lessons we've learned over the years through the ups and downs of our first orphan care community, the Kasana Children's Center, we will explore various cultural issues in leadership and what the leadership of any orphan ministry around the world should pursue on a local and cross-cultural level. We will also address various cross-cultural issues that nonnationals and nationals alike need to understand and overcome to function in true partnership and relationship.

I say *we* and *our* because I am writing this chapter with two co-authors. Jonnes (pronounced "Jones") Bakimi is a Ugandan and Jay Dangers is an American (more of an American who is now part Congolese-Ugandan), and together they have been laboring side by side for over twenty-five years to bring God's Fatherhood to countless fatherless children. We desire that through this chapter orphan care communities and advocates everywhere will gain a solid vision and practice in the area of national leadership and healthy cross-cultural relationships. Not just for the sake of *ministries* to children, but for *the good of the children* whom we are seeking to love and serve.

We believe that healthy leadership should be nationally driven, discipleship based, and servant oriented. This type of leadership is then set free to raise up its own leadership and function in *genuine* partnership and relationship with other staff, children, locals, and foreigners according to God's diverse and varied calling.

Let's dive into our journey together by meeting Jonnes.

FROM THE CITY TO THE BUSH

I (Jonnes) grew up in Western Uganda as an orphan. My parents separated when I was five years old, leaving my siblings and me broken, confused, and deeply wounded. My father went on to take many wives at one time, abandoning us to the care of aging grandparents and an auntie. My mom ended up having seven children by three different men. Because of this, I grew up questioning my identity. I felt like I belonged to neither of my parents.

In February of 1985, the Lord came into my life and powerfully saved me. He placed me in a church in Kampala that became family to me. I knew that God owned my life and I wanted nothing less than to live for my Redeemer. After my first ministry experience, I knew in my heart I wanted something big, with pomp and good cash. I wanted to settle down, get a good job, make good money, and get married, all in order to do ministry "well." But my concept of what I thought I needed was all backwards and upside-down.

The following year I met Jay Dangers at a prayer meeting. He asked me to prayerfully consider joining him deep in the bush where he was starting a children's center for orphans. I offered to pray about it, though I felt like telling him straight up, "Sorry, I cannot!" Jay and his wife, Vicki, did not look like wealthy Americans. In fact, they looked like they themselves were below the "poverty line." So I wrote down reasons why I could not join them and presented them to God. Among them were: Jay looked too poor to pay me a salary that would meet my dreams; Jay drove a car that barely fit his own family—confirming my first reason; Jay had no visible company, like World Vision; and Jay had nothing that would fit my training in chemistry/biochemistry.

Despite my argument, after just a few days in prayer, the Lord made it clear to me that I should join Jay. I was convinced Jay was a genuine servant of God and that God would provide for me as I pursued His calling on my life. When I next saw Jay, he asked me if I had an answer for him. I said, "I am afraid it is a yes!" And that began a lifelong partnership in ministry together.

What we did not know, however, was that our initial concepts of leadership were quite different from each other. Both of us came from cultures that had very different understandings of leadership in ministry.

CULTURAL LEADERSHIP

When a ministry to orphans or an orphan care community forms, there are already cultural forces at work that will determine much of what will actually be portrayed and lived out in the leadership context, regardless of what the ministry desires or speaks about how its leadership is to function.

To give you an idea of what some of these cultural forces might look like in your respective cultures, here is a quick understanding of what many Ugandans grow up believing about leadership and its leaders, and how those beliefs impact their culture and perceived ideas about leadership.[2] These reigning paradigms are what we were up against when starting New Hope many years ago, and what we continue to be up against today in our pursuit of excellence in leadership.

Leadership means dictatorship

In Uganda, leaders are not to be questioned; they are to be obeyed. The Ugandan Chief is the ruler. It is the job of everyone else to do his bidding, to receive his word, commands, and laws without dispute. If you question him, he will "chase" you (fire you or run you off).

In this context, while it might be agreed upon that there should be freedom for others to approach leaders with questions or concerns, it is understood by the leader and his "subjects" that this simply will not happen. As much as people are told to relate with a leader, they will avoid getting near "the big man."

Leadership means power

Power is not to be relinquished and is to be maintained at all costs. It is the leader's job to keep himself looking good and keep everyone else dependent on him.

In this context, a leader might be encouraged to treat people with care, but in reality his posture, tone, and actions all communicate to those under him that he is in charge and not to be crossed. Staff will give lip service and appear outwardly compliant while harboring inward rebellion. Mistrust of leadership and a leaders' mistrust of others is the unfortunate result.

Leadership means knowledge

Most Ugandans also believe leaders must have "secret" knowledge (i.e., they must have more training, information, and understanding than everyone else), so they are careful not to allow others to gain knowledge that might usurp their authority.

In this context, while training and continuing education are seen as necessary, leaders will feel the pressure to stay "one-up" on those under them. Subordinates with more training will resent and look down on their leaders with less training. There will always be a gap, perceived or real, in knowledge or experience that will not allow for true mentorship or for the leaders to raise up others from within their organization to take their place.

Leadership means status

To be in leadership in Uganda means having respect from other workers and community members based solely on the position. Advice is naturally sought from those in leadership, and a superior air surrounds those on whom others depend.

Hiring for leadership positions might include talk of calling and serving, but the driving factor behind application for leadership roles often is the status it offers. When dealing with issues of sin or compromise, a leader's natural tendency will be to deny as much as possible because his highest goal is to maintain face with others. If things get too bad, he will often simply run away.

Leadership means corruption

Of course, few actually use the word *corruption* or think directly in those terms. Nevertheless, in Uganda, corruption generally is not seen as a moral issue grounded in right and wrong—it is simply part of life. Leadership means access to wealth accompanied by an expectation to make use of resources for personal use. It is also normal to gain from those who are under you or to ask for "food money." If you do not gain directly from your position and those under you, then you are looked down upon by your family, community, and everyone else.

In this context, while talk of integrity and accountability in leadership is used, subtle theft or the receiving of bribes will still take place. This is viewed as normal and right. Historical justification for this belief dates back to colonial days and beyond.[3]

These flawed views of leadership infiltrate all aspects of Ugandan life. Under them, whether in government, education, or children's ministry, to wield the power of leadership is to maintain cultural status and control access to information and monetary gain for one's (and relatives' and friends') own benefit.

BROADER CULTURAL LEADERSHIP

Every nation on Earth faces similarly flawed cultural views and practices of leadership. For example, in the West, while they may manifest themselves differently, power, authority, and control are still central issues in leadership. While maintaining secret knowledge might not drive Western leadership, education and specialization are integral parts of being accepted as an authority in any area. Though Western leadership might not come with an expectation of corruption, it is a culture that still expects and basks in preferential treatment and benefit packages.

Orphan care and other ministries around the world face these same challenges from flawed views of leadership every day. Further, working with wounded children and broken people carries with it an added degree of difficulty that too often leaves leaders, parents, teachers, and laborers in these ministries wounded and burned out. Compound with this the reality that if leadership is unhealthy or driven by false, cultural ideologies, there will be no life-giving help available to others laboring in the delicate area of the heart.

It takes leaders who are healthy themselves to be sources of health to those working under them. Healthy leadership cultivates health among others. Unhealthy leadership breeds *un-health*, and survival becomes the norm.

In the face of these challenges and realities, how can we avoid un-healthy leadership in orphan care communities?

HEALTHY LEADERSHIP

Fortunately, virtually every culture also has healthy leadership views and practices to counter its unhealthy ones. To have best practice when it comes to leadership, an orphan care community (and all organizations) must thoroughly examine, understand, and appropriately deal with (debunk, when necessary) all of the cultural leadership ideas and practices, good and bad, which are relevant to its context. The root foundations of worldview relating to leadership, good and bad, need to be identified and discussed. After such examination, through humble submission to God's calling for leadership, the community will be much closer to a healthy view and practice of leadership.

Recognizing that healthy leadership involves much more than dealing with cultural views and practices, however, we now are going to share with you three things that we have learned to be essential to excellence-driven leadership in any orphan care community. To be healthy for staff and children, the leadership must display each of the following characteristics:

* Nationally driven

* Discipleship based

* Servant oriented

All three of these are grounded in Scripture, which confronts our cultural ideas and practices and provides the clearest direction for seeking best practice in the area of leadership.

Nationally Driven

A few years ago, as I (Keith) traveled through one particular country that was strongly opposed to Christianity, I was surprised to stumble upon an orphan ministry run by Christians. Passing through their gates, I was happy to leave the hot sand behind. As I looked around, I saw children dressed in American casual wear. A large group of kids were playing basketball. I stepped into a building and found others watching old American reruns from the 80s. It was a surreal experience and all felt so out of place.

When I met the ministry's leadership, things began to make sense. American missionaries. Huge heart for orphans. Dedicated over twenty years of their lives to bringing the love of Jesus to needy children. Few national staff. No national leadership.

The reality is the children were being raised in a way that made them feel like they no longer fit in their native land. They were lost somewhere between two cultures. When children in these situations grow up, they often feel like their only viable choices are to stay and work with the ministry or move to the United States to study and live. The foreign leadership had clearly passed on more than the love of Jesus. They had passed on a completely foreign culture and value system. In so doing, they failed to raise their children with hearts and visions for their home culture or their place in the future of that country. Indeed, upon leaving the ministry, they will face a huge struggle to find a place in their home country. When national leadership is missing, the impact is much greater than we often think.

Why National Leaders?

All of us need to remember that the orphan care problem in any nation is *primarily a national problem*. It is therefore *very* important for nationals to be active in the solving of their own problems, especially if the proposed solutions are to be locally impacting and sustainable long-term. This means that it is imperative for orphan care communities and ministries to raise up high-capacity national leadership.

There are a variety of reasons as to why national leadership is so important:

* Nationals usually have better insight into cultural matters than foreigners and need to be in positions of responsibility so they can help steer policy and methodology.

* Nationals understand how best to impart the positive aspects of culture into the lives of children so they can be fully integrated with their communities.[4]

* Nationals have a voice into their community that foreigners do not.

* Nationals better understand the broader impact of decisions and policies on the children and on the community directly.[5]

* Nationals are essential for helping foreigners see and understand the cultural "baggage" they carry with them and its impact on the children and community.

* It is important for children to see nationals as key parts of the solution to the problems around them. If they do not see this, they will have a hard time seeing the possibility of one day being a part of the solution.

* If children do not see nationals as key parts of the solution, they likely will begin to look down on their own culture and the people from their own country. They will believe that the only true solutions, hope, resources, wisdom, and similar things, only come from the West.

* For children to grow up and become leaders in their communities and nation, they must see true leadership modeled and celebrated from among their own people.

* Foreigners do not have all the answers to the problems, and often the answers that they do have are not the best in terms of longevity or local context.

* Foreigners may have to leave and return to their countries of origin for a number of reasons including health, family, age, finances, and security. Without strategic planning and the raising up of nationals, those ministries will likely move into chaos or end with the departure of the founders.

Paul, the apostle, further encourages us to raise up national leadership. While establishing churches among various peoples, he did not keep returning to Jerusalem to find Jewish Christians who could lead the new churches. Instead, he raised up leadership from within the local context. When in Crete, Paul saw national leadership to be of such importance that he appointed Titus to make sure that local leadership was established in each church in the towns he had left behind (Titus 1:5).

He did not bring in foreigners to do the job "their way," even if it would have been more convenient and would have gotten things done "faster."

Servant Oriented

When Jay first took me (Jonnes) to the site where the ministry was to be established, it was a jungle! I expected to find hired workers clearing the land, but instead I found this *mzungu* (white man) rolling up his sleeves, working, cutting brush, and clearing the land. I had to make a decision. Was I there for a nice title or was I there to serve? By the grace of God, I joined him and it was the beginning of a lifetime of serving together, side by side.

Servant leadership is counter-cultural all over the world. In many African cultures, where it is the job of everyone else to serve "the big man," the concept of servant leadership is confronting. Leaders want to be served, and they will use leadership as a badge that says it is everyone else's duty to serve while he or she manages. Of course, Jesus has a completely different understanding of leadership. Jesus revealed that the greatest leader is the one who is the greatest servant, the one who comes down the lowest and is willing to do even the most menial tasks.[6] I love to tell people that Jesus would have cleaned the dirtiest toilet or latrine for the glory of God—with joy in His heart and thankfulness to His Father.

Jesus' leadership model is truly the *best model* for leadership in orphan care communities. Servant leaders *must* be willing to get down on the level of the children[7] and be willing to radically confront culture (and reveal God's culture). From King David to the disciples of our Lord, God's greatest leaders are measured in the heart and are servants first and always. This concept of leadership will only be *taught* and *caught* when it comes from leadership who understand and live out the gospel. This is true gospel-driven leadership.

These are characteristics that I (Keith) have enjoyed seeing in both Jay and Jonnes. I have witnessed them both repenting publicly for mistakes they have made, a practice that is *counter*-cultural. I have seen them laugh and cry together and with others—again *counter*-cultural. I have enjoyed living life together with them as we mutually love each other and encourage each other on the journey of faith and ministry. This is the heart that they have always led with, hearts committed to servant leadership and genuine discipleship.

Discipleship Based

As Jay and I (Jonnes) drove back and forth to the ministry site, those six hours in the jeep were precious to me. Jay envisioned me for the ministry, but more than that he envisioned me for manhood, fatherhood, and family. He discipled me. And I discipled him. I helped him to understand Uganda, her culture, and her people. We became partners in the work, but more than that, we became brothers. Family and discipleship became the foundation of our ministry.

In the early years, we made it clear to staff that it was never about the job. It was about family. It was about growing in the Lord, together. As our ministry grew, though, it became harder and harder for us to disciple everyone. We knew that we had to be strategic and raise up other leaders who could disciple others as they themselves were being discipled. One way we have sought to accomplish this goal is through the New Hope Institute of Childcare and Family, which trains and disciples men and women so that they can train and disciple others. And together we disciple the children for whom we are caring. Over the years we have also met with strategic groups of people for discipleship and prayer and to read through good books together.[8] This type of discipleship must be intentional and lifestyle oriented. It goes beyond the job and work site, to walking together on the journey of spiritual formation.[9]

CULTIVATING NATIONAL LEADERSHIP

What if you don't have a man like Jonnes in your ministry—a strong national leader who can mentor and raise up other high-capacity national leaders? How can you find and go about developing national leaders, especially when you feel like you do not have any in your midst and do not even know where to begin looking for one? Though the principles and practices discussed throughout this chapter implicitly respond to these questions, we quickly want to address the issues raised by them.

When a ministry lacks a strong national leader, its existing leadership first needs to firmly understand and believe that very competent, high-capacity leaders likely exist in the nationals surrounding them—in their surrounding communities and even in the staff of their ministry. As Robert Lupton said, "The poor, no matter how destitute, have enormous untapped capacity; find it, be inspired by it, and build upon it."[10] With that understanding, it is crucial to pray consistently with others for God to bring the right person or people to the ministry and to pray for wisdom and discernment in identifying that person. Then, when the leadership finds potential candidates, it should get opinions and perspectives on them from as many trusted sources as possible, including following up references and pastoral/church recommendations. Finding a trusted national who can assist the ministry in this process is strongly recommended.

Additionally, orphan care communities should seek partnerships with local churches, which can watch for people whom it would be good to invest in for future ministry. At the same time, strategically give children from within your own community opportunities to develop and grow in leadership. Leaders should make developing leadership in children who can one day step into leadership roles in the ministry a high priority.

When looking to raise up leadership from within, be sure to strategically *invest* in the people under you. Doing life together and building trust in relationship can go a long way in terms of discovering who is able to take on leadership responsibilities. Part of strategic investment should include extensive training in worldview and the other areas mentioned in the spiritual formation chapter of this book. This will make it easier to identify men and women who really "get it" when it comes to ministry and leading others. It is also helpful to observe how various leaders or potential leaders respond under stress and when corrected. How *voluntarily* accountable are they? The answer to this question will prove to be very important.

One last thing . . . do not get stuck on what you think the leader you are looking for "should look like." Instead, allow God to surprise you and raise up the leader that is actually needed according to his or her personality and gifts. It is crucial to release leaders to lead in their particular area according to their own gifting and calling. Founders or directors can end up micromanaging everything, which in the end will limit the ability of others to take "ownership" of the heart and vision of the ministry or to make long-term investment in it.

Ultimately, understanding, developing, and implementing healthy leadership in an orphan care community is a very difficult, ongoing, and long-term process that likely will have obstacles and barriers over time. What are some of the barriers to the healthy establishment of national leadership and how can we work to overcome them? Let's take a look together.

OVERCOMING BARRIERS

Mark Johnson[11] and his family came to Uganda to establish a work among orphans. He had contacts through his local church and a local church in Uganda. A Ugandan friend helped him find a piece of land where he could begin his ministry, and the local government had orphans who desperately needed care. All seemed well. And then the problems began.

Over the next year, issues came up with the land. People demanded more money at every turn to settle one "problem" or another. Government leaders were no longer helpful. Instead, they gave him the run around, purposefully bringing problems in order to receive a bribe for their "help". People Mark had trusted began stealing from him. He felt betrayed, wounded, and his family began to suffer. His son began to despise all Ugandans, refusing to come out of his room during the day. His wife's emotional and physical health spiraled downward. He desperately wanted a Ugandan partner that he could trust, but he felt helpless and alone. Finally, after feeling completely isolated and unable to trust anyone, he and his family decided to leave Uganda.[12]

While many might agree in principle that national leadership, servanthood, and discipleship in leadership are important, each cultural context will provide many reasons that could ultimately trump sound reason. Mark had a desire to raise up national leaders, but he became convinced that his context did not allow for it. Over the years we have heard many people say, "You just do not understand our context." The truth is that while every context is unique, the issues tend to be similar. After all, cross-cultural ministry to orphans is about the most difficult area to engage in and thrive. Building on the cultural ideologies discussed above, what are some of the various issues or beliefs orphan care communities and Western organizations face that make the raising up of national leadership a challenge?

* The undergirding belief that nationals *cannot* be trusted or that they are not competent, qualified, or simply "aren't ready" to lead

* The undergirding naïve belief (and desire to believe) that *all* nationals *can* be trusted

* Western leadership micromanaging from afar, dictating practices, policies, and procedures

* Western lack of humility or teachability when it comes to culture and cultural issues

* Belief that nationals lack what Westerners desire to see instilled in the children

* Belief that Western culture has better solutions and money is the answer

* Belief that bringing money or position to nationals will breed corruption

Knowing that there is a lot more to these barriers that simply can't be covered in this short chapter, we expound on each of them and invite your input at ThinkOrphan.com. Each one of these beliefs and others like them fall short of our greater calling to pursue national leadership and effective cross-cultural relationships. The cultural issues faced in all ministry contexts are both within and without, ranging from tribal issues to cross-cultural issues. Excellence for national leadership constitutes understanding and dealing with these issues with wisdom and grace. Excellence also demands that foreigners understand these same issues so that national leadership can be free to function in *genuine* relationship and partnership with Westerners.

How do we get there? One thing we absolutely need to reach such excellence is solid commitment to the intentional pursuit of unity in the midst of diversity.

Multiethnic Commitment

All cultures face barriers and divisions—ethnic, tribal, cultural, economic, generational, to name a few. Whether we are speaking about male to female, tribe to tribe, or ethnicity to ethnicity, the division and mistrust created by dividing walls of hostility ultimately cripples ministries. This crippling occurs between leadership and staff, right to the parents and children involved with the ministry. The gospel demands that we expose the lies, forgive the wrongs, pursue love, and then walk together in the beauty of relationship that reflects the glorious Savior who gave His life that we might truly be one. One people from many. One people. A multiethnic bride purchased by the blood of the Savior.

At New Hope, to raise up national leadership that will seek multiethnicity and facilitate a commitment to multiethnicity among our diverse staff from over fifteen tribes and six nations, we have very intentionally created opportunities for our various team members to learn about each other. We work hard to do life together, living in community side by side and ministering together. We encourage cross-cultural interaction, fellowship, and friendship. We visit each other, play sports with each other, attend church and fellowships together, and have water fights and cultural meals together.

We also give opportunities for people from different tribal or ethnic background to speak about what they have heard or know about *them* (i.e., others). Sometimes the revelations of how we perceive each other are very hurtful, shocking, and potentially devastating. Instead of taking the easy way out and breaking relationship, however, our commitment to humility, repentance, and forgiveness frees us to be able to go on together. False unity dissolves as we get well below the superficialities that characterize so many cross-cultural and cross-national relationships. Freedom comes into hearts that have been held captive by the bonds of unforgiveness or the lies about other cultures and peoples that were passed down to them. We are then free to share with our children a true commitment to Christ-centered reconciliation and relationship with all peoples.

One look around New Hope today and it is almost too good to be true. Tribes that used to despise and kill one another are now loving and serving one another. Ugandans and foreigners, so long divided by the colonialism of the past and the paternalism of the present, are living and laboring side by side as equals. *It is amazing to see what God does in all of us when we get real with each other and value each other as brothers and sisters in the Lord—not as "them" and "us."* It becomes a taste of heaven!

But, of course, the reality of the world we live in also carries with it many issues that all of us must face to be able to establish and grow in relationships with one another. None of these issues are harder to overcome than the ones that are cross-cultural. It is paramount for national leaders and foreigners seeking best-practice to understand and overcome these issues.

Cross-Cultural Issues

Over the years I (Jay) have frequently been viewed by Africans with suspicion and resentment even while being deferred to and given special privilege or undue recognition. In one crowd of Ugandans, there are typically at least two views of whites[13] and Americans as a whole.[14] There are those who look down on whites and resent them for what *they* (the colonial masters) did to *our* people and *our* continent. Then there are those standing right next to them who almost slavishly defer to the Westerners who *seem* to have the upper hand in every way—economically, educationally, technologically, and spiritually. We can be both demonized and idolized, and at times you can find both going on in the same person, at the same time. This presents serious challenges for locals and foreigners seeking to develop partnerships and genuine relationship.

A Need to be Needed

Unfortunately, this all tends to be compounded by the fact that many foreigners coming into a third-world country have an underlying *savior* mentality. The foreigner generally has more education, and advantages in a variety of technical and communication skills, along with a broader world perspective. And the foreigner usually has the funding. They naturally tend to view themselves as the *haves* and the locals as the *have-nots*. They are the *needed* ones, and the locals are the *needy*, the *"less fortunate"* ones. They come from *advanced* nations and have come to serve in an *underdeveloped* country. Because of these advantages, even while loving the local people with hearts full of good intentions, many foreigners end up having a relationship with nationals that stem from a *superior* mind-set and becomes paternalistic in nature.

On the flip side, nationals are frequently very aware of their own deficits. They recognize the educational, technological, and economic advantage of the foreigners and often tend to view the foreigner as their superior. After all, he is white—he must be highly educated and he must have unlimited funding. The foreigner carries better technology, "validating" his superiority. It is assumed that the white man should be up front, the speaker, the decision maker, and the holder of the purse strings. Nationals may resent all of this, but they can still help perpetuate the problem by participating in a codependent relationship with the foreigners who at their own core often enjoy the feeling of being needed and treated preferentially.

Peer Leadership and Ministry

It will be very difficult for foreigners seeking to raise up national leadership to succeed as long as these vast issues go unaddressed or remain unacknowledged. So, after acknowledging these realities, how can we work to overcome them? We believe that if foreigners choose to be peers instead of patrons, and if nationals choose to be peers instead of dependents, we can learn to work together effectively for the kingdom of God. It is not easy but it can be done. From our experiences, we want to help you learn how.

Cultivating Partnership in Relationship

When I (Jay) came to Uganda, I faced all of the above issues (and have continued to face them over the years) and easily could have assumed the "savior" role and ruled as "boss man" over the ministry, staff, mission, vision, and operations. After all, the vision was mine. I was the founder of this fledgling ministry. I was the white man. I was the boss. And that was the normal way of things.

But that would not have been a genuine partnership. That would not have made the most of the significant gifts and abilities of my new partner, Jonnes. That would not have made good use of his significantly superior knowledge of culture, language, national history, and national identity.

What was important was to establish a *genuine* partnership where each of us could bring what he had to the partnership, and where the contribution of each was valued and given opportunity to find full expression. I call this *peer ministry*: the foreigner and the Ugandan working in a peer relationship, under which neither person defers to the other simply because of nationality, education, or other real or perceived advantages.

From the beginning, our goal was to establish a ministry where we as both American and Ugandan lived and labored side by side, as true partners in ministry, seeking to honor and respect one another. Many foreigners as well as Ugandans who have watched Jonnes and I interact and work together have no idea who is the boss—and that is a really good thing—it isn't a hierarchy relationship, it is a peer relationship.

The Sharpening of Peer Ministry

Jonnes and I (Jay) often disagree on matters, important and trivial. When we disagree, we discuss. Sometimes the debates become emotional and sometimes there is no conclusion or agreement for days or even months. But when agreement comes, it comes because one of us has proven his position to the other and the other has accepted it. Then we move on together. My experience is that the majority of the time

Jonnes is right. He is very intelligent, very godly, very wise, and very persuasive—but he has to convince me, just as I have to convince him.

Neither of us views our culture as superior to the other; we both love to honor each other's culture. My "foreign" perspective forces Jonnes to really think through his position and to judge his perspective objectively, just as Jonnes's superior cultural insight and wisdom constantly challenge me. But at the end of the day, we both submit ourselves and our cultures to God's Word.[15] This peer ministry relationship enables both of us to bring to the table our unique perspective, though like a guest in someone else's home, I will consistently defer to Jonnes's culture above my own as I simultaneously seek to conform to it as much as possible.[16] It really is "iron sharpening iron," and we and the ministry are better off for it as we raise our children in a redeemed Ugandan culture.

As national leadership is sharpened by foreigners, foreigners also have the privilege of being sharpened by national leaders. One of the most important things a Westerner should bring into an orphan care community context is a humble desire to learn from and be molded by what God is doing through national leaders.

Coming Under National Leadership

Shalom. That was the word written across the front of the note handed to me (Keith) by my Ugandan leader. I was aching. It was the culmination of years of ministry and one very painful experience. I had mentally packed my bags. I was ready to leave Uganda. At that moment, his words to me were more than words from a boss; they were words from a father's heart:

> *This comes to be a whisper of Shalom into your heart! The accuser may use different avenues to judge and blame you; even where you have poured out your heart to love without measure. But today we want you to know: You are our delight and joy. You mean much to us as a beautiful model of sonship and family. Your labor is not in vain. The One you serve is faithful to reward your labor. And He is well pleased with you. I am very blessed to have you in my life and as a part of our Dad's team. From my heart, Shalom! Jonnes*

One of the greatest privileges of my life has been living and serving in Uganda. Indeed, I have had the great privilege of being both led and mentored in ministry by a Ugandan whom I deem to be one of the wisest men I have ever met. I recognize and am quick to tell anyone willing to listen that I have learned much more from what God is doing in and through Uganda, from Ugandans sharing and imparting to me, than anything I have had to offer in service to them. This is the beauty of the body of Christ on display, the partnership of relationship in the give and take found in His people submitting themselves one to another.

Jay and Jonnes have modeled peer ministry for those they are raising up. It is exciting to see nationals and foreigners follow their example by having very deep and genuine relationships that are deeply personal, are cross-racial, and share mutual accountability.[17] It is also exciting to see foreigners with Ugandan leaders, and Ugandans with foreign leaders working together in ministries that cultivate lasting friendships.[18]

With this said, how long should Westerners plan to be involved in cross-cultural ministry? After all, shouldn't they seek to work themselves out of a job in their foreign land?

Do Not Work Yourself Out of a Job

There is a mentality in Western missions that lends itself to the goal of: *Come in, get the job done, raise up nationals to continue doing the job, and get out.* While this is a good way to avoid establishing a paternalistic, dependence-based ministry, it is also very un-Ugandan and terribly flawed in a Ugandan context for many reasons.

Ugandans (like much of Africa and the Global South) value relationship above all things, while Americans tend to be efficiency minded and task oriented. Americans tend to value getting the job done and see reaching the goal as the most important accomplishment. For Ugandans, the satisfaction and value of accomplishing the task is secondary and subservient to the satisfaction and value of relationships. In fact, the time given to relationship is more important than the time given for the accomplishing of a task.

So, the moment a Ugandan hears an American say that he or she has come to accomplish a job, what he or she really hears is: *I do not value you. I am not here for relationship. I am here for a job. I do not desire relationship.* It is an immediate barrier in the heart.

I (Keith) once asked Jonnes, "Shouldn't we Westerners be here to work ourselves out of a job?" He strongly rebuked me, looking me in the eye and saying, "The job is not the greatest reason that God brought you here. It is the secondary reason. Relationship is the primary reason." I was stunned. His words did not fit my paradigm.

Most Westerners do not know what to do with this. After all, without a job, would we even be there? Then there is the performance pressure and expectations placed on us from results-oriented donors. *Aren't the people supporting me paying me to do a job?*

It is not that accomplishing the task has no value, but for a Ugandan, relationship is *always* more important. These dynamics must be understood and overcome or foreigners will be crippled from the beginning. If they can understand and overcome, they will go much farther in cultivating genuine relationships. Nationals who understand and know how to communicate this will also be able to show more grace and develop greater working relationships between locals and foreigners.

So how long should we stay? As Jonnes would say, "Stay until Dad says it's time to go."

CONTINUALLY MOVING FORWARD TOGETHER

National leadership is not something that can be produced by our own efforts. It takes God Himself to redeem a heart and equip that person for ministry in a local country and community. Yet God has given leaders in His multiethnic bride around the world, His Church, to be a part of the equipping of the saints for the work of ministry (Eph. 4:11–12). All of us are called to pursue national leadership, just as we are called to pursue healthy cross-cultural and cross-national relationships. This chapter has sought to lay a foundation in this area on which orphan care communities around the globe and their partners can build. It is our great desire that orphans everywhere will grow up with respect and honor for their national and local "heroes" who form a part of a God-centered vision for leadership that is nationally driven, servant oriented, and discipleship based. That will allow all of us to produce, by the grace of God, the kind of leaders from among our children that our countries, cities, and villages so desperately need.

Going ☼ Deeper

1. Spend time thinking through your own cultural context. What are aspects of leadership that are being culturally driven? How do those things play out on a practical level?

2. Which reasons for national leadership stood out to you most? Why do you think those are so important?

3. What did you think about Jay and Jonnes's relationship? What made it so unique? What can you learn from it?

4. What struggles have you found relating to people of different background, culture, or ethnicity? How does the truth of the gospel impact that and help you overcome the struggles?

Chapter

11

WANTED: ENTREPRENEURIAL MINDS (SELF-SUSTAINABILITY)

"Again and again we are finding that when it comes to global needs in organizational development and human development, the granting of money creates dependence and conflict, not independence and respect. By changing the equation to other means of exchange, we find that we are empowering people based on shared responsibility, mutual support, and accountability." —Robert D. Lupton

"[M]aterial poverty alleviation . . . involves the much harder task of empowering people to earn sufficient material things through their own labor, for in so doing we move people closer to being what God created them to be."—Steven Corbett and Brian Fikkert

As recent books like *When Helping Hurts*, *The Poor Will Be Glad*, and *Toxic Charity* bring to light, economic self-sustainability is a necessary component to any child's, organization's, and/or program's *long-term* results and successes. Orphaned and vulnerable children, and orphan care communities are not exceptions to this rule.

At the organizational level, there needs to be real ownership and buy-in by the community serving and being served by the project. Some ways to achieve such ownership and buy-in are through revenue-generating businesses, other entrepreneurial ventures, in-country fundraising by the nationals, and "sweat equity." The important thing is that the ownership and buy-in happens so that the project does not reinforce an unhealthy dependency on outsiders that is ingrained in so much of the developing world.

Of course, consistent with the rest of this book, our primary goal in considering and implementing any sustainability ventures should be to affirm and support God's design for sustainability, where moms and dads are the primary providers for their children. Therefore, our programs need to emphasize organizational and personal sustainability, *and* aim to keep children and their biological parents together in healthy environments whenever humanly possible.

In seeking self-sustainability, we seek economic self-sustainability, not relational self-sustainability. In fact, as discussed in the chapter on community integration, relational interdependence, i.e., teamwork, is essential for any community, and any human being, for that matter, to thrive. Therefore, collaboration and deep and authentic relationships, working in conjunction with projects that work toward that community's economic independence, are critical to a community's development toward self-sustainability. Collaboration, hard work, and deep, authentic relationships that work toward economic independence are also critical to any child's ability to thrive as an adult.

In this chapter, we have the privilege of joining a conversation on the why, what, and how of self-sustainability with Keith and Peter Greer. Peter Greer is president and CEO of HOPE International, a global nonprofit organization focused on Christ-centered job creation, savings mobilization, and financial training.[1] I invite you to learn, as I have, from their collective wisdom and firsthand experience about how we can develop and implement self-sustainable orphan care programs and communities with excellence.

Self-Sustainability
(Keith McFarland and Peter Greer)

Sylvia lost her parents at a young age.[2] Her grandmother took in Sylvia and her three siblings and looked after them as best she could. Sylvia rose each morning at four thirty, and walked the half mile each way to fetch water for cooking and washing. During the rainy season, before heading off to school, she spent an hour in the garden digging or weeding. After returning from school, she immediately returned to the garden. She knew that if she did not work hard, her family would not have the food needed to get through the following dry season. After digging, Sylvia helped gather firewood before preparing dinner. After finishing these tasks, she finally began her homework.

Because of her diligence and hard work, Sylvia did well in school. She was promoted to upper-level high school where she excelled in math and science. Though Sylvia wanted to pursue teaching, a lack of available funds and the need for her to help provide for her family forced her to quit school and stay home. After a few years, when her relatives saw that she was not going to bring future profit into the family, they forced her to marry so they could receive cows in exchange for her. Needless to say, she never became a teacher.

Stephen also lost his parents at a young age, but he grew up in very different circumstances than Sylvia. Stephen grew up in an orphan care community seeking best-practices in many areas described in this book. He planned to one day become a lawyer. He knew that education was key to that plan, so his daily life revolved around school. When he got home from school, he was allowed some time to rest, but the remainder of the evening centered on homework and study. Because of the suffering of his past (and the suffering of other children like him), the founders and financial backers of the ministry made sure that he was sponsored under their child sponsorship program and the ministry catered to all of his needs (and the needs of the other children). Meals were prepared for him, laundry was washed for him, and most of the cleaning was done for him. He did a few chores, but very little else.

After Stephen graduated from high school, he struggled to adjust to living on his own. He did not know how to handle money. He refused to get a job to help pay for school, choosing instead to wait for someone to sponsor him. Up to that point in his life everyone had catered to his needs. He finally tried to get a job, but because he lacked a genuine work ethic and was unwilling to do what he deemed "menial" jobs, he was unable to keep a job. Needless to say, he never became a lawyer.

These two stories represent very different ends of the spectrum when it comes to work and self-sustainability in the lives of orphans. Of course, there are a multitude of scenarios in between these examples. Yet both of these serve to typify a glaring problem in orphan work today: the lack of opportunity for orphans to develop a foundational work ethic, followed with the means to develop to the fullest potential of their God-given talents and abilities.

And these children's lives have something else in common: they both are intimately connected with and are microcosms of self-sustainability issues at the organizational level. Let me (Keith) explain.

SELF-SUSTAINABILITY AND SELF-SUFFICIENCY

When we speak about self-sustainability in the context of an orphan care community, we are talking primarily about a ministry's ability to currently maintain and to continue to meet its own needs apart from outside sources or dependence on the West. While the term can have a broader scope,[3] this chapter primarily focuses on economic independence, which factors in the positive and negative impact of choices and practices on the ministry and community as a whole.

While many of you may think this type of self-sustainability is impossible in the short-term, best practice in this area demands that we understand the need for and continually work toward the goal of self-sustainability. We also need to understand that reaching the goal of self-sustainability likely will require the development of strategic partnerships, through which ministries strategically use relationships with outside individuals and other organizations to establish projects that will continually move the ministry toward self-sustainability. Self-sustainability is a long-term venture that requires strategic thinking, planning, and "bridge" projects in the short term, and commitment to the strategic plan and execution in the long term.

A common synonym used to speak of self-sustainability is the term self-sufficiency. Self-sufficiency, like self-sustainability, has to do with the ability to supply one's own needs without external assistance. But self-sufficiency also carries the idea of having extreme confidence in one's own resources, powers, and abilities.[4] While self-sustainability is primarily speaking to a ministry's ability to function independent of outside sources, self-sufficiency carries the idea of having all that is needed within oneself in terms of adequacy and necessity.

We use the term self-sufficient primarily in relationship to the children that we are seeking to care for, as our goal is to provide fatherless children all that they need to stand and succeed in life. While the term carries the idea of complete independence, we do not mean to imply that all sufficiency comes from within or that a person should be able to live independent of other people. This is where the gospel confronts and defines our terms for us.

CHRIST-CENTERED SELF-SUFFICIENCY

While self-sufficiency as a goal might seem to imply that we have all that we need within ourselves to accomplish whatever we want, the truth of the gospel declares that in ourselves, apart from the grace of God, we lack all things necessary to stand and succeed in life. The reality is that we can do nothing that is of lasting value apart from Jesus. As the apostle Paul has stated, "Not that we are sufficient in ourselves to claim anything as coming from us, but our sufficiency is from God" (2 Cor. 3:5). Jesus made it clear to His disciples: "Apart from me you can do nothing" (John 15:5).

We also resonate with Peter's words that inform us that in God, we have all that we need. In fact, He has already given it to us. "His divine power has granted to us all things that pertain to life and godliness, through the knowledge of him who called us to his own glory and excellence" (2 Peter 1:3). The key is *knowing* the One who has called us and living in dependence on Him.

The beauty of both of these truths is that the beginning point and the end point is Jesus. We depend on Him to provide for our needs, while we use the hearts, minds, skills, and talents that He has granted to us. As we live in dependence on Him, we are able to trust that He is going to provide for our needs and use us to care for others in need as well.

What does ministry sustainability have to do with the children we are caring for?

Everything.

REFLECTING MIRRORS

If all funding from the West was suddenly cut off, would your ministry survive? The stark reality for most orphan care communities and ministries is that without outside funding, they simply could not survive. The impact of this reality is felt with every economic downturn, every threat of inflation in local currency, and every insecurity in a local context, whether from internal strife or cultural instability. And because of this, many ministry leaders believe that there is simply too much to think about "on the ground"—too much need and not enough provision—to spend time thinking about hypothetical situations and "needs" that seem so far away.

On the other hand, some ministries love to talk about self-sustainability. *Someday, we would like to* . . . fill in the blank with any money making idea. Ideas and business proposals are discussed, but when it comes to implementation, virtually nothing happens. After all, it is much easier to depend on funding from outside than to generate it from within. That takes time, resources, staff, business know-how, and great effort on many levels. And the sad reality is that it simply is not easy to establish an income-generating project in most contexts that actually proves profitable.

With this said, what is the connection between ministry self-sustainability and personal self-sufficiency? The connection is a close one. If a ministry is *completely* dependent on outside funding for survival, then children growing up there will assume that their own ability to survive is also dependent on outside funding, regardless of what words are spoken to them to the contrary. Child sponsorship usually becomes the main source of income, at times leaving children with four or five sponsors at once![5] This quickly creates a *sponsorship mentality* that will ultimately drive both the ministry and the children. The West is seen as the great source of funding, and therefore all Westerners are a means to more funding. Like Stephen, success in life is simply a matter of finding the right sponsor.

When a ministry is striving to provide for itself, when it utilizes local resources, works with others to develop resources, and continually displays the importance of and dignity of work, there will be more ownership by both staff and children as they recognize their abilities to help meet their own needs. In this context, work becomes a community project and a means of real-life discipleship. When a community diligently works *together*, not regulating work to one specific group of people while the others stand by and "manage" or participate only in "easy" jobs, that community fosters a sense of family, teamwork, and servanthood.

So what can we do in the here and now in orphan care communities to implement best-practice and excellence in self-sustainability and self-sufficiency? While we cannot possibly address all the ways to pursue excellence in this short chapter, we are going to share with you some ideas that we've learned and encountered around the world.[6]

EXCELLENCE FRAMEWORK

What does excellence in self-sustainability, working toward Christ-centered self-sufficiency, look like in an orphan care community context[7] or the wider spectrum of orphan care? Four foundations are crucial:

1. God-centered vision of work
2. Positive community impact
3. Local sustainability
4. Integrity and witness

God-Centered Vision of Work

Through my experience on the continent, I (Keith) have learned that many cultures in Africa view work as a curse. Others in Africa and beyond view work as a punishment. The worldview surrounding work in any culture will impact ministries and the children being served. What vision of work should we be promoting?

Work was created by God as a beautiful means for mankind to experience God's grace and love in relationship to Himself and other people. Before man sinned, before the curse and punishment for sin, God placed the man in the garden to *work it and keep it.*[8] Man was to reflect the God who Himself works and thus to participate with Him in His work.[9] Work was relational and experiential. Man enjoyed God's goodness and beauty reflected in the garden and through the receiving of God's good grace in the provision of his needs. When God created woman, she, too, became a participant in this experience of God-centered work.

Of course, with the fall came sweat and thorns and thistles and pests and drought and famine and every other disruption to the work of our hands. Nevertheless, in Christ we are still free to participate in work in dependence on Him to care for our needs as we continue to experience His grace and love through work and as we share with others out of God's great provision.[10]

Pursuant to this view of work, each of the family groups at the Kasana Children's Center, a ministry of New Hope Uganda, work between three and five acres of land, which helps to provide for the needs of the family through the growing of maize, beans, peanuts, cassava, bananas, and potatoes. The children who attend school also help to maintain school gardens. Over the years, we have experienced consistent resistance to hard work, yet many kids continue to come back and thank us for teaching them how to work. They say things like, "Out there, people don't know how to work." Others have shared how their willingness to do *anything* and to *serve* has gotten them a job that others with higher qualifications were denied. We find children who have grown up at New Hope and go on to higher education *consistently* rise to leadership and are relied upon as the "responsible" ones in class. Many have told us that they are often asked, *"Where* did you grow up? You are different!" While more than having a God-centered view of work comes into play in these situations, work remains as the foundation.[11]

Positive Community Impact

It can be easy, especially for foreigners, to develop good ideas of income generation that can negatively impact a community. For example, while it might seem like a good idea to ship secondhand clothing into an area where it can be sold for a modest profit, it can also flood the market with low-cost and low-quality goods. The effect is that of driving out all local efforts in textiles and tailoring. Best-practice self-sustainability will look for means to generate income that will have a positive impact on a local community.

For example, in 2007, New Hope Uganda wrote a proposal to a European charity that wanted to invest in self-sustainable ministry as opposed to simply giving funds that would be quickly consumed. New Hope proposed the establishment of a maize mill. This made sense because the major crop that the family groups, schools, and the ministry grow is maize. The nearest place providing milling was thirteen kilometers away, and the cost of transportation on top of service made milling maize less economical than it could have been. New Hope's proposal would allow locals in the community and the ministry to save money while providing a service and jobs for the community. This venture would indeed have a positive impact on the community.

Local Sustainability

While foreign aid and charitable giving can be a great means of beginning an income-generating project, it can also set a project up for failure if the project has not proven to be locally sustainable. For instance, one church wanted to help a ministry get a farming project going. So they raised money and purchased an American-made Massey tractor for the project. While things started out well, the project went downhill quickly once the tractor broke down. Why? Because most of the parts were not available in-country and the parts that were available were wildly expensive. So, the tractor sat unused and the project folded.

Westerners also tend to want to establish something "big" right off the bat, a good intention that can flop if not tested first. Thus, scaling is critical. For example, a few years ago, some people gave funds to help establish a poultry project for the New Hope Pastoral Training Institute. Instead of using all of the funds to develop the entire proposed operation, we first developed a trial project of three hundred hens to see if the business was indeed sustainable and profitable on a local level. Only after it proved successful did we increase the number of hens to one thousand. The income sustained the project and also provided the funds needed to support the week-long training of pastors each month.[12] The success of this project has also helped us on the agricultural/animal husbandry side of the pastoral training, as we seek to equip pastors with the practical skills needed to provide for their family's needs.

Integrity and Witness

In the world of business and amid the pressure to turn a profit, it is easy to lose sight of the greater purpose of it all: making known and building the kingdom of God. Losing sight of this goal is not acceptable. Excellence in self-sustainability requires all involved to remain centered on the truth of the gospel, conducting business as a reflection and witness of Jesus.[13]

When New Hope began maize milling, what began as a simple milling service quickly expanded to include the buying of maize on the open market for resale as *posho* (corn flour). New Hope then branded its *posho* with its own label and increased retail sales. While the overall goal was to make money that would provide support and lessen the burden on the ministry financially, along the way it also provided a safe and fair environment for business, while also empowering the local farmer. A new level of righteousness was introduced to the local marketplace as the ministry weighed their flour accurately, providing integrity that the consumer could count on. This practice has required others in our surrounding community to maintain a higher standard in business practices as well.

The integrity of the business and the workers has been a witness of the gospel in the community. Where these foundations are laid, business is able to meet ministry and ministry flows out and is supported through self-sustainable business.

WHEN BUSINESS MEETS MINISTRY

Several years ago, one American couple acted on their passion to establish family-based orphan homes affiliated with neighborhood churches for discipleship and support. In so doing, they started their ministry in a South American country riddled with extreme poverty, a high rate of child abandonment and death through exposure or drowning in the Amazon River, and a low rate of orphanages. To begin addressing those issues, the couple partnered with churches to build family homes with Christian parents and up to ten orphaned children. And once the homes were built, they immediately began working toward self-sustainability by creating and running businesses to fund the ongoing needs of the homes, rather than simply seeking donations from churches and individuals.

This story is one of many similar examples of business and mission mixing in our world today. *Tentmakers* use their business or trade to get into countries closed to Christians. *Bivocational* pastors and church leaders care for their flocks while working outside because of the inability of their congregation to provide for the pastor's needs. *Microbusiness* or "Mustard Seed" loans help meet the needs of impoverished Christians in struggling economies, while encouraging believers and teaching biblical stewardship. A recent movement called *Missional Business* is encouraging the 65 million working Christians in the United States to consider their place of employment as their personal mission field. And less common are the Christian businessmen and women who feel called to dedicate a significant part, or in some cases all, of their business to the great commission. For lack of a better term we call this a *Commissional Business*, created and commissioned to fund a ministry.

Creating strategic partnerships with local churches and businesses that are then able to partner relationally and/or financially is also a growing part of best-practice self-sustainability. Christians and non-Christians alike should be continually engaged to give back to the needs in their own country and to be a part of the solution to those problems. Whether through hosting seminars or fundraisers, the long-term value of these partnerships is paramount for the long-term vision of self-sustainability. These partnerships are also helpful in addressing the greater issue of poverty that plays a major role in the global orphan crisis.

POVERTY AND MICROFINANCE

A very critical area for establishing long-term self-sustainability and self-sufficiency, particularly as a bridge from the realities of today to long-term goals, is the area of microfinance. I (Keith) can think of no better person to give us examples of what gospel-driven microfinance can look like than Peter Greer. Fortunately, he has done just that for us in the pages that follow. I first met Peter Greer in 2002, when my wife and I were newly married and working with street children in Rwanda. I was blown away by Peter's love for Rwanda and her people, as well as his knowledge and ideas in the area of business and microfinance. It has been such a joy to read his books and learn from what God has entrusted to him. I expect that you will feel the same way after learning from his experiences.

I (Peter) was shocked when I read a study by the Better Care Network describing the connection between poverty and the orphan crisis. The study described the high percentage of children living in orphanages with at least one surviving parent in five different countries. Liberia: 98 percent; Sri Lanka: 92 percent; Azerbaijan: 70 percent; and Zimbabwe: 40 percent.

Prior to this research, I was under the false impression that children were in institutional care primarily because they had no living relatives. This research opened my eyes to the fact that many of the world's orphans are actually economic orphans (i.e., poverty has pushed them out of their homes and into orphanages). Poverty is one of the largest underlying causes of the global orphan crisis.

When we listen to parents around the world, we find that they desperately want to care for their children, but poverty forces them to make decisions that no parent should ever make. *Poverty should never be a reason why children are put into a home.*

Given these statistics, we need to find supplemental approaches to traditional orphan care, solutions that equip orphan care communities to take responsibility for their needy and vulnerable, *and* help parents take care of their children.

Microfinance is a newer approach helping to address the needs of the global orphan crisis by helping parents increase their income and care for their children. What we have found is that lives are changed by simply providing entrepreneurship training, financial literacy, a safe place to save small amounts of money, and access to loans for people who have a business idea. When this is done with discipleship and in a way that points people to Christ, entire communities are changed, starting in the home.

It is simply a better option to provide a hand up, rather than a handout.

We have also found that entrepreneurs don't stop at success. Motivated by Christ's love and empowered to give through their increased profits, many are practicing "true religion" by adopting orphans within their local communities.

Here are just three case studies from sub-Saharan Africa:

Democratic Republic of Congo

When her husband died during the Second Congo War, Mama Atiya—along with her six children—was stripped of her land and estate by her husband's relatives. According to tribal tradition, a husband's family possesses the rights to the land, not the widow.

Left destitute, Mama Atiya temporarily stayed with her parents in Kisangani, dreaming of saving enough money to buy her own house again. After meeting with a HOPE loan officer, she knew that a HOPE loan was just the opportunity she had been praying for.

Taking out a $55 loan, she decided to venture into the smoked fish business. Successful, Mama Atiya became a wholesaler, increasing her profits. And today, life is no longer a daily struggle for survival. Mama Atiya has realized her dream as the proud owner of an apartment, who is able to send all of her children to school.

Beyond this, she has taken four orphaned children into her home, providing for them and paying for their education like they are her own. Atiya is but one example of how a starting $55 loan is enough to get someone on her feet, providing for her family and enabling her to take care of others in the community.

Burundi

A woman with an eye for entrepreneurship, Anastasia first took out a $50 loan to buy twenty chairs, which she rented out for community events. Today she is known as a successful wedding planner in Bujumbura. Her expanded inventory now includes two hundred chairs, a stereo system, baskets, plates, and three wedding dressings in three different sizes (small, medium, and large).

Because of her increased income and her recognition of Christ's call to care for the vulnerable, she adopted two girls whose parents were killed in the recent civil war. Looking toward the future, Anastasia dreams of saving enough money to send both of the girls to university.

Rwanda

Esperance is a skilled weaver. With an initial loan of just $35, Esperance purchased colorful thread and used bed sheets and bed covers. Through her intricate, woven designs, she transformed used bedding into beautiful home decor, increasing its resale value and affording her a healthy profit margin.

As her husband was injured in an accident, Esperance became the sole provider in the household. Through her business acumen, Esperance was able not only to provide for her six children, but she also had enough to put glass in the frames of the windows in her house.

Known as a woman with a heart for God and for others, she began a sewing workshop on her front porch for underprivileged women so that they too could provide for themselves and their families. Her home became a classroom where the women met to learn, pray, read the Bible, and grow together in community. Each of the five women can now provide for her family using the skills she learned from Esperance.

Beyond that, she has brought seven orphans into her home as her own. Today, she is paying for the education of all thirteen children, five of whom are at the university level.

An Alternative Approach

Microfinance is not just a way of helping individuals increase their income. It is also a powerful tool that empowers women (and men) like Mama Atiya, Anastasia, and Esperance to address the orphan crisis by working hard and using their profits to show Christ's love in their communities. Supporting these three mothers helped to keep their children in their homes and allowed them to experience the dignity of work. It allowed these mothers to bless their children with a vision for *their* future, by providing an example of how hard work can pay off. It also allowed them to bless their communities, even to the extent of helping other orphaned children in their neighborhoods. Our efforts in sustainability must focus on avoiding dependency on foreign donors, but it must also affirm God's design for the family, where parents are providers for their children.

What are some other practical ways that we can turn the concepts of this chapter into realities in orphan care communities?

PRACTICAL IDEAS FOR ORPHAN CARE COMMUNITITES

Vocational Training

There are two great ways to implement vocational training in an orphan care community context. The first is to offer high-level training in areas of labor that are needed on a local level. The New Hope Vocational Institute, for example, has been able to provide vocational training for young men and women who are not gifted or called to pursue higher academic education. Through gardens and by providing services to the surrounding community, much of the school is able to pay for itself, while providing skilled laborers with a vision for God-centered self-sufficiency in the local community.

Another, less direct way to offer vocational training is by providing internships and placements for young people interested in certain fields of work. Such opportunities will simultaneously give the young men and women much-needed experience in a trade or profession and enable them to discern whether they are gifted or truly called to work in that area.[14]

Enterprise Farm

In countries where land is available and crops can be grown, agricultural projects are a great means for providing impact on a local level while generating income for the ministry. Lifesong for Orphans' project in Zambia, Lifesong Farms, is impacting a community where only 30 percent of adults are employed. By growing strawberries and selling them to local grocers, the ministry is providing the gift of a job and self-worth to an orphaned child's caregiver, allowing him or her to care for even more orphaned children. The farms are also able to provide temporary employment to the children as they transition into adult living. Through the creation of a sustainable business, providing micro-loans, and providing empowerment training, the employment rate among the caregivers of Lifesong students today is 92 percent.[15]

Creative Businesses

Over the years, I (Keith) have enjoyed watching creative business ventures in action. One street children project I visited kept rabbits and fed them through gathering leftover lettuce and cabbage from the local market venders. They were then able to provide meat for themselves or sell the rabbits for a small profit. Another venture catered to my American taste buds through the provision of hamburgers and fries delivered to my doorstep by a child earning money for school.

Students in New Hope Uganda's Investment Year program, which provides discipleship, vocational guidance, and internships,[16] have created a working store that provides basic necessities, purchases fruits and vegetables from local growers for resale, and also serves as a hangout spot by selling soda products and small baked goods.

Coffee Business

Many creative business efforts are centered on coffee. New Hope's Investment Year students purchase coffee in bulk and repackage and market it with their own unique label.

Other organizations roast and sell coffee as a vehicle to care for orphaned and abandoned children with excellence. In most situations, one hundred percent of the proceeds from the coffee sales go toward the care of the orphaned children in the particular ministry's care.[17]

Orphan Crafts

Ministries around the world also are beginning to utilize the creativity and local materials available to create various crafts and jewelry for sale both locally and in foreign contexts. Pearl Ministries has created a seasonal niche that allows them to provide fair trade, hand-crafted African ornaments to support orphaned children in Uganda.[18]

Saving and Investing

Ugandans by and far tend to live hand to mouth. Recognizing the need to introduce and create a culture of planning and saving, the leadership of New Hope Uganda established what is known as Seed Savers. The program functions as a basic savings and loan, teaching economic principles and biblical stewardship, while also providing a means of generating interest and income on money saved and shares purchased for investment in local projects. The impact of this small ministry is being seen throughout the community as men and women who have never understood savings or had a means to do so in a profitable way are not only saving money for themselves, but are learning to give to others out of the little that they have been entrusted with. The Chalmers Center for Economic Development, founded by Dr. Brian Fikkert, is a tremendous training resource on how to establish community-based savings programs like this.

Work Scholarships

A few years ago New Hope began requiring each child going on for vocational or further study to pay a certain percentage of their education. The amount increases with each level, with University level as the highest. The ministry commits a certain portion as scholarship, but it is up to the children to come up with the rest. Whether through relatives' contributions or through work projects, the kids are mentored in wise planning, investing, and generating income.

CONTINUALLY MOVING FORWARD

Our ultimate goal is neither self-sustainability, nor self-sufficiency. Ultimately, our goal is to honor our great God and Father who has given us the gift and calling of work and entrusted us to raise sons and daughters who will look to Him for all things. We desire to see our children live lives dependent on Him above all else, while working diligently where He has planted them until they reach the fullness of their potential and gifting. While this chapter may seem like a mountain of ideas and information, at the heart of it all is a calling for strategic thinking, planning, and implementing. What works in one context might not work in another. But you are not alone on the journey. The more we are able to corroborate efforts, the better for us, the better for the parents, and the better for the children who we are all seeking to serve. Thanks for joining the conversation.

Going ☀ Deeper

1. How has your view of work and self-sustainability been challenged and/or changed after reading this chapter?

2. What are various forms that Christ-centered self-sufficiency can take in your life and the lives of orphaned and vulnerable children around you?

3. What are some practical ways to establish a God-centered view of and practice of work in your own context or in any orphan care communities in which you're working?

4. What creative ways can Westerners and other "outsiders" strategically partner with orphan care communities to help promote and work toward excellence in self-sustainability?

Chapter

12

It Starts in the Heart
(Spiritual Formation)

"These words that I command you today shall be on your heart. You shall teach them diligently to your children, and shall talk of them when you sit in your house, and when you walk by the way, and when you lie down, and when you rise."—Deuteronomy 6:6–7

"For we are his workmanship, created in Christ Jesus for good works, which God prepared beforehand, that we should walk in them."
—Ephesians 2:10

As David used his gifts to serve "the purpose of God in his own generation" (Acts 13:36), God created every child with a unique set of skills, talents, and passions to be used to fulfill specific purposes in this world. That is why an integral part of the best-practices framework is spiritual formation for each and every child in an orphan care community. And it's so much more than simple evangelism—simply sharing the gospel with the children and asking them to pray a prayer. It's about lifelong intentional discipleship.

Home, church, and school stand as the three greatest pillars of spiritual formation, and any excellence-driven orphan care community must work together with these pillars to help children establish their identity as children of God—sinners saved by grace who get to work with Christ to bring renewal to the world.

In fact, for spiritual formation to be effective, it must be interwoven through each of the other best-practice aspects covered in this book (e.g., providing children with Christian, gospel-driven parents; effective psychosocial care grounded in the gospel; a Bible-based education; and gospel-driven national leadership). When God is restricted to one area or sphere of life or when He is not intentionally and fully brought into every sphere, compartmentalization is the dangerous result. This is one of the greatest enemies of spiritual formation that we must protect against.

In this chapter, Keith draws from his years of spiritual formation experience at New Hope Uganda and the New Hope Institute of Childcare and Family, as well as contributions by Dan Cruver[1] and Johnny Carr,[2] to walk us through different ways we can develop orphaned and vulnerable children's (and every other child's) spiritual lives and identities in Christ.

Spiritual Formation
(Keith McFarland with Johnny Carr and Dan Cruver)

"At the heart of the central idea of Christianity lies the reality that Christians will know the Father and the Son."—Donald Fairbairn

Agnes is a double-orphan who lived each day in fear. Death. When would it come for her? She would wake in the dark of night, *What was that? An owl! The announcer of death. Who will be next? Could it be me?* She believed in Jesus, but she thought that Satan held the power of death. She went to church and prayed, hoping to earn God's favor and blessing. She believed the Bible was true, but she also believed what she read in the newspaper, saw on television, and heard on the radio. She once heard someone on the radio say that we are all like people hanging over hell by a spider's thread—one little sin and *snap*.

Agnes attended a youth rally where she heard people talking about demons and family curses. People told her, "If you hear a knock on your roof at night, it is a demon. If your family was involved in witchcraft, you are under a generational curse. You need to get saved if you want to be free from these things." Others told her that the gospel of salvation had to be accepted before the gospel of deliverance could be applied. She wondered, *How many gospels are there?*

While Agnes was being raised in a Christian environment, the culture that she was a part of was also having a profound impact on her view of God, herself, and the world in which she lived.

What was she missing? What are we missing?

The answer lies in spiritual formation.

WHY SPIRITUAL FORMATION?

Have you ever thought about the first physical orphan in the Bible? He was raised by his grandfather and later his uncle. He heard the gospel and believed,[3] but his orphan heart[4] remained. He lived independently. He did not trust God for his provision and protection. He walked a path of compromise, tormented in his soul yet unable to break away from the influence of the world in which he lived. It cost him his family. In the end, he lost everything.

This is Lot. And his story is far too common in our world today.

Lot is often viewed as a side character in the story of Abraham. Yet God strategically places him in the story, side by side on the journey of the man of faith, Abraham. Lot's story stands out as a contrast to Abraham's life—a life saturated with living faith and that faith's impact throughout his lifetime. Lot's story is a genuine tragedy.

Tragedy is the inevitable result when spiritual formation is lacking in the world of orphan care.

This chapter is a rallying cry for orphan advocates, orphan care providers, and orphans themselves to think deeply about spiritual formation. If we fail in spiritual formation, then we will fail the children we are seeking to love and serve.

What Is Spiritual Formation?

Spiritual formation is ultimately the work of the Holy Spirit; His delight to change His people into the image of Christ. It is Christ formed in you, in me, and in orphans who then cease to be orphans. They have relationship with their Father, which enables them to become growing children in His family and world.

It is a journey.

When Jesus told the rich young ruler to sell all of his possessions and give them to the poor, the selling and giving was not an end in itself. Jesus had a great goal for him: "And come, follow me" (Luke 18:22).

The calling to self-abandonment leads to the rich discovery of a lifetime—a lifetime of walking with Jesus. This is spiritual formation, a call to a life of discovering Jesus, relating to Jesus, *knowing* Jesus. It is a Jesus-saturated life.

We need to lead orphans on a journey of spiritual formation as together we seek to truly *know* and *follow* Jesus, the One who *is* Truth. This journey of discovering truth is ultimately a theological journey, as we get to know God Himself. This is where it begins.

STUDYING THEOLOGY FOR THE SAKE OF THE ORPHANS[5]

"There must be knowledge of God before there can be love to God; there must be a knowledge of divine things as they are revealed before there can be an enjoyment of them."—Charles Spurgeon[6]

Christians frequently ask us, "Do we really have time to study theology when there is so much to be done for orphans now? Scripture commands us to care for orphans, so isn't that enough?" Or, "Do we really have the time and resources for teaching theology to orphans when they have so many material, physical, and educational needs to be filled?"

If we think of theology merely as information about God—as the mental collection of facts about the Father, Son, and Holy Spirit—then these questions are legitimate. But if by theology we mean a real knowing of God, an ongoing and growing relational engagement with God Himself (which is what we do mean), the questions are quite misguided.

Theology is *never* merely or even *mainly* information. We know there is much more to the ocean than the fish it contains. In the same way, there is so much more to theology than all the information is contains.

Theology has always existed in the Father's eternal knowing of the Son and the Son's eternal knowing of the Father in the personal fellowship of the Holy Spirit. For all of eternity, the Father has known the Son and the Son the Father, and they have enjoyed this in the joyous fellowship of God the Spirit (2 Cor. 13:14). Understood like this, theology is a gracious gift to humanity, because our delight in theology is actually a sharing in the eternal love story of the Father and His Son in personal bond with the Spirit. It is a never-ending participation in the communion of love that the Trinity is ("God is love"). There is no greater gift in the universe that can be given to man!

So, do we really have time for theology *now* when orphans need our help *now*? Yes, an emphatic yes.

Do orphans legitimately need theology when they need so many other things now? Yes, an emphatic yes.

Whether we are working "hands-on" with orphans or simply have a heart for orphans and are seeking a way to live out James 1:27, we must be committed to a life of growing deeper in our commitment and love for theology.

Because theology is the beginning point for spiritual formation, one of the worst things we can do is neglect or overlook theology. If we neglect it, we and the orphans God places before us are the poorer for it. But if we embrace theology as those who live in daily, vital, loving communion with the God who is love, we and the orphans with whom we share life and theology will be all the more relationally richer for it.

What orphans and orphan care communities most need, then, is Christians who do not merely know and share true statements about God. Rather, orphans need Christians who freely participate (by the power of the gospel) in the mutual knowing and loving of the triune God and freely share that experience with everyone they come in contact with, including orphans.

Ultimately, spiritual formation is more than an evangelism that involves simply telling others about the gospel and praying prayers; orphaned and vulnerable children, as every other human being, need to be discipled and spiritually formed by Christians who are deeply theological, both intellectually and experientially. If we are to fulfill James 1:27, we must have and practice both. Look at the life of Jesus. His knowing of God was both intellectual and experiential and no one did more for the poor and marginalized than he did.

How do we get to the place of this kind of spiritual formation? How do we lead orphans there? It all revolves around the gospel.

THE CENTER POINT OF THE GOSPEL

Agnes was confused about the gospel. She is not alone. Many cultures around the world promote different "versions" of the gospel: the prosperity gospel (accept Jesus and God will make you healthy and wealthy), the pray-this-prayer-to-get-out-of-hell gospel (accept Jesus and get a ticket to heaven), the gospel of deliverance (accept Jesus so we can deal with your curses and demons), and the gospel of works (accept Jesus but also do this and this and this and this to get to heaven). Of course, there are many more, and we often blend various versions together. But in reality and in truth, there is only one gospel in the midst of many distortions.

When the apostle Paul wrote to the Galatians, he was writing to a church that was turning to a "different gospel" (1:6). Paul emphasized there is only *one* gospel, adding that any promoters of another version of the gospel should be accursed! Getting the gospel right is that important!

What is the gospel? If we miss this fundamental truth, then all spiritual formation will be affected, and we ultimately will build our lives and instruction on the wrong foundation.

The Gospel of Mark begins with the words, "The beginning of the gospel of Jesus Christ, the Son of God." In Mark's mind, all that he wrote about the birth, life, death, and resurrection of Jesus *was* the gospel. Jesus is the center. As John Piper has written, "God is the Gospel."[7]

We could summarize the gospel by saying: The gospel is the "good news" that Jesus Christ, the unique, eternal Son of God, was born of a virgin; lived a sinless life; died on a cross; rose again on the third day as the victor over sin, death, and Satan; and ascended to heaven where He reigns with all authority in heaven and on earth.[8]

How should we respond to this incredible good news? How do we lead orphans to respond?

RESPONDING TO THE GOSPEL

A right response to the gospel includes a biblical concept of faith and repentance. The gospel demands more than simple mental assent. Right response incorporates belief and a complete reorientation of one's life around the truth of Jesus. This is where faith meets repentance.

As David Platt wrote:

> *Repentance* is a rich biblical term that signifies an elemental transformation in someone's mind, heart, and life. When people repent, they turn from walking in one direction to running in the opposite direction. From that point forward, they think differently, believe differently, feel differently, love differently, and live differently. . . . Jesus' call to repentance, then, was a summons

for them to renounce sin and all dependence on self for salvation. Only by turning from their sin and themselves and toward Jesus could they be saved.[9]

Ultimately, faith and repentance are like the doorway into a life of spiritual formation. Moving forward, proper application of the gospel to sin, death, and Satan is also crucial for a right view of God, ourselves, and the world in which we live.

APPLYING THE GOSPEL: THE CROSS AND SIN

"For our sake he made him to be sin who knew no sin, so that in him we might become the righteousness of God."—2 Corinthians 5:21

Jesus took our sin and God's wrath for sin upon Himself that we might be given the gift of His righteousness. This is what is known as justification, and it is God's free gift to sinners who turn to Him in faith (Eph. 2:8–9).

Shepherding the hearts of orphans into this glorious truth is one of the greatest challenges in spiritual formation. The heart is revealed through every action and every word of a child.[10] Be it selfishness, pride, deceit, or even compliance, it is difficult and time-consuming to take the time to identify the sin in the heart behind the actions and deal appropriately in that place. Leading orphans to the place where Jesus is continually invited into those heart places, where faith and repentance become a lifestyle, is the first step in dealing with sin and shepherding the heart.[11]

APPLYING THE GOSPEL: THE CROSS AND DEATH

"'Death is swallowed up in victory.' 'O death, where is your victory? O death where is your sting?'" . . . But thanks be to God, who gives us the victory through our Lord Jesus Christ."[12]—1 Corinthians 15:54–55, 57

Orphans, like most children, fear death.[13] It is the enemy that swallowed up their parent(s) and changed their lives forever. Every culture has various beliefs about death, what causes death, and how to keep death away. Yet the Bible reveals Jesus as the one who holds the keys of death and Hades and who delivers us from our lifelong slavery to the fear of death.[14] This is good news for orphans! The gospel alone sets us free from the fear of death. Jesus' resurrection brought victory over the grave and alone provides the hope of life.

Importantly, though, we must be sensitive to how near the pain of death is to an orphan's heart before seeking to lead them into this glorious truth. Simply asking questions and praying with a child can go a long way in leading them away from the pain of death to the hope of life and freedom from fear.

APPLYING THE GOSPEL: THE CROSS AND SATAN

"Since therefore the children share in flesh and blood, he himself likewise partook of the same things, that through death he might destroy the one who has the power of death, that is, the devil, and deliver all those who through fear of death were subject to lifelong slavery.[15]—Hebrews 2:14–15

In many parts of the world, fear of Satan or spirits is a normal part of life. Yet living in fear is counter to living in the truth of the gospel. According to the Scriptures, Satan was cast out, disarmed, and destroyed at the cross.[16] He has no power over the lives of Christians. While we still see Satan moving around "like a roaring lion," and as we await God's final crushing of the serpent's head (Rom. 16:20; Rev. 20:10), we have assurance that the enemy of our soul has no power over us. As we stand firm in faith in the truth of the gospel, resting in Jesus' victory over sin, death, and Satan, we are able to experience freedom from fear.[17] We must lead orphans into the glorious freedom of this reality.

PILLARS OF SPIRITUAL DEVELOPMENT

Applying the gospel to sin, death, and Satan was life changing for Agnes. As she lived in the reality of the gospel, she was set free from fear of death and Satan. The sin that had gripped her heart lost its hold and she began growing in her love of God and others. But this was just the beginning. She had the foundation in place, but in order to become a pillar "carved to adorn a palace,"[18] she needed further grounding. For Agnes to grow as a daughter of God and to understand what it means to live as a real woman of God in her generation, it would take intentionality and care.

In order to help us move forward on our journey of spiritual formation, here are five pillars (among others[19]) that constitute a base for best practice in spiritual formation in any orphan care community:

* Worldview formation

* The Word of God

* Biblical sonship

* Manhood and womanhood

* Strategic discipleship and investment

As we examine these pillars, we will also look at practical ways to implement each in any orphan care context.

Pillar One: Worldview Formation

Worldview is the lens through which we view and make sense of all of life and reality. In actuality, it is how we understand ourselves, others, God, and the world in which we live. Each of us has a worldview.[20] From the time we are born into this world, shaping forces have been at work that impact how we think, act, and live.[21] Family, friends, teachers, religion, and media have all powerfully formed our outlook on everything.

If we are to help children understand how our cultural worldview impacts all areas of our lives, we must dig deeply into the realm of worldview.[22]

Ultimately, God should be the definer of how we view the world and live in it. He must be the One to confront our fallen worldviews and give us *His lens* through which to view life and each other. This means that the kingdom of God must become the driving force behind values and pursuits, or we risk our children and ourselves living like Lot in the world.

We desire that orphans everywhere be not conformed to the world, but instead be transformed by the renewal of their minds (Rom. 12:2). For this to happen it takes a life saturated in the Word of God.

Pillar Two: The Word of God

Throughout Scripture, syncretism comes naturally for the people of God. It also comes naturally for each one of us. Syncretism happens when we combine the worship of God with the worship of the world and its gods. It happens when we read the Bible through the lens of our cultures and "fit" it into our cultural ways of thinking. Or even worse, we do the opposite and keep the two in separate compartments as if they have nothing to do with one another. Leading orphans on the journey of spiritual formation means the Word of God is accepted as the standard and test for all of life. It exposes all fallen cultures, whether American, European, Asian, African, or any other culture.

One key concept for combating syncretism is that of authority.

Authority

Agnes, like many Christians around the world, believed the Bible to be authoritative. The problem was she believed the Word of God was *an* authority among many others, instead of *the* authority to which all others must conform. Spiritual formation will be weak where it is accompanied with a low view of the Word of God or where the Bible is seen as one authority among many.[23]

One of the most helpful means of establishing the authority of all of Scripture is to have a firm grasp on the entire story of the Bible.

The Big Picture

The Bible is God's story and each of us has a role to play in this unfolding drama. At the center of God's story (and our story) is the Lamb who was slain from before the foundation of the world (Rev. 13:8). The entire Old Testament gives us the foundation for that story. It is a shadow of the coming Christ, the unveiling of our desperate need for a Savior, and God's gracious provision for that need. All of us need to have an understanding of the "big story" of the Bible, the covenants and promises, and the redemptive themes throughout what scholars call salvation history, if we are ever going to understand our place in this chapter of the story and lead orphans to discover their greatest purpose in life as a part of His story.

Asking ourselves and answering four simple questions will serve to equip us and the orphans we are seeking to lead when we study the Old Testament together (I've included more discussion about application of these questions in the footnotes):

  1. What does this story reveal about God?[24]

2. What does this reveal about man's heart (and my heart)?[25]

3. How is the gospel unveiled?[26]

4. What is my response?[27]

Three resources for teaching the story of the Bible to children (and adults) are: *In the Beginning . . . Jesus: A Chronological Study for Children on Redemptive History* found at childrendesiringgod.org; *The Jesus Storybook Bible* by Sally Lloyd-Jones; and *The Big Picture Story Bible* by David Helm. These story Bibles complement each other very well as each carries a different focus and theme. We have used all of these in Uganda, adapting things culturally.

Bible-Saturated Communities

Excellence in spiritual development means cultivating a culture where the Word of God is a normal part of life. It means that the Word is not restricted to church or devotion time. This means the reading of God's Word takes place throughout the day. Conversations and discussions centered on the Scriptures are happening everywhere—e.g., during mealtime, in the garden, at school. But this doesn't just happen—it takes effort and intentionality to cultivate such a lifestyle.

One way to achieve this is to have staff-and-child-led Bible studies, or to read the Bible or the New Testament through in a year. This can be done as a family, community, church, school, or combination of all.

New Hope Uganda worked to cultivate a Bible-centered culture recently by reading through the entire Bible in a year as an entire ministry.[28] Teachers set aside class time in school for daily reading. Offices took time to read together. New Hope's radio station provided daily readings in the local language. The church preached through the big story of the Bible. Over what ended up being a year and a half, the spiritual practice saturated the whole community in God's story, laid foundations for the gospel, and changed lives.[29]

Pillar Three: Biblical Sonship

One of the greatest challenges of spiritual formation is leading orphans to discover and walk in the fullness of their identity as sons and daughters of God. This was the hardest thing for Agnes to overcome. In her mind, God the Father was like her earthly dad had been. She had little contact with her dad in the early years, unless she needed something. And even then, she would only approach him very humbly, on her knees, in hopes that he might grant her request. That was the extent of the relationship. But that is not the relationship that Jesus has with *His* Father.

At the core of Jesus' relationship with the Father is an intimacy that goes back for all of eternity. It is an intimacy seen at His baptism and expressly revealed in Jesus' prayer to the Father in the garden of Gethsemane. At the height of his agony in facing the coming cross, Mark tells us that Jesus fell on the ground and prayed, "Abba, Father, all things are possible for you. Remove this cup from me. Yet not what I will, but what you will" (Mark 14:36).

The *Abba* cry of Jesus is one of relationship, familiarity, and intimacy. It was a word that no typical Jewish man or woman would have uttered as an address to God. Yet Jesus, in the darkest hour of his life, cried out in the most familiar and intimate title for Father His language offered. The closest English translation would be "Daddy" or "Papa," yet even these fail to communicate the significance and intimacy of the original "Abba" cry.[30]

Incredibly, because of the glorious gospel, this same intimacy with the Father is now offered to us.

In light of all of this, we could summarize the story of the Bible the way theologian Graeme Goldsworthy likes to put it: "*God's* people in *God's* place under *God's* rule" (italics mine).[31] But we like to tweak Goldsworthy's words slightly and offer it this way:

The ultimate destination of the Grand Story of Redemption is *the Father's children in the Father's home under the Father's care.*[32]

Can you see how the entire sweep of the Story of Redemption can be described as climaxing with *the Father's children in the Father's home under the Father's eternal care?*

Our justification (i.e., being declared righteous because of Jesus' sacrifice and the removal of guilt and the penalty of sin) and adoption into God's family are two foundation stones that, if missing or distorted, will cause our attempts at spiritual formation to be empty, weak, and misleading. We are leading children somewhere on their journey of faith, and that somewhere should be into a growing relationship with God the Father, through the Son, and by the Spirit.[33]

There are many practical ways to lead orphaned and vulnerable children (and all of our children) on this journey of growing intimacy with the Father.[34] At New Hope, one practice that we have found to be very helpful is to ask children what words come to mind when they hear the word *father*. Have them explain why or draw pictures to express their feelings. Pray with them where earthly fatherhood has meant pain and disappointment. Ask God to make His fatherhood known to their heart.

Another practice is to read John 14 (or the entire Gospel of John) and take note of how Jesus describes His Dad. List the characteristics of Jesus demonstrated through the gospels, and remind children that this is what God the Father is like. Is this the kind of Father we all long for? Why?[35] (For more ideas on deepening children's intimacy with God, read footnote 34 and visit ThinkOrphan.com.)

The journey into spiritual sonship is a growing relationship of trust and dependence on God. While this is a lifelong journey, it is also one where we are maturing in our faith to become the men and women that God has purposed us to be. That is what makes the next pillar so important.

Pillar Four: Manhood and Womanhood

The world is full of competing visions of what it means to be a man or a woman. Ever since the fall, God's design for manhood and womanhood has been turned upside down. The cultural worldviews related to *what it means to be a man or a woman* are designed to keep us in bondage, living as immature boys and girls even when wearing adult clothing.

Various cultures also have confused the roles relating to manhood and womanhood, either making women subservient to men (or even to cows!) or subtly valuing them above men. The beauty of the biblical vision of manhood and womanhood is that both genders are equal before God as those made in His image, and both have been given roles to guard and promote the unique identity He has given mankind by making us male and female.

It is Jesus alone who can lead us to maturity as the men and women that He has designed us to be, and Jesus alone can redeem the roles of men and women reflecting His glory, the image of Christ, today.

Excellence in spiritual formation seeks to identify and promote biblical manhood and womanhood in the life of each child, as opposed to simply focusing on the children as a general group. This looks beyond putting girls and boys through the same training, experiences, schooling, etc., and expecting them to somehow come out different. It means individualized teaching, training, and discipleship that leads to maturity and wisdom in the living out of redeemed manhood and womanhood. When this occurs, orphans are raised with a clear understanding of what it really means to be a man or a woman while watching it modeled and lived out in the context of family, church, school, and community.[36]

Practical ways that New Hope Uganda is seeking to implement the pillar of manhood and womanhood are through requiring all parents and staff to attend teachings that uncover unbiblical views of manhood and womanhood within their culture, and how they are playing out on a personal and community level. Teachings examine Old and New Testament passages that unveil God's design for men and women, as well as Jesus' display of genuine manhood lived out.

In African fashion, but in a redeemed way, we offer a calling into manhood and womanhood that solidifies God's calling of His people to maturity in redeemed manhood and womanhood. We set aside specific days for manhood and womanhood that confront various cultural lies and practices while pointing to the beauty and truth of what God has designed.

New Hope has dedicated full-time staff working toward developing and implementing the manhood and womanhood initiative across the ministry and across the country. As part of the ministry, Musana Camps (a manhood, womanhood and family camp on the shores of Lake Victoria) exists as a place where orphans or various groups can come and receive solid biblical teaching on manhood and womanhood.

Pillar Five: Strategic Discipleship and Investment

Agnes has walked a long road from the pain of loss to the healing of family. After she discovered God's Fatherhood, she began finding healing from the wounds of her past and the orphan heart she had carried. She found security in God as His daughter and began walking in mature womanhood, calling her young sisters to follow her in that calling. Yet through it all, she would say the most important thing God brought into her life was fatherhood and motherhood, men and women committed to walking with her on the journey of spiritual formation. She found family who laughed and cried with her and who stuck it out with her through thick and thin. A family to walk with her through the ups and downs, the joys and pains, the victories and defeats of day-to-day life, pointing her to truth and shepherding her heart. This is *real* spiritual formation.

Lasting spiritual formation takes strategic discipleship and investment. For discipleship to be strategic, every child needs to be *known*. This means her story, her life, and her journey are shared with someone who cares about her and who is committed to walking alongside of her.[37] Orphans do not need someone simply doing good deeds *to* them or *for* them; they need people to live life *with* them, giving sacrificially of their time, energy, input, discipline, prayer, and encouragement.

The goal of spiritual formation is not to "change" anyone, but to walk with each child *one step closer to Jesus*.[38] This is done through day-to-day life and can be as simple as praying together, reading Scripture, listening, asking questions, visiting, appropriate physical touch, and other means of care. This also requires parents (and staff) who are committed to long-term relationship, as rapid staff turnover only adds to the wounding of an orphan's heart.

Here are some key things to keep in mind when it comes to strategic discipleship and spiritual formation:

* *Cultivate a love for the church.* It is easy for organizations to think they are islands in themselves. Cultivating a love for the local church will provide crucial lifelong fellowship, discipleship, family, and submission to godly authority and the Word.

* *Enjoy God in His creation.* Opening up children's eyes to the glory of God revealed through all of creation is a way to cultivate lifestyle worship of God and keeps fresh the spiritual lens through which we should view the world.

* *Enjoy God in work.* Learning to do all things for the glory of God includes gaining a healthy view and practice of work.[39]

* *Practice spiritual disciplines.* It is in the context of doing life together that the spiritual disciplines taught and practiced by Jesus become more than simple external religious practice. Prayer, Bible reading, fasting, memorizing Scripture, as well as caring for the poor and needy, become a natural outflow of walking in relationship with Jesus, wanting to become like Him, and desiring to make Him known.

Jesus was clear that because of His authority in heaven *and* on earth, Christians are to make disciples of all nations, teaching them to observe all that our Lord commanded.[40] The beauty is that when discipleship is intentional in orphan care communities (and everywhere else), these five pillars of spiritual formation will naturally all work and flow together. When that happens, it is not just children's hearts and lives that are transformed, but entire ministries, communities, and even nations.

LIVING IT OUT

What are practical ways an excellence-driven orphan care community can incorporate the journey of spiritual formation into its day-to-day practices and operations? Here are some ideas from things we've experienced at New Hope over the years.

Most evenings, the various family groups of New Hope Uganda have a time of worship and sharing of the Word together. These times are led by the family father, other "aunties" or "uncles" (i.e., staff members), or the children themselves. Testimonies, games, or just times of unstructured fun are also important parts of the gatherings.

When the children of New Hope reach a specific age or place in school, they take a "gap year" during which the New Hope staff invests strategically in them. Our IY (Investment Year) department uses that time to help the children solidify a biblical worldview, and they seek to find out what gifts and talents God has put in them and what calling He has on their lives. This is done in relationship with the parents and families of the children with the goal that each son or daughter gain a clearer picture of the direction the Lord is taking them in life, not based on spur of the moment decisions or exam-based results. Through prayer, service opportunities, and work experience gained through three ten-week internships in the areas they are interested in pursuing in the future, children are better prepared to move into their future.[41]

New Hope Uganda also provides a number of ways that children can receive strategic investment while giving to others. The church provides service opportunities in prison and hospital ministries, as well as involvement in the worship team. The youth lead a youth-oriented discussion program on the local radio station where they talk about issues young people are facing, while they share what God's Word speaks into those areas. Our young people also started Emmanuel Youth Outreach

(EYO) as an outreach ministry. Under the authority of the church, it continues to be youth led and operated, organizing community outreach projects, evangelism, discipleship, and youth rallies.

Whatever your situation in the particular country and culture in which God has placed you, there are incredible opportunities all around you to strategically invest in orphans by helping them to simply live out the gospel as the light of Christ in their communities.

JOY IN THE JOURNEY

Spiritual formation is a journey on which we have the privilege of leading orphans as together we heed Jesus' words: "Come, follow me." May we remember that the calling to self-abandonment, the calling to spiritual formation, is a call to a life of discovering Jesus, relating to Jesus, and *knowing* Jesus. The greatest thing that we have to offer orphans is found completely outside of ourselves. It is the treasure of God Himself. And we cannot offer what is most precious if it is not most precious to us.

In order to help others on their journey to maturity, our faith needs to be built on the reality of the gospel. Are we living lives of faith and repentance, finding the freedom Jesus offers based on His defeat of sin, death, and Satan? Ultimately, Jesus is the transformer of our worldviews,[42] the great teacher of His Word,[43] the Father of the fatherless,[44] and the true Man.[45] All of our strategic discipleship and investment must be grounded fully in Him, because His glory is our ultimate goal and He alone can bring ultimate healing, transformation, and renewal to the heart of an orphan.

May you stay the course and enjoy the journey of spiritual formation as together we see orphans across the globe set free to bask in the fullness of their identities as sons and daughters and full-grown men and women of God who then pass it on to their own families and other fatherless children.

Going ☀ Deeper

1. How has your understanding of spiritual formation been challenged as a result of this chapter? List some ways and then share them with someone.

2. What are ways you can apply the gospel to your life as you walk with and lead others on the journey of spiritual formation?

3. What does it mean for you to view spiritual formation as walking with others "one step closer to Jesus"? How can you practically apply this in your context?

Chapter 13

WHERE DO WE GO FROM HERE?

We have discussed a lot in this book. Together, we have explored the issues surrounding orphaned and vulnerable children and orphanages, why we care about orphaned and vulnerable children, why orphan care communities are necessary at this time in history, why excellence is needed in every area of orphan care, including orphan care communities, what best-practice care entails and looks like in practice around the world, and steps we can take to move toward establishing and sustaining thriving orphan care communities around the world. As we've seen, excellence in orphan care in our world today goes way beyond adoption and involves the same things and often more than what we need in order to raise our own children.

In the end, it is quite simple . . . we need to treat every child as if he or she is our own child and love and care for him or her accordingly. If we would not be willing to have our own children (or a loved one's children, if you don't have children) raised in a particular orphanage or orphan care community if they were orphaned, we need to make any necessary, culturally appropriate changes to make the community reach the level of excellence that we demand for our own family and home.

I pray that you have taken the time to read this book in its entirety, process it, and think about how it applies to your life, both personally and corporately with others around the world. After reading, processing, and applying, I hope that you have concrete ideas about how you can advocate for orphaned and vulnerable children, and feel, as I do, that together we have taken a major step toward answering the question posed at the beginning of this book: "While holding onto the permanent, legal family as ideal and constantly working toward that ideal, how can we develop orphan care communities with as much excellence and best practice as possible?"

Given the scope of the crisis and myriad problems associated with it, we know that we don't have all the answers, and we will not likely have them during our lifetime. But, as you finish this book and realize this reality, I hope that you are not left discouraged. I hope that you don't, in any way, feel like giving up or stopping the hard work involved in figuring out the answers and continually seeking to improve the care we are providing to every single orphan and vulnerable child in our world.

To the contrary, I hope that the conversation in this book, and the great work going on all over the world encourages you to continue pursuing orphan excellence in whatever capacity you are called, whether that be as a national, a field worker, a church leader, a worker with an orphan care organization, or an individual who stumbled upon this book and became a brand-new orphan advocate. If we're going to make a dent in the orphan care crisis, all of us need to act now, in the place where we are, and in the ways we are able. And we all need to collaborate and act together.

* As an individual, if you're not called into full-time ministry, your excellence-driven action might include (but absolutely is not limited to) participation with others in ThinkOrphan: an Immersive Experience,[1] adoption, foster care, actively sponsoring a child, advocating for orphaned children with governmental and other authorities, taking a short-term trip (in accordance with the recommendations in this book), or partnering in prayer, financially, and/or in other ways with a family-model orphan care community or other orphan care organization furthering best practices.[2]

* If you're a national in a developing country, your excellence-driven action might include advocating for and working to enable healthy family reunification, domestic adoption, quality foster care, working with your church to love orphaned and vulnerable children in your community, and/or working to ensure that local orphanages and orphan care communities are furthering the best practices and excellence discussed in this book (e.g., providing families for orphaned and vulnerable children, partnering with churches and others in the local community, working toward self-sustainability, and developing national leaders).

❋ If you're a church leader in the United States, it might include regular preaching on excellence and best practices in orphan care, creating an orphan care ministry and adoption fund in your church, leading short-term trips, encouraging long-term partnerships with orphan care communities locally and globally, engaging church participation in ThinkOrphan: an Immersive Experience, and/or promoting adoption, Safe Families for Children,[3] and healthy foster care in your church.[4]

❋ If you work with an orphanage or orphan care community as a national or foreign missionary, seek to ensure that your organization is continually working to provide excellence-driven care for each and every one of its children in a manner consistent with the principles and framework provided in this book. Ask and answer the hard questions, and do not compromise or settle for anything less than gospel-driven excellence.

❋ Regardless of who and where you are in the world, one way that all of us can stay connected, engage the conversation, and collaborate on best practices and excellence in orphan care is through ongoing involvement with the discussions and resources on ThinkOrphan.com (which I invite you to visit now if you haven't already), the companion website to this book.

By engaging in one or more of these wise, excellence-driven actions, and by participating in other civil, educated conversations in your circles, all of us working on this project hope that you actively become part of our team, join our conversation, collaborate with us, and advocate with excellence for beautiful children around the world who currently have no advocate in their lives. Because we have so far to go in our pursuit of orphan excellence, we need everyone working together as companions, not competitors, to love each and every one of these children as God loves them.

Some Real-Life Examples

As we act together, it's important to remember that your action will look different from my action. Let's be honest . . . most people reading this book aren't called to full-time ministry. Many will never adopt or provide foster care to an orphaned or vulnerable child. And nobody is called to do everything on the spectrum of orphan care.

But we are all called to love the orphaned and vulnerable in some way. We are called to *do something* with excellence. Knowing that, Keith and I want to share our stories with you to show how God uses ordinary people (yes, even lawyers) in different ways to fulfill His desire to love orphans with excellence. Hopefully they will encourage and help direct you as you seek your "place" in our collective pursuit of orphan excellence.

Phil's Story

Born and raised in Southern California by two loving, Christian parents, orphaned and vulnerable children didn't cross my mind during my childhood except when I watched *Annie* or *Oliver Twist*. I grew up going to church and responded to God's call (my dad baptized me) when I was nine, but I don't feel like I really started responding to God's call on my life until my junior year of high school when I joined up with a group of young men for a Bible study. (Those young men—now a bit older—are still some of my best friends to this day.) Despite growing in my faith and intimacy with Christ through that Saturday night Bible study, caring for orphaned or vulnerable children still wasn't on my radar when I left home for college. It's just not something that was talked about in the suburbs and on the beaches of South Orange County.

During college and law school, God confirmed in my heart and mind my calling to be an attorney (no, not an adoption or family law attorney). At the time, I thought it was simply because "I was good at it" since I had analytical skills and an argumentative nature. As time went on, however, I began to realize that I was called to be an attorney for a season to prepare me for something other than simply practicing law.

After law school, God blessed me with an amazing first job in Hawaii, where I worked for a federal judge for one year. Incidentally, my future wife, Becca, was on staff with Athletes in Action at the University of Hawaii at that time. And to make a very long story extremely short, God brought Becca and I together in paradise, where we eventually fell in love, and as they say, the rest is history.

After leaving Hawaii, getting married, starting my career as a lawyer in Atlanta in late 2000, and becoming a father to my first daughter in October 2001, I began to understand even more how God wanted me to balance my life between work, my family, and other things. In so doing, I worked very hard at work, while making every effort to eat dinner with my family, play with my kids, put my kids to bed, and spend time with my wife every night. God also used me outside the office to lead community Bible studies and help plant a church in a racially and socially divided city.

You may have noticed that caring for orphaned and vulnerable children still hasn't been mentioned as part of my story, and we're up to 2004. If you think that you missed something or you're mistaken, you're not. Orphan care wasn't even on my radar at that point in my life, and hadn't been on my radar before then. I am living proof that God can even use a lawyer with a rhetoric and communications degree, who has never adopted and has two living parents still married after forty years, to impact the lives of orphaned and vulnerable children. So how did it happen?

In 2004, my family (four of us at the time) and I moved back home to California, where I joined another law firm and God showed me amazing ways that He could use me to glorify Him through my legal skills. Not only at work by seeking to be a worker beyond reproach and a model of Christ's love, but by ensuring that justice was served in my community and throughout the world.

At that time, God captured my heart with a passion to help the oppressed throughout the world, including orphans, widows, the sick, and the poor. And He did this through a "back door" by using various "non-orphan-care" books, including *Desiring God*, *Good News about Injustice*, *Terrify No More*, and *Don't Waste Your Life*. After reading the books,

I felt compelled to do more with my skills and talents to fight against the depths of the horrible slave trade that plagued (and continues to plague) our world. As I researched the trafficking issues deeper, I kept seeing that the vast majority of trafficking victims were orphans, widows, and the poor.

As a result, a passion was ignited within me to keep orphans, widows, and at-risk children from ever being oppressed in those ways. Experiences on mission trips to Brazil and Honduras in 2006 also showed me the world's "deep need" in a real, firsthand way. So, I looked into doing pro bono legal work to fight oppression. I did end up doing pro bono work, but it has looked a lot different than what I thought it would look like.

For starters, the lessons learned through the above research and experiences and my wife's and my desire to adopt from China led me to start an Orphans and Missions Ministry at my church with a few others. As part of that ministry, we began a partnership with La Providencia Orphanage in Honduras, which led to my involvement on the board of directors of Providence World Ministries. After active participation for several months, Providence's board asked me to be the organization's research and development ("R & D") director. Through much prayer, an open heart and mind, and conversations with Becca and several others who knew me well, I discerned that God was calling me to leave my legal career to fill the position of R & D director in the fall of 2008.

How did I know? In short, the position required a blend of (a) the skills and talents with which God has blessed me, including the legal background and (b) the passion to help the world's orphans, widows, sick, poor, and oppressed with which God had captured my heart. Additionally, from the beginning of my legal career, I had felt that God was preparing me for a job where I could use my legal, communication, writing, and analytical skills to further His kingdom. I just had no idea that the job would involve working for a nonprofit orphan care organization—and I would have called you crazy if you had suggested that future for me back in 2003, just eleven short years ago. Much has happened since then—I now serve as Providence's president, have cowritten this book, still get to call Becca my bride, have five beautiful children (three girls and two boys), and get to work with amazing people every day to love orphaned and vulnerable children with more excellence than we did the day before.

And just think . . . my orphan care journey all started by reading a book. Just sayin'.

Keith's Story

I grew up in the rolling hills of West Virginia attending a little church that my grandfather built. When I was fourteen I responded to the gospel and a few years later found myself heading off to Moody Bible Institute in Chicago to study the Bible. My heart was drawn to work with the inner-city kids in the housing projects of Cabrini-Green. It did not take long for my small-town culture and worldview to be exposed and expanded, as this country-talking young man had his eyes opened up to an entirely different world. I fell in love with the children and they deeply impacted me during the years I served in their community. One young boy especially impacted me, and I "adopted" him as my little brother (or did he adopt me as a big brother?), spending between three and five evenings a week together. He remains an intimate part of my life to this day.

While at Moody, my eyes were also opened up to the broader world through friends who were passionate about missions, as well as international students who exposed me to foreign cultures. I was drawn particularly to those from Africa. By my senior year I was cutting class to read books on street children, AIDS orphans, children of war-torn countries, and sexually exploited children. I wrestled with God about the reality of suffering in our world. I walked around in a daze for much of that year, often bumping into a beautiful young lady named Laura Beth, who though she did not understand what I was going through, sought to be a friend nonetheless.

Finally, through His Word and Spirit, God made it clear to me that He is not distant or removed from the suffering children of the world. In fact, He has entered into this suffering and died to redeem it. He showed me that He sends His people to engage the suffering and be His agents of transformation—beauty from ashes. I was in. So after graduating in 1999, I headed to Zambia where I lived with a Zambian family and worked with AIDS orphans and street kids for four months. I then took trains and buses around East Africa researching various ministries and organizations working with at-risk children. Though the trip was perilous at times, it was an incredible faith builder and served to affirm in my heart my calling to work with children in Africa.

I returned to Chicago where I interned and was grounded in a local church, and where I also began hanging out with the same young lady, Laura Beth. I was drawn to her heart for the nations and enjoyed becoming part of her family. She was third born out of eight—I had never seen a family that big! We were married a year and a half later, and eight months after that found ourselves heading to Rwanda to work with street children. From there we headed to New Hope Uganda to be a part of their first class in the Institute of Childcare and Family. We were hungry for mentorship and discipleship from those working directly with orphaned children, but we had no idea what God had in store for us.

Those twenty weeks were life changing, as we were confronted and challenged in just about every way. Starting with our own Western worldviews, moving to the depth and complexity of an African worldview, we unpacked a God-centered worldview that permeates all areas of life. Some of these areas included manhood and womanhood, marriage and family, and healthy ministry as an outflow of all of them. We worked hands-on with orphaned children in the context of a family group, and we fell in love with New Hope's vision to bring the Fatherhood of God to the fatherless by raising up Ugandan men and women to be fathers and mothers to orphans.

After returning to Chicago, we welcomed our first son into our home and began raising support in order to return to Uganda full time. On April 1, 2004, we touched down at Entebbe Airport with nine pieces of luggage and far too many carry-on bags for three of us. We can honestly say it has been a delight to work with New Hope Uganda and the Institute for the past ten years. We love being a part of equipping others for effective work among the fatherless. I also have the joy and privilege of working toward family and church-based orphan care and prevention through our Pastoral Training Institute and village initiatives. We live and work side by side with Ugandans in a community that is very unique and beautiful. It is a privilege to "do life" with the kids from Samuel Family (one of New Hope's family groups) and the other kids around us.

God has graciously given us five biological children (four boys and one girl)—the last two born in Uganda. We also have a Ugandan daughter that we have walked with from our days in the Institute and had the joy of helping to raise into womanhood as a part of the New

Hope family, as well as other "sons" and "daughters" who are a part of our family, even while living elsewhere.

It's Time To Act

So where do we go from here?

We know that there are about 153 million children in the world who have lost at least one parent.

And about 18 million children have lost both of their parents.

This is not new information. We haven't given you novel or modified statistics on the number of orphans in the world. You've seen these numbers in this and other books, and you've heard people talk about the statistics. If you've been a part of the orphan care movement for any time at all, you may even skip past the sections with numbers and percentages because you know the stats so well.

You know the data.

You know the facts.

With that knowledge comes a big risk—a risk of apathy or a feeling that we can do little to change anything. I pray that our knowledge doesn't have that effect and that these numbers never become mundane for any of us. Rather, I pray these numbers invoke a deep compassion and urgency to take action far beyond the ease of donating old shoes, toys, and clothes.

Remember . . . in our world today:

Children are harmed.

Children are violently abused.

Children are killed.

Millions of children do not have a family.

Millions of babies, children, and teenagers do not have a single person in their lives willing to really take care of them.

Millions of children are not loved as we love our own children . . . as those of us with parents were loved as children . . . as God loves them.

It is time to act to change this reality.

It is time for all of us, individually and corporately, to love and act with excellence as we visit orphans in their affliction.

APPENDIX A

CHRISTIAN ALLIANCE FOR ORPHANS' WHITE PAPER: ON UNDERSTANDING ORPHAN STATISTICS[1]

If we are to communicate with humility, credibility, and integrity, Christian orphan advocates must both accurately understand and carefully present orphan-related statistics. Failure to do so undermines the strength of our advocacy and can misguide the actions that organizations, churches and individuals take on behalf of orphans. Meanwhile, an accurate grasp and communication of the true nature of the need provides a strong foundation for an effective, well-focused response.

Current Global Estimates

Although reflecting only broad projections, the estimated number of orphans globally currently reported by the US Government and UNICEF include:

* 17.8 million children worldwide have lost both parents ("double orphan").[2,3]

* 153 million children worldwide have lost *either* one parent ("single orphan") *or* both parents.[4]

Missing From the Estimates

There are many inherent limitations to any data that claims to be truly "global" in nature. While such data can help us gain a clearer picture of the size and scope of need, it can also be misleading.

One of the greatest weaknesses in these global orphan estimates is that they include only orphans that are currently living in homes.[5] They do not count the estimated 2 to 8+ million children living in institutions.[6]

Nor do current estimates include the vast number of children who are living on the streets,[7] exploited for labor, victims of trafficking, or participating in armed groups. *Thus, global orphan statistics significantly underestimate the number of orphans worldwide and fail to account for many children that are among the most vulnerable and most in need of a family.*

Many of these children who live in orphanages or on the streets are known as "social orphans." Although one or even both of their parents may be alive, social orphans rarely see their parents or experience life in a family. Some never do. Global orphan statistics shed virtually no light on the reality of the vast number of social orphans who have one or more living parents, yet experience life as if they did not.[8]

Finally, these global statistics reveal nothing about the distinct needs and vulnerabilities of individual children. Losing one or both parents increases a child's vulnerability greatly. But seeking the best outcome for each child requires knowing far more about him or her.

Priorities in Response to Orphan Need

The Christian Alliance for Orphans affirms the historic Christian understanding—conveyed in Scripture and affirmed by social science[9]—that God intended the family as the essential environment for children. We believe the ideal outcome for every orphan is to know the love and nurture of a permanent family.

Our world's brokenness at times makes this goal unattainable. Thus, alternative forms of care are sometimes necessary. This reality calls us to affirm two seemingly opposing truths at the same time.

First, that amidst the deeply painful and complex situations facing orphans around the globe, there are times when care outside of a permanent family may be the best that can be attained. This can be especially true in countries in which war, disease or other factors have done great harm to the fabric of society. In such situations, the Christian Alliance for Orphans affirms the convictions articulated in its "Core Principles" document (see end of document).[10]

Second, that the need for triage measures should not obscure the ideal or diminish our pursuit of it. This includes:

1. **Preserving Families.** *We must work to aid widow-and-orphan and widower-and-orphan families, as well as other*

families at risk of disintegration. This includes offering opportunities and support that enable these families to remain safely intact—and providing the community and other resources to help them thrive.

2. **Reuniting Families.** *Whenever it can be done safely and responsibly, we must work to rejoin in a timely manner families that have been sundered by war, natural disaster, poverty or other crises, including situations where children have been temporarily placed in residential care—and provide the community supports and other resources to help these families thrive.*[11]

3. **Expanding Families.** *When birth parents have died, or are unwilling or unable to provide adequate care even with outside support, we must work to place orphans in permanent, loving families—and provide the community and other resources to help these families thrive.*

Implications of the Data

In light of the information presented above, it is important to understand that:

✳ *Millions of orphaned children have a surviving parent and are part of a one-parent family that needs help to remain together and to thrive.*[12] There are certainly times when a surviving parent is unwilling or unable to provide adequate parental care, but to the fullest extent possible, we place priority on efforts to preserve struggling families and to re-unify those that have been separated.[13] Research suggests that single orphans—especially those who've lost their mother—are much more vulnerable than non-orphans to a wide range of dangers, including HIV, teen pregnancy, depression, suicide, alcohol and drug abuse, institutionalization, malnutrition, and death. The relational, physical and spiritual support of the local church community are vital to helping single orphans and their surviving parent to thrive.[14]

✳ *Millions of orphans and other vulnerable children are in need of help to reunify with their birth families.* While estimates vary, studies consistently reveal that a large percentage of children living in orphanages and on the streets have at least one living parent.[15] Not all of these parents are willing or able to provide adequate parental care. But in many cases, it is possible to reunify families that have been split apart by extreme poverty, disaster, war or other crises. Further, even when both parents have died, finding a permanent home with a caring relative is often the most desirable outcome for a double orphan, particularly when it can be ensured the child will be treated as a full and equal member of his or her new home.[16] Both family reunification and "kinship care" represent vital aspects of the church's response to the needs of orphans worldwide.

✳ *Millions of children are in need of families that are willing and suitable to adopt them.*[17] Each year only a tiny fraction of children that need families are adopted within their own countries or internationally. In much of the world, major barriers stand between these children and permanent family. These barriers include cultural biases against adoption, proclivity toward non-adoption care models by some government and NGOs, apathy towards orphans in the church and broader society, and government policies that make adoption difficult or impossible. In addition, a large percentage of children in need of adoption are considered particularly "hard to place" because they have special needs, are over age 4, and/or are part of sibling groups. An essential aspect of service to orphans is working to remove these barriers and to grow a culture within the church in every country that affirms and embraces adoption. Well-crafted safeguards must always be set to guard against unethical adoption practices, as with all services to children. But the need for such safeguards must never become an excuse for systems that, in effect, relegate children to life without a family. Placing these children in permanent, safe, loving families should be our unequivocal goal whenever possible.

Conclusion

In all of this, it should be clear that statistics regarding orphans, and even the definition of the term "orphan," have inherent weaknesses. This does not mean they are not important. Good data can help us understand the nature and extent of the need. And the term orphan itself helps a society—perhaps especially those that have been influenced by Judeo-Christian values—to connect the needs of vulnerable children with the clear mandate in Scripture to protect and care for the "fatherless" and the "orphan."

At the same time, we should understand that the biblical concept of the "orphan" and "fatherless" includes more than just the boy or girl who has lost one or both parents. Rather, it describes the child who faces the world without the provision, protection and nurture that parents uniquely provide. No statistical analysis will ever perfectly capture the global number of children fitting this description. Regardless, God calls His people to reflect His heart and character in choosing to "defend the cause of the fatherless,"[18] to "visit the orphan and widow in their distress,"[19] and to "set the lonely in families"[20]—whatever the details of his or her situation may be.

In living out this high calling, it is our firm desire to see the local church in every region increasingly play the central role in meeting the needs of orphans in distress—from family preservation and adoption; to provision for specific physical, social emotional and spiritual needs; to advocacy for government policies that combat systemic injustices and help advance the priorities expressed in this paper.

For western Christians, this includes a distinctive call to foster, mentor and adopt children within their local foster systems. In addition, when there are more orphans in need of adoption than local families available in any country, children can find loving homes through intercountry adoption. Western churches and nonprofit organizations also can continue to play a vital supportive role globally—humbly aiding local churches and ministries.

Ultimately, our final hope is this: that Christians in every nation will rise as the primary answer to the needs of the orphans in their midst, glorifying God as a reflection of His great love for the orphan and for us.

CHRISTIAN ALLIANCE FOR ORPHANS
CORE PRINCIPLES

God's Heart and Ours. God is vested, deeply and personally, in the plight of the orphan—and in all who are destitute and defenseless (Deut. 10:18; Ps 10:14; Ps. 68:5-6, Is. 58:5-12). He calls His people to join Him in this, sharing His passion for orphans and bringing to each child the love of Jesus Christ in both word and deed (Is. 1:17; Ja. 1:27; Mt. 25:40).

Responsive Love. To act upon God's call to care for orphans is not merely a matter of duty or reaction to need. It is first a response to the Gospel: the loving Father who sought us, adopted us, and invites us to live as His sons and daughters (1 Jn. 4:19; Eph. 1:15; Gal. 4:6).

Commitment to the Whole Child. To meet only spiritual or only physical needs of an orphan is incomplete (1 Jn. 3:17; Jm. 2:16; Mk. 8:36). Christian love seeks to address both. Even a cup of water given to quench the momentary thirst of a child is of eternal value (Mt. 10:42). Yet of surpassing greatness is to know Jesus as Lord (Phil. 3:8). So, just as in the ministry of Jesus, we should always hold together the meeting of physical need with the Gospel and our hope that every child will know God's love deeply and personally.

Priority of Family. God created the family as the ideal environment for every child, and the best outcome for an orphan is to know the love of a permanent family. Given the vast and complex needs facing orphans worldwide, this is not always possible. However, priority should always be placed on family-based solutions, and any long-term care should be as *permanent, nurturing* and *close to family* as is feasible for the particular situation.

Role of Residential Care. Crisis situations sometimes demand residential care for children, including orphanages. To the fullest extent possible, however, residential care should be viewed as short-term and transitional. In general, the goal for each orphaned child should be to seek a solution as far as feasible along a "continuum" toward permanent family: large group homes, small group homes, foster care, kinship care, and, ultimately, full adoption whenever willing families can be found.

Family Preservation. Whenever possible, children classified as "orphans" that have one surviving parent or other relatives should be helped to remain with family members. Efforts that enable families to stay together and prevent children from ending up in orphanages or on the streets are a vital part of response to the global orphan crisis.

Central Role of Local Church. The local church in every nation possesses both the Christian mandate and many other resources needed to care for the world's orphans in a nurturing, family-based environment. Every initiative to care for orphans should prioritize and honor the role of the local church, carefully pairing what foreign resources may be necessary with indigenous believers willing to open their hearts and homes to orphans in their community.

APPENDIX B

GLOSSARY OF KEY TERMS

Any productive conversation surrounding the concept of how to improve orphan care must begin with working definitions of key terms.

The definitions provided below are a product of research, biblical study, and conversations with orphan care providers around the globe. However, I am by no means saying that they are perfect definitions of the respective terms. So, if you disagree with anything in this book, definitions or otherwise, everyone collaborating on this project hopes that you will engage the conversation and intelligently challenge any of the definitions, premises, or conclusions. On the other hand, if you agree with what is propounded in this book and have specific examples to confirm and bolster the definitions, theories, and principles espoused, we invite you to share them with us through the online community at ThinkOrphan.com.

Ultimately, while these definitions are by no means exhaustive, set in stone, or universally accepted amongst orphan care providers, they reflect an understanding of the terms in the context of the current orphan care conversations and research. It is necessary to provide these working definitions because we risk "talking past each other" or misunderstanding each other in this book and future conversations in their absence.

* **Adoption:** The official transfer through the court system of all of the parental rights that a biological parent has to a child, along with an assumption by the adopting parent of all the parental rights of the biological parents that are being terminated and are being assumed in their entirety by the adoptive parents. These include the responsibility for the care and supervision of the child, nurturing and training of the child, providing for the physical and

emotional health of the child, and financial support of the child.[1] Additionally, the adopted child assumes all the rights of a biological child to the adoptive parents, including "inheritance rights." Earthly adoption is modeled after the biblical concept of adoption, which includes "full rights as sons" and "heirs with Christ."[2]

❋ **Community Integration:** The process of being made equals in society.

❋ **Development:** "[A] process of ongoing change that moves all the people involved—both the 'helpers' and the 'helped'—closer to being in right relationship with God, self, others, and the rest of creation. In particular, as the materially poor develop, they are better able to fulfill their calling of glorifying God by working and supporting themselves and their families with the fruits of that work. Development is not done *to* people or *for* people but *with* people. The key dynamic in development is promoting an empowering process in which all the people involved— both the 'helpers' and the 'helped'—become more aware of what God created them to be."[3]

❋ **Family-Model Orphan Care Community:** A community caring for orphans that places orphaned children from institutions or other nonfamily settings into homes with families, that is, with mothers *and* fathers and siblings. Typically, there are multiple family homes in the community (i.e., a cluster of homes), but not always.

❋ **Family Reunification:** When a child returns from temporary out-of-home care (e.g., orphanage, foster care) to his or her family of origin.

❋ **Foster Care:** Placing a child in the temporary care of a family other than its own as the result of problems or challenges that are taking place within the birth family, or while critical elements of an adoption are being completed.[4]

❋ **Gospel-Driven (or Gospel-Centered):** Guided by Scripture and the model of Christ, seeking to do everything for the glory of God, not for our own glory, because we are worse than we could ever know but undeservedly far more loved by God than we could ever imagine. Driven by a love for Jesus, a deep gratitude for His sacrifice on the cross that saved us from our sins, and our role as co-laborers with Him to be agents of renewal. When the gospel is the center and driving force in one's life.

✳ **Institutional Orphanage (or Orphanage or Institution):** An institutional orphan care setting where the orphaned children have no family and/or other permanent parental figures caring for them and typically are housed in a dormitory-style setting.

✳ **Intervention:** Care for orphaned and vulnerable children after taking them off the streets, rescuing them from prostitution, other trafficking situations or the drug trade, or removing them out of other negative situations.

✳ **Justice:** "Justice" is about making things right, from a biblical perspective. To bring shalom to the world. Stephan Baumann, President/CEO of World Relief, covers the definition well in his article, "Justice 2.0":

Two words are used for justice in the Old Testament. The first, *mishpat*, means "rendering judgment" or "giving people what they are due" and is sometimes referred to as "rectifying justice." The second word, *tsedeqah*, means "the right thing" or, especially, "right relationships" and is referred to as "primary justice." These words are often paired together in Scripture as "justice and righteousness" and, in some rare instances, one means the other. The Book of Isaiah even uses the word *justice* to mean "the sum total of what the Lord has deemed right"—or, in essence, the very will of God. . . . Taken together, mishpat and tsedaqah present a relational definition of justice, an important dimension that has been overlooked for too long. In its fullness, justice is about right relationships— relationships that work. Injustice is about relationships that don't. Justice for what some call the "Quartet of the Vulnerable"—the orphan, the widow, the immigrant and the poor—is especially important to God, due to its prevalence in Scripture. Injustice occurs when these people are left out, oppressed or exploited. . . . The Old Testament vision of justice carries through to the New and converges in the life and message of Jesus. Jesus not only teaches justice, but he becomes justice. Through the Cross, the very possibility of justice is made available to all, and the incarnation is both a mandate and an example to us. . . . Justice is best incarnated by the people closest to those who suffer, not only geographically, but culturally too. When we live out justice in our relationships, we give witness to the person of Jesus and effect change. When we empower others to become the hands and feet of Christ in their own communities, we create heroes who, in turn, bring justice to a suffering world.[5]

This book highlights several such heroes that are humbly co-laboring with Christ to bring justice and shalom to our suffering world by seeking to love orphans and vulnerable children with excellence, as God loves them. All of this book's authors hope and pray that you are inspired, encouraged, and equipped by their stories to "do justice" yourself.

* **Orphan Care Community:** A community caring for orphans that places orphaned children from institutions or other nonfamily settings into homes or villages with permanent caregivers. Typically, there are multiple family homes or huts in the community (i.e., a cluster of homes), but not always.

* **Orphans (or Orphaned Children):** Children without both parents ("double orphans") and fatherless children in situations where the mother is unable to adequately and properly advocate for and/or care for her child/children. Currently, it is estimated that there are approximately 18 million double orphans in the world, and approximately 8 million children who are in need of adoption, foster care, an orphan care community, or other care from someone other than an immediate or extended family member.[6] (Notably, this definition differs from the more commonly used UNICEF definition, which defines an orphan as any

"child who has lost one or both parents. By this definition there were over 132 million orphans in sub-Saharan Africa, Asia, Latin America and the Caribbean in 2005. This large figure represents not only children who have lost both parents, but also those who have lost a father but have a surviving mother or have lost their mother but have a surviving father. Of the more than 132 million children classified as orphans, only 13 million have lost both parents. Evidence clearly shows that the vast majority of orphans are living with a surviving parent, grandparent, or other family member. Ninety-five percent of all orphans are over the age of five."[7] The current estimated number of orphans under the UNICEF definition is 153 million.[8])

✳ **Prevention:** To the extent that children have been orphaned, care for the orphans with excellence as early as possible in their lives, before they are abused or otherwise scarred by the world. To the extent that children are "vulnerable" children, equip the parents and/or other family members to care for the children with excellence so that they do not become orphaned children (i.e., work to strengthen families, men and women, and communities in such a way that orphans are not produced).

✳ **Rehabilitation:** "Seeks to restore people and their communities to the positive elements of their precrisis conditions."[9]

✳ **Relative/Kinship Care:** Care of an orphaned or vulnerable child by an extended family member.

✳ **Relief:** "The urgent and temporary provision of emergency aid to reduce immediate suffering from a natural or man-made crisis. . . . The key feature of relief is a provider-receiver dynamic in which the provider gives assistance—often material—to the receiver, who is largely incapable of helping himself at that time."[10] (Notably, "one of the biggest mistakes that North American churches [and ministries] make—by far—is in applying relief in situations in which rehabilitation or development is the appropriate intervention."[11])

＊ **Social (or Economic) Orphans:** Children who are driven out of their homes and into orphanages or onto the streets due to poverty and other negative factors, such as drug use, imprisonment, or disease.

＊ **Village Model Orphan Care Community:** A community caring for orphans that places orphaned children from institutions or other nonfamily settings into homes with other children (usually 10–15) and a single parent or multiple house parents. Typically, there are multiple homes or huts in the community, but not always.

＊ **Vulnerable (or At-Risk) Children:** Children in extreme poverty, children whose parents have abandoned or relinquished them, motherless children, street children, and any other children who do not have someone in their lives to adequately advocate for their rights—that is, any child who faces the world without the provision, protection, and nurture that parents uniquely provide.

APPENDIX C

The Orphan's Heart
Paul Kusuubira and Keith McFarland

I (Keith) sat with Paul and asked him to define these different characteristics of an orphan heart according to his own experience, some of which is shared in chapter 4. Many of these attributes overlap and none of these exist in isolation from the others. Yet, it is still good to look at each one individually as each is a distinct part of the larger puzzle. To effectively minister to orphans, we must truly understand what's going on in orphans' hearts, and this list of attributes is a great starting point toward any such understanding. The list also helps us make sense of how we, too, often operate out of an orphan heart.

* **Abandonment:** The deep feeling of having no one to turn to for answers or help. One has to make his own way because those who would help are not there. Even when people are there, they cannot be trusted because they will probably leave too.

* **Anger:** Anger is always present in the heart because of what has been experienced in the past and comes out over even a small thing. It often seems like an eruption that has come out of nowhere, but it has always been there, only suppressed. Fighting at a moment's notice among children is a very common outflow of this anger that is constantly present in the heart. Another aspect is that there is always someone to blame for anything bad that happens.

* **Deceit:** Constant lies are told to make sure that the heart remains safe and protected. Truth will hurt and pain is to be avoided at all costs. The memory becomes selective and only exposes what will provide safety in the situation.

✳ **Escape:** Pain in the heart leaves it continually unsatisfied. Therefore the heart seeks satisfaction in things that give it temporary value or identity—things like sports, drugs, sex, and alcohol. At times the false world created by the heart can be more real than the painful one that is a reality, and thus the false reality is sought after at all costs and at all times. In the West, entertainment, video games, pornography, and the Internet become some of the favorite modes of escaping reality in addition to the ones listed above.

✳ **Fear:** This defines life. Anything that has the potential of causing pain or the memory of pain is to be fearfully avoided. Fear of what "could be" or "could happen" is always on the mind. It pushes the heart to pursue safety at all costs. Obedience does not flow out of what is good for me or out of love for the person asking, but because of the fear of what could happen if I fail to obey.

✳ **Greed:** Tied into poverty. The constant need for more and more whereby the heart is never satisfied but is driven to be. Care is not given to whether others have what they need so long as individual needs are met. There is no consideration of others, or if there is it is only in what can be gotten at their expense.

✳ **Hiding:** This is both physical and emotional whereby one does not really want to talk about real things, but he or she is free to talk about things surrounding the real issue, always careful to make sure no access is given to the real issue. Authority figures are suspect and kept away because of the fear of experiencing the pain they might cause. Any correction means rejection and the heart retreats away from the corrector. Accountability is very difficult to accept, as the true problem is never dealt with, only surface problems.

✳ **Hopelessness:** Because the present is so unstable, one cannot even imagine what the future will hold. There are no dreams. Life becomes a puzzle of trying to put pieces

together again to make sense out of life. One just exists
with no sense of purpose or meaning.

✳ **Independence:** The heart posture of doing what is desired
without being questioned. If questioning comes, then rebellion will follow. Things have to be done "my way" and
anyone who gets in the way of that is an enemy. Accountability is rejected and life is lived according to what is best
in one's own eyes.

✳ **Insecurity:** Tied into fear. A sense of feeling unprotected
all the time and therefore feeling unsafe. The result is great
care given to make sure that the heart is protected. A defense mechanism is constantly employed where one is quick
to interpret what people say and do, whether in trouble
or safe. One often reads intentions into statements and
actions that were not there. Offense is easily taken where
none was intended.

✳ **Loneliness:** The loss of identity in family leaves the feeling
of being out of place and isolated, even when surrounded
by people. The preference is to be alone in a self-made "co-
coon" rather than to be involved with people. The feeling
of loneliness is often both hated and enjoyed. It is hated
because the heart longs to be free to relate and enjoy relationships, but is enjoyed when it is able to gain sympathy
from people without the tie of strong relationship. Self-
protection is at the heart of this.

✳ **Loss of Identity:** Tied into worthlessness. In the African
culture, people are identified by their fathers. Children are
a priority because a man's name and identity is continued
in them. To die without children is to "perish". On the
other side, to lose a father is to lose the one in whom that
identity is found. "Who is his Dad?" is asked of every child.
If the father has died the reply is, "He's just an orphan."
A result of this loss of identity is that one cannot identity
himself with anyone (especially male figures who can easily
betray). One cannot lift his or her head—it stays "down"
because the father, the source of identity, has died.

✳ **Manipulation:** Using the situation one is in to convince people to give you what you want. Emotions, sadness, loneliness, all are used for the advantage of the suffering one. Life is a drama where acting becomes the key to gain.

✳ **Mistrust:** It is hard to believe and trust what people say and do. Because one is alone, without value, and abandoned, one can have no confidence that people are truly there to help or that they are not trying to use him or her for their own benefit. The heart will ride out the relationship to the point of what one can get, but it is always ready to leave as soon as there is reason to suspect any kind of rejection. The heart is careful to select who it will allow to enter into its sphere. It operates in comfort zones.

✳ **Poverty:** A feeling of constant scarcity that says there will never be enough even in the midst of plenty. The goal is therefore to get what is needed NOW, because what will happen the next day is unknown. The now becomes the focus without thought or hope for the future. Decisions are made based upon what seems temporarily best for needs in the moment. Hoarding becomes a lifestyle.

✳ **Rejection:** The feeling of being unwanted by people. One feels like a misfortune whose presence is a burden for those around you. The thought is, "Why should I even exist if I'm an inconvenience to others?"

✳ **Sadness:** Tied into loneliness and the outflow of the hurt in the heart. Happiness can come for a moment, but it always gives way to the feeling of sadness. Even in the midst of a conversation, one's entire demeanor can suddenly change as the heart reconnects with its deep sadness. It is unexplainable by the person feeling sad, but it is the fruit of pain. It can also be a tool to keep people around to bring comfort, but without the commitment of relationship.

✳ **Striving:** This defines life. Since there is no one that cares, one has to do what it takes to make sure that things will work out for good. One will try at all costs to do anything possible to make life better, even overworking, yet without finding satisfaction in it. Often, identity is tied into what is being strived after. The need for success can even be with an attitude of revenge—"After I have succeeded then those who have rejected me will turn back to me and I'll get them back!" One's value is attached to the accumulation of what he or she has.

✳ **Superficiality:** Tied into hiding, it becomes the guard of all relationships. One can never know the true heart as it is guarded and protected. Relationship is kept at a distance for fear that the true heart will be revealed. When the heart is pursued intentionally, the person will end it all together.

✳ **Worthlessness:** A conviction that says I am of no value. If a person comes who seeks to bring value to you or to appreciate you, it is denied and the person rejected.

ENDNOTES

INTRODUCTION

1 See Appendix B for definitions of key terms, including "orphan" and "orphaned children."

2 For deeper discussion of the "God complex" and the concept of help that is hurting, read Brian Fikkert and Steven Corbett, *When Helping Hurts: How to Alleviate Poverty Without Hurting the Poor . . . and Yourself* (Chicago: Moody Publishers, 2009).

3 See Appendix A, Jedd Medefind, "Christian Alliance for Orphans' White Paper: On Understanding Orphan Statistics," Christian Alliance for Orphans (CAFO), last accessed on December 16, 2013, http://www.christianalliancefororphans.org/wp-content/uploads/Christian-Alliance-for-Orphans-On-Understanding-Orphan-Statistics.pdf.

4 See Appendix B for definitions of "vulnerable children" and "at-risk children."

5 See Appendix A, Medefind, "CAFO White Paper: On Understanding Orphan Statistics." For a deeper examination and analysis of the statistics surrounding adopted and nonadopted orphaned children, reasons why all orphaned children are not adoptable at this time in history, and some of the issues underlying why some of the adoptable orphans are not adopted, read Diane Lynn Elliot, *The Global Orphan Crisis: Be the Solution, Change the World* (Chicago: Moody Publishers, 2012); and Johnny Carr, *Orphan Justice: How to Care for Orphans Beyond Adopting* (Nashville: B&H Books, 2013).

6 See Appendix B for definitions of "gospel-driven" and "gospel-centered."

7 Eugene Peterson, "What Are Pastors Good For?" National Pastor's Conference 2007, General Session.

CHAPTER 1
In Pursuit of a Dream

1 See Appendix A, Jedd Medefind, "Christian Alliance for Orphans' White Paper: On Understanding Orphan Statistics," Christian Alliance for Orphans (CAFO), last accessed on December 16, 2013, http://www.christianalliancefororphans.org/wp-content/uploads/Christian-Alliance-for-Orphans-On-Understanding-Orphan-Statistics.pdf.

2 For a deeper examination of why children are not adopted in our world today, listen to Smith, K., "The Unadoptable Orphan 201- Octopi Care," CAFO Webinar, http://vimeo.com/46399383 (accessed on December 16, 2013).

3 See Appendix B for this book's working definitions of key terms used in orphan care.

CHAPTER 2
Why Should Anyone Care about the Plight of Orphaned and At-Risk Children?

1 Timothy Keller, "The Beauty of Biblical Justice – Isaiah 58 on the importance and meaning of justice," The Aquila Report, October 28, 2010, found at theaquilareport.com/the-beauty-of-biblical-justice-isaiah-58-on-the-importance -and-meaning-of-justice/ (accessed on January 9, 2014). See also, Timothy Keller, *The Prodigal God: Recovering the Heart of the Christian Faith* (New York: Dutton, 2008), 126: "[H]e is saying that the inevitable sign that you know you are a sinner saved by sheer, costly grace is a sensitive social conscience and a life poured out in deeds of service to the poor."

2 Eph. 2:8-9.

3 Gary Haugen, *Just Courage: God's Great Expedition for the Restless Christian* (Downers Grove, IL: InterVarsity Press Books, 2008), 63.

4 Keller, *The Prodigal God*, 127.

5 Haugen, *Just Courage*, 65.

6 For an exposition of these concepts, read Fikkert and Corbett, *When Helping Hurts*.

7 Keller, *The Prodigal God*, 133.

8 Tyler Charles,"Fostering Hope: How the Church Is Changing the Face of Foster Care and Adoption in the U.S.," *Relevant*, July/August 2012, 84.

9 C. S. Lewis, *Letters of C. S. Lewis (July 18, 1957)* (Harcourt Books, 1988), 467.

10 Eph. 2:10.

11 "Strong's Greek," accessed December 16, 2013, http://bibleapps.com/greek/2041.htm.

12 Parliament of the World's Religions, "Declaration Toward a Global Ethic," September 4, 1993, http://www.parliamentofreligions.org/_includes/FCKcontent/File/TowardsAGlobalEthic.pdf (accessed December 16, 2013).

13 "Abandoned to the State: Cruelty and Neglect in Russian Orphanages," Human Rights Watch, 1998, 198 (citing UNICEF, "Children at Risk in Central and Eastern Europe: Perils and Promises," Regional Monitoring Report No. 4 [Florence International Child Development Centre, 1997], 89), found at http://www.hrw.org/sites/default/files/reports/russ98d.pdf, accessed November 7, 2013.

14 David Kinnaman, *You Lost Me. Why Young Christians Are Leaving Church . . . And Rethinking Faith* (Grand Rapids, MI: Baker Books, 2011), 46.

15 John Sowers, *The Fatherless Generation: Redeeming the Story* (Grand Rapids, MI: Zondervan, 2010), 36–37.

16 Ibid.

17 An example of pop culture discussing the impact of fatherlessness on a child's life is the song, "Just Like You," by Lecrae, which can be found on Phil Darke's

Providence mix on Spotify, and can be downloaded through iTunes, Amazon.com, and many other locations.

CHAPTER 3
Why Excellence for the Fatherless?

1   Philip Darke, "Why We Do What We Do," *Providence Blog*, January 23, 2013, https://providenceworld.com/blog/2013/01/why-we-do-what-we-do-re-visited/.

2   See, e.g., John Williamson and Aaron Greenberg, "Families, Not Orphanages," Better Care Network Working Paper, (Better Care Network, September 2010), http://www.crin.org/docs/Families%20Not%20Orphanages.pdf (accessed December 16, 2013); The Way Forward Project, "The Way Forward Project Report," November 2011, http://filecdn.s3.amazonaws.com/thewayforwardproject.org/Final%20Report%20Uploaded%206.27.13%20Reduced%20Size.pdf (accessed December 16, 2013); "Abandoned to the State: Cruelty and Neglect in Russian Orphanages," Human Rights Watch, 1998, 198 (citing UNICEF, "Children at Risk in Central and Eastern Europe: Perils and Promises," Regional Monitoring Report No. 4 [Florence International Child Development Centre, 1997], 89), found at http://www.hrw.org/sites/default/files/reports/russ98d.pdf, accessed November 7, 2013.

CHAPTER 4
Family Matters (Family)

1   Dan Cruver, *Adoption Is Bigger Than You Think*, Desiring God Blog, September 18, 2013.

2   See http://www.christianalliancefororphans.org/orphanstats/ and http://www.unicef.org/media/media_45279.html for information on statistics and related orphan terminology.

3   I used to say "formerly fatherless," but I like the phrase "fatherless no more" that Lifesong for Orphans and Lifeline Children's Services have been using (http://www.lifesongfororphans.org/fatherless-no-more/).

4   Ps. 68:5-6.

5   I love to tell people that as a newly married couple we learned more in those twenty weeks and were impacted more deeply than four years of Bible college! For information on the Institute see http://newhopeuganda.org/programs/institute-of-childcare-and-family/.

6   Gal. 5:19–21 & 2 Tim. 3:1–5 show many of the same tendencies describing the sinful human heart. Each tendency of the orphan heart is drawn out in various ways depending on the story and experience of each fatherless child.

7   See Col. 1:19–20; Eph. 1:7–10; and 1 Cor. 9:16–23.

8   Eph. 1:3–6.

9   See John 8 and John 14 as two incredible examples of Jesus making known the Father.

10   J. I. Packer, *Knowing God* (Downers Grove, IL: IVP Books, 1993), 186–88.

11   Ibid., 201–2.

12   See Rev. 5:9–10; Rom. 8:15; and Gal. 4:6.

13   For Scripture references unveiling God's family, see Eph. 1:3–14; John 14, 17; Rom. 8:15–17; Gal. 4:4–7; Phil. 2:5–10; and Heb. 2:11–15.

14   Cruver (quoting John Piper from an undisclosed benefit concert in 2007), *Adoption Is Bigger Than You Think*, Desiring God Blog, September 18, 2013.

15   See chapter 9 on Psychosocial Care.

16   See Johnny Carr, *Orphan Justice* (Nashville: B&H Publishing Group, 2013), 69–72; (or do a simple internet search).

17   Julie Gilbert Rosicky et al., The Way Forward Project Report 2011, "Section 1: Family Preservation and Reunification," 23.

18   Lorraine Sherr et al., The Way Forward Project Report 2011, "Section 2: Interim Care Alternatives and Foster Care," 38.

19   Ibid., 38–39.

20   Carr, *Orphan Justice*, 71.

21   David Blankenhorn, *Fatherless America: Confronting Our Most Urgent Social Problem* (New York: HarperPerennial, 1996).

22   John Sowers, *Fatherless Generation*: Redeeming the Story (Grand Rapids, MI: Zondervan, 2010).

23   Barack Obama's Speech on Father's Day, June 15, 2008, http://www.youtube .com/watch?v=Hj1hCDjwG6M (I first saw this quoted in Mark Stibbe's book *I Am Your Father: What Every Heart Needs to Know*, Monarch Books, 2010); Mark adds statistics from the UK that echo these findings in the context of the UK (pgs. 23-24).

24   Kevin Leman, *What a Difference a Daddy Makes* (Nashville: Thomas Nelson, Inc., 2000), 5, 7.

25   Quoted in Leman, *What a Difference a Daddy Makes*, 7–8.

26   Eph. 3:14–15.

27   You can listen to Paul's song in its entirety (and read its lyrics) on ThinkOrphan.com.

28   Carr, *Orphan Justice*, 63.

29   Douglas Wilson, *Father Hunger: Why God Calls Men to Love and Lead Their Families* (Thomas Nelson, 2012), 158–59.

30   For biblical examples of Adoptive Family see Ps. 68:5–6; 1 Sam. 3:1–6; 2 Sam. 9:11; 1 Kings 19:19–21; and Est. 2:5–7, 15.

31   Jesus was known as the "son of Joseph" while fully aware that His true sonship was in God (John 6:42; Luke 2:49).

32 For biblical examples of Extended Family see Gen. 12:5; Ruth 1–4; Est. 2:5–7, 15.

33 World Orphans and Lifesong for Orphans are two such ministries laboring in this area.

34 See ThinkOrphan.com for New Hope Uganda's ministry points.

35 For an interview with one of the children formerly abducted by Kony and the power of the gospel and forgiveness to change a heart and life, see http://newhopeuganda.org/2012/03/20/nhus-response-to-the-kony-2012-initiative/.

36 The names of the children have been changed for their protection.

37 For more details about life at La Providencia, visit providenceworld.com/La-Providencia.

38 For example, The Mentoring Project and John Sowers are doing a great work of developing partnerships between churches.

39 1 Tim. 1:2; 1 Cor. 4:14–15; Titus 1:4; and 3 John 4.

40 I do recognize that ultimately eternal life with the Savior is the most important thing for each human being on the planet. My intention here has been to draw attention to the bigger picture that we as Christians are called to represent and the place to which we must seek to lead orphans. This "bigger picture" will drive the way we view and practice ministry to orphans.

CHAPTER 5
It Takes a Village (Community Integration)

1 Kate Borders is in a leadership role at World Orphans and oversees all of WO Mobilization. She has a Sociology Degree from Wheaton College and came to WO in 2009 after serving at a ranch that provides a Christian home, education, and counseling to children in crisis situations. She also has developed a biblically based sports curriculum. Kate was drawn to WO by its commitment to care for children around the world through the local church. She enjoys riding her motorcycle, hiking, camping, reading, playing the violin, and a good cup of coffee. She and her husband reside near the mountains of East Tennessee with their daughter.

2 Rom. 12:1; Eph. 2:10.

3 https://providenceworld.com/la-providencia/.

4 Name used with permission.

5 Name used with permission.

6 Tyler Charles, "Fostering Hope: How the Church Is Changing the Face of Foster Care and Adoption in the U.S.," *Relevant*, July/August 2012, 84.

7 See Appendix A, Jedd Medefind, "Christian Alliance for Orphans' White Paper: On Understanding Orphan Statistics," Christian Alliance for Orphans (CAFO), last accessed on December 16, 2013, http://www.christianalliancefororphans.org/wp-content/uploads/Christian-Alliance-for-Orphans-On-Understanding-Orphan-Statistics.pdf.

CHAPTER 6
Masters in Education (Education)

1   Voddie Baucham, "Education: The Forgotten Key to Discipleship," http://www.gracefamilybaptist.net/topics-and-issues/education-forgotten-key-discipleship/ (accessed on January 20, 2014).

2   Andy has been with Lifesong for Orphans since its inception in 2002, serving as vice president and orphan advocate, developing partnerships, growing church relationships, launching new initiatives, speaking, and global advocacy. He also serves on the board of directors for the Christian Alliance for Orphans and the Orphan Sunday campaign, has been a guest on numerous Christian radio programs, and has authored articles for Focus on the Family and elsewhere. As a couple, he and his wife have also served as house parents at Gateway Woods, a Christian children's home for at-risk youth. He and his wife, Jill, have four children (two through adoption)—Travor, Haley, Caleb, and Hope.

3   Born on a little offshore island on the south of England, Katharine was brought up in an established Christian family; grandparents, parents, and siblings all being involved in Christian ministry and evangelism in many parts of Africa and the United Kingdom. Her grandparents played an integral part in the East African revival in Uganda and Rwanda and her parents were missionaries in Ethiopia. Her family has also had strong links with education over many generations. Katharine earned her BEd (Hons) in education at Oxford University. Over the last thirteen years, she has taught in schools in Uganda, UK, and Honduras, gaining valuable experience in working in and establishing centers of Christian education in a variety of different cultures. At the heart of all her endeavors is the single aim of bringing the love of Jesus to each child through educational experience of the highest possible quality.

4   You can read more about education principles from Andy Lehman and Katharine Marrow, including Katharine's article on Education at La Providencia in its entirety, on the education page of ThinkOrphan.com.

5   For more information about Lifesong for Orphans, visit lifesongfororphans.org. And for more information and resources about Lifesong's education projects in Ethiopia, Honduras, and Zambia, visit ThinkOrphan.com's education page.

6   For more information about Academia La Providencia, visit providenceworld.com/la-providencia.

7   Many of these orphaned and vulnerable children live with a relative or neighbor who has taken them in, but cannot really afford to give them the necessities of life (food, education, medical care, nurturing). Often they are treated as slaves to the rest of the family. If there are biological children present, the child who is taken in by the family is usually a servant to the biological children. The biological children may get to go to school or get the good food, but the "taken in" child often does not get these benefits.

8   In 2009, there were 230 students in the new schools; today there are nearly 1,000 students in the schools. They are on their way to building a school system

that can generate 140 leaders a year, who will be equipped to transform their country and continent from the inside out, drastically altering Africa's orphan and vulnerable child cycle in the region.

9   Each week every student memorizes a Bible verse both in English and Amharic. At the end of the school year they have tucked away thirty-six verses in their hearts. Additionally, even at their young ages, many of the students at our primary school in Ziway have voluntarily joined prayer and Bible study clubs/groups on our campus.

10   Jorge's name is a pseudonym for his protection. Another example was when we took our football team to the bilingual school in town for a friendly match. They wiped the floor with us and beat us with an embarrassing score, but at the end of the day we saw that we have far more than just a love for football. The host school was very generous and invited our children for a snack, to allow them to talk to their pupils, to mix with them. The children got their snack and drink and the other school kids tucked in whilst our kids just sat there with it in front of them. I rushed over to ask one of them why they weren't eating. She looked me straight in the eye and said, "But we haven't prayed." So in front of both schools little Gracia (name changed) stood and prayed for the food and then they all tucked in. They seemed genuinely shocked that the others would even consider eating without saying grace. It amazes me how much they take on board.

11   Having said all this, one of ALP's biggest struggles has been finding a principal that fulfills our requirements (including being bilingual), meets the needs of the job, has a heart for the ministry, and is willing to work for less than they can get at a public school.

12   "Hope Springs a Trap," *The Economist*, May 12, 2012.

13   At ALP, we are trying to educate our parents about how to help their children at home—in education, discipline, and spiritual formation. To do this, we work to make the most of our termly parent/caregiver meetings. Our parents come in to collect their child's report cards and we hold our meetings then. We find speakers to talk to them about how to help their child at home in the three areas listed above, choosing different topics to approach each time. As time goes by, the parents are becoming more open and engaged in these meetings and starting to put things into practice.

14   By Western standards the school fee is very low (less than $4.40 per month in Ziway and less than $1.40 per month in Adami Tulu), and they do very little to cover the actual cost of educating the child. The fees serve a different purpose: they make the caregivers appreciate more the worth of the education. Simply receiving everything for free from the foreigner builds a feeling of entitlement by the student and dependence upon the foreigner.

15   Some of the children from wealthier homes pay tuition for their schooling.

16   A rotation of duties, for you non-British folks out there.

17   For more information on proper nutrition, see the nutrition chapter of this book (chapter 7).

18   Just a few years ago, only about 30 percent of children's caregivers (adults) were gainfully employed. Now, we have helped create jobs for 92 to 98 percent of all the adult caregivers, through Lifesong Farm's sustainable agri-business, micro-loans, empowerment programs, and other similar projects. Some examples are: making Vaseline, carpets, and shoes to sell. There are many vocational and cultural skills that must be considered when providing a quality education. There must be opportunities for hands-on learning and skills training that are practical and helpful for everyday life.

19   Attachment deficits are covered in more detail in chapter 9 on psychosocial care.

20   Orphan care communities likely will see many more special needs than we possibly could address in this short book. We simply want to ensure that you are aware of the issues presented and seek appropriate and excellent ways to address them. Further, orphan care communities not specializing in special needs likely will be unable to adequately address the needs of some children with more severe special needs, and we encourage the communities to seek outside support and care for those children. At La Providencia, we have done just that with one of our children. Because our school is not equipped to address his educational needs with excellence, we send him to another school that is better equipped to teach children with his special needs.

21   Behind every child who misbehaves and underperforms in school there is a story, and the story is acted out in the classroom. For some it is a temporary glitch in their lives from which they quickly recover; others need support and intervention. But in the most complex and challenging situations, it can be a long history of intergenerational adversity which the child trails into school and presents to the staff in alarming ways. Teachers are exposed to this stressful experience daily—adding to classroom tensions and challenges." (www.youngminds.org/uk/training_services/young_minds_in_schools/wellbeing/attachment)

22   According to Nancy Thomas (2004), children with Reactive Attachment Disorder require educators who are 'loving leaders', teachers who combine the best from Arnold Schwarzenegger and 'grandma'. They need tight structure and firm limit setting that is provided by an empathetic adult who models 'supercharged' expectations for their learning." Carey McGinn Ed.D., CCC/SLP, "An Open Letter to Educators Who Work with Students Who Have Been Diagnosed with Reactive Attachment Disorder or Have Suffered Early Trauma," accessed January 21, 2014 at http://www.attachmentnewengland.com/documents/educators.pdf.

23   We recognize the value and importance of our children interacting with the teams, to learn about cultures, to speak with different people—and to practice their English. Likewise, it is good for visiting people to learn more about our children and to build relationships. Rather than interrupting our classes, we do this through recess times and lunch times. Teams are invited to eat lunch with us—previously informed to help us keep the children calm while eating and in the dining room—and to build relationships. Then they come out to recess and just play with them. It has worked really well.

CHAPTER 7
You Are What You Eat (Nutrition)

1   Kristina DeMuth is a registered dietitian and currently a candidate for her masters in public health nutrition at the University of Minnesota. She graduated from the College of Saint Benedict in 2011, *summa cum laude*, with distinction in both Psychology and Nutrition. Upon graduation from college, Kristina received the honor of dietetic student of the year in Minnesota through the Academy of Nutrition and Dietetics. From 2011–12, Kristina completed her dietetic internship through the University of Minnesota and the Emily Program, with an emphasis in eating disorder therapy. In 2011, Kristina took her first trip to Haiti on a ten-day mission trip. She took three subsequent trips over the course of one and a half years before deciding to spend a year serving as a dietitian at an orphanage in Haiti. Kristina blogs about nutrition-related topics at for-i-was-hungry.blogspot.com.

2   World Health Organization (WHO), "Nutrition challenges," http://www.who.int/nutrition/challenges/en/. Also, in 2011, 165 million children were considered stunted and 52 million children were considered wasting (see UNICEF—WHO—The World Bank Joint Child Malnutrition Estimates (2012), "Levels and Trends in Child Malnutrition," http://www.who.int/nutgrowthdb/jme_unicef_who_wb.pdf.)

3   WHO, Nutrition challenges, http://www.who.int/nutrition/challenges/en/.

4   V. Matins, T. Florencio, A. Swaya, (2011), "Long-Lasting Effects of Undernutrition," *International Journal of Environmental Research and Public Health* 8, no. 6 (June 2011): 1817–46, http://www.ncbi.nlm.nih.gov/pmc/articles/PMC3137999/?report=reader.

5   UNICEF—WHO—The World Bank Joint Child Malnutrition Estimates (2012), "Levels and Trends in Child Malnutrition," http://www.who.int/nutgrowthdb/jme_unicef_who_wb.pdf; Matins, Florencio, and Swaya, "Long-Lasting Effects of Undernutrition," 1817–46.

6   B. Popkin, L. Adair, and S. Wen Ng, "Now and Then: The Global Nutrition Transition: The Pandemic of Obesity in Developing Countries," *Nutrition Reviews* 70, no. 1 (2012): 3–21, http://www.ncbi.nlm.nih.gov/pmc/articles/PMC3257829/; See more about The Nutrition Transition on the University of North Carolina website: http://www.cpc.unc.edu/projects/nutrans/whatis.

7   See video podcast: Christian Alliance for Orphans (2013), "Preventing Malnutrition in Residential Care," http://vimeo.com/77233341.

8   For more discussion of macro- and micronutrients and their impact on our bodies, as well as more details on practical, real-life applications of this chapter's discussion, visit ThinkOrphan.com.

9   J. Brown, *Nutrition through the Life Cycle*, 5th ed. (Stamford, CT: Cengage Learning, 2014), chapter 1.

10   Id.; see also Reed Mangels, "Protein in the Vegan Diet," www.vrg.org/nutrition/protein.php; V. Young and P. Pellett, "Plant Proteins in Relation to Human

Protein and Amino Acid Nutrition," supplement, *American Journal for Clinical Nutrition* 59 (May 1994): S1203–12, ajcn.nutrition.org/content/29/5/1203S. long. For more discussion on proteins in plant-based, vegan, and/or vegetarian diets, visit ThinkOrphan.com.

11   Brown, *Nutrition through the Life Cycle*, chapter 1.

12   Brown, *Nutrition through the Life Cycle*, 297; "Raising Vegetarian Children," American Academy of Nutrition and Dietetics, http://vegetariannutrition.net/ vegetarian-kids/; "Frequently Asked Questions about Vegetarian and Vegan Nutrition," Academy of Nutrition and Dietetics, http://vegetariannutrition .net/faq/.

13   For more examples like these, visit the nutrition section on ThinkOrphan.com.

14   The peanut butter–based product's moderate amount of carbohydrates and protein to a relatively high fat ratio, as well as the fortification with phosphorus, potassium, magnesium, and sodium made the product ideal for treatment of the refeeding syndrome. For more on the refeeding syndrome, see eRefeeding Syndrome: What It Is, and How to Prevent and Treat It," http://www.ncbi.nlm .nih.gov/pmc/articles/PMC2440847/.

15   See WHO Child Growth Standards: http://www.who.int/childgrowth/en/.

16   The additional five hundred calories were especially helpful for several of the older boys in the orphanage who were below the third percentile on the WHO body mass index growth charts.

17   See ThinkOrphan.com for a discussion of the consequences of micro- and macronutrient deficiencies, as well as ways to treat chronic and acute malnutrition; see also the United Nations Standing Committee on Nutrition (2011), "Module 3: Understanding Malnutrition," http://www.unscn.org/en/gnc_htp/ modul.php?modID=5&docID=17 (accessed on January 28, 2013).

18   Learn more about changes in dietary patterns and the influence of foreign rice in Haiti at http://www1.american.edu/TED/haitirice.htm; see "Old Ways to Learn about Healthy, Cultural Eating," http://oldwayspt.org/; read more about "The Nutrition Transition" on the University of North Carolina website, http:// www.cpc.unc.edu/projects/nutrans/whatis.

19   Even fully vegetarian diets, when properly planned and adequate in variety and calories, can provide all the essential vitamins and minerals for maintaining health. Particularly if one eats foods rich in protein, iron, zinc, iodine, omega-3s, calcium, vitamin D, and vitamin B12 deficiencies can be avoided. See ThinkOrphan.com for more discussion about how to properly plan and implement plant-based diets and their benefits; see also American Dietetics Association, "Position of the American Dietetic Association: Vegetarian Diets," *Journal of American Dietetic Association* 109 (2009): 1266–82, https://www.vrg. org/nutrition/2009_ADA_position_paper.pdf; "Vegetarian Nutrition: Frequently Asked Questions," *Academy of Nutrition and Dietetics*, http://vegetarian-nutrition.net/faq/; and TED (2009), "Dan Buettner: How to Live to Be 100+," http://www.ted.com/talks/dan_buettner_how_to_live_to_be_100.html.

20 The change in diet made an impact on the children's health almost immediately. For examples, several months after implementing changes to the menu, when a dentistry team came to do cleanings on the children's teeth, the dentist told us that it was evident that there was some sort of healing on the teeth that likely resulted from the increased fruits and vegetables and decrease in refined sugars in the children's diet. He stated, "The improved diet in [the orphanage] appears to be making a big difference for tooth health. Many serious decay area seem to have stopped and 'healed' to some extent because the sugary meals they had been eating have been shifted to fruits and vegetables. They all seem so vibrant too."

For the "rest of the story" about the resulting positive impact of the dietary changes, in conjunction with other environmental changes in the children's lives (e.g., new home, better hygiene, psychosocial care, more social interaction, better medical/dental care), and similar stories about diet's impact on health and development, visit ThinkOrphan.com.

21 In Haiti, two such nutrient-dense foods I've discovered from elders are moringa tree and purslane.

22 http://en.wikipedia.org/wiki/Food_politics.

23 See Jonathan M. Katz, "With Cheap Food Imports, Haiti Can't Feed Itself," http://www.huffingtonpost.com/2010/03/20/with-cheap-food-imports-h_n_507228.html; "Food Sovereignty Prize," http://foodsovereigntyprize.org/about-fs/; Marion Nestle,"Learn More about Food Politics," http://www.foodpolitics.com/.

24 See L. Blinkhorn and M. Davis, "Tackling the Weight of the World: What One African Woman Taught Us about Global Obesity," *Health Affairs* 32, no. 4 (2013): 813–16.

25 E. Satter, "Ellyn Satter's Division of Responsibility in Feeding," (2013), http://ellynsatterinstitute.org/cms-assets/documents/105500-525938.dor2013.pdf.

26 Id.

27 E. Satter, "The Satter Eating Competence Model," (2014), http://ellynsatterinstitute.org/other/ecsatter.php.

28 Identifying drivers for people's current behaviors may be useful for determining what will motivate desirable behavior change. For outsiders helping in this area, establishing rapport and deep relationships with the children and staff will increase trust and respect for cultural differences. Humility, respect, and a listening approach to the identified issue or behaviors in need of change will further enhance ability to motivate changes. Creating a system of social commitment for the behavioral change (i.e., putting their name on a board) and recognizing the desirable behavior with appraisal and positive attention (i.e., words of encouragement, putting their picture on the wall) can continue to maintain and reinforce desirable behavioral changes. See more on motivational behavior change at ThinkOrphan.com; "Touching Hearts, Touching Minds," http://www.touchingheartstouchingminds.com/overview_project.php; "Getting to the Heart of the Matter," http://www.gettingtotheheartofthematter.com/; and Pam McCarthy,"Tapping into the Power of Influence," http://www.doh.wa.gov/Portals/1/Documents/Pubs/961-962-ConnectingtoInfluenceHandout.pdf.

CHAPTER 8
What's Up, Doc? (Medical and Dental Care)

1   John F. Campbell, MD, is a board-certified internist who has practiced internal medicine and emergency medicine for twenty-two years. Since 2002, he has been actively involved with a mission called Asia's Hope, which has twenty-six orphan homes based upon a family model in Cambodia, Thailand, and northern India. He has established and initiated medical and dental protocol and policies in those countries. He has made over twenty trips to Southeast Asia and Asia in the last ten years. Dr. Campbell lives with his wife, Bobbi, in Charlotte, North Carolina. They have raised four children, now adults, two boys and two girls, the girls being Korean-born adoptees.

2   Brent Phillips and his wife, Leah, have been serving in Uganda with Cherish Uganda (www.cherishuganda) for the past three and a half years as the Village Pastor/COO. This village of orphaned children, all of whom have HIV, is bringing hope to not only the children in their ministry, but also to the surrounding villages and other parts of the country. Brent and Leah have been married for twenty-two years, have five children, ages two to twenty (two of them adopted) and have pastored churches in California and Texas. Serving Jesus is their passion, and leading others in their understanding of the love of God and loving people motivates them each day.

3   Visit ThinkOrphan.com for more discussion on the issues orphaned and vulnerable children face.

4   We are making the assumption here that the child living with the extended family would not be a healthy situation for the child.

5   Unfortunately, extended family members sometimes bring children to orphan care communities because they feel that they are unable to care for the children for a variety of reasons. Health care information may be available from the family members in these situations. If they were the health care provider for this child, there may be legal issues that arise regarding authorization for medical treatment. So, it is important to get any necessary signatures from extended family members, obviating the need to be placed into a significant dilemma later.

6   The "home kit" should contain things such as home first aid kits accompanied by basic first aid instructions, Tylenol, decongestants, antihistamines, and guidelines for their use.

7   The "crash" box should contain more supplies for first aid, an EpiPen, and gauze pads and rolls for managing more serious wounds. Also, if spiders, snakes, or other critters that have the potential for being poisonous or lethal are in the area, materials related to these bites should be placed in this crash box as well. This would include basic instructions about immediate first aid care for a bite and instructions about simple measures such as ice and analgesia.

8   We have found that some governments, either through national or regional channels, will supply vaccines serum free, or at their cost, though often with a number of restrictions. The cost/benefit ratio of using their serum with restric-

tions may not be in your favor. Every community needs to take time to evaluate and discern the best route, given their circumstances.

9   If governments provide conflicting recommendations, it is important to know that there is no "correct" immunization schedule. If governments cause undue delay with their arbitrary suggestions, an excellence-driven community should simply start an immunization program that it is comfortable with and make any necessary amendments later.

10 Good record keeping is very important. If you work with an orphan care community, do not ignore this oft-neglected area of administration as you take care of immunizations. Duplications of immunizations are neither safe nor financially wise. Come up with a good system, keep the group of record keepers small and record all immunizations at the time they are dispensed. This will save you much time, money, and headaches down the road. You won't find anyone who felt that their records were too well kept.

11 Immunizations given on your site are a good place to utilize short-term mission team personnel who usually are happy to hold and coddle during this experience.

12 Interestingly, the snakes in the same area were manageable even though poisonous. The boys loved getting the better of a snake. The campus's local record was a fifteen foot python over which the staff argued to see who could have a pair of boots made from the skin. (I don't know who got the boots.)

13 Examples of child protection policies can be found online with a simple search. Also check with the arm of government that manages childcare in the particular community's country. Most countries, even developing countries, have this policy already written. New personnel will receive the training and regular personnel will be updated, possibly recertified, at retraining intervals. I cannot overstate the significance and importance of this policy!

14 Securing resources requires much research and as does seeking out medical networking and specialties. Much of this work involves beating the bushes, talking, discerning, reviewing, observing available medical options, and making contractual decisions about who are the best practitioners to take care of our children. This is an essential part of providing excellent care.

15 One way to use short-term teams is to allow the "expert" doctors from the teams to assist and train doctors on-site. If short-termers just do tasks, their ministry will end when they leave. If they train, then their ministry can continue for years to come.

16 Visit ThinkOrphan.com for more discussion about what should go into an orphan care community's long-term health care plan.

17 Orphaned and vulnerable children often can receive favorable benefits from their government and/or other agencies. But one needs to ask to receive many of the benefits. So, if you're part of an organization, be relentless in your questioning. Question all governmental officials. Question everybody who might know something relevant to the issue. Get the answers and act on them.

18   PEPFAR is the US President's Emergency Plan for AIDS Relief, an initiative that works to alleviate suffering from HIV/AIDS around the world.

19   In Asia's Hope, the regional director is informed of all emergencies beyond home care, will conference with houseparents to determine the best course of action, and one of his responsibilities is to immediately advise the representative of the sponsoring body or church. An advantage of this chain of command is that within twenty to thirty minutes a treatment decision has been made and this child is being raised up in prayer across the world. At Cherish Uganda the house mother will contact the "on-call" leadership staff member who will assess the situation and make necessary calls to nursing staff and decide the next course of action. Everyone in your home/ministry/organization must know who to call and have those contact numbers easily accessible.

20   The examination can include some of the following questions: What has transpired in the last period of time? What's different now? What are we doing well? What are we doing poorly? What can we improve? How does our chart review look? How is our medical record? Is it recorded in a common language? Dare I ask, is it legible? What are we doing about medical record security? What does excellence mean today compared to what it meant six months ago?

21   For more stories like these, visit ThinkOrphan.com.

CHAPTER 9
Beautiful Hearts and Minds (Psychosocial Care)

1   K. Purvis, D. Cross, and W. L. Sunshine, *The Connected Child: Bring Hope and Healing to Your Adoptive Family* (New York: McGraw-Hill, 2007), 26.

2   Dr. Karen Hutcheson is a licensed clinical psychologist, a pastor's wife, and a mommy to four children within two years by adoption and birth. Karen has over a decade of professional experience working with children and families living in underserved populations, residential treatment facilities, foster-reunification programs, and crisis-stabilization units. Karen has a master of arts in clinical psychology and a doctorate in clinical psychology from Spalding University, where she specialized in the assessment and treatment of children, adolescents, and families. Karen completed her predoctoral residency through the Chicago Area Christian Training Consortium. She completed her postdoctoral fellowship with Behavior Associates in Kentucky, specializing in the assessment and treatment of children, adolescents, and adults living in residential care facilities diagnosed with intellectual disabilities and pervasive developmental disorders. Karen is professionally trained in TBRI®, and has a wide range of experience in areas of child development, relationship-based traumas, and pre- and postadoption psychological services, including psychological evaluation. Karen also provides clinical consultation and training in orphan care settings domestically and internationally.

3   Child's name and specific details modified for privacy.

4   UNICEF, "The Importance of Families."

5   Purvis, *The Connected Child*, 26.

6   Ibid.

7   *Id.*, 34.

8   Marinus H. van IJzendoorn, Maartje P. C. Luijk, and Femmie Juffer (2008), "IQ of Children Growing Up in Children's Homes A Meta-Analysis on IQ Delays in Orphanages," *Merrill-Palmer Quarterly* 54, no. 3, (July 2008): 341–66.

9   The remaining concepts on this list can be found at ThinkOrphan.com.

10   In a best-case scenario, an infant receives reliable responsiveness from a caregiver, and the bond is secure or, in other words, healthy. Through this secure bond, an infant learns to explore and interact with his environments. Secure attachment provides the best opportunity for healthy development, and provides a healthy model for future relationships. A child who is secure in her attachments is more likely to have healthy social functioning, have fewer be-havior problems at school, and is more likely to be a competent leader in social settings. ("Trust-Based Relational Intervention," Instructor Workbook, 2012 TCU Institute of Child Development [ICD]).

     On the flip side, however, insecure attachments develop when a caregiver responds to an infant without warmth or consistency. There are several reasons an insecure attachment may develop, but here are some of the main identified ways. A caregiver simply may be unable to meet the emotional needs of a child or may meet the emotional needs of a child inconsistently. A caregiver may provide care in ways that scare an infant, or the caregiver may be scared when attempting to meet the needs of an infant. In all of these situations the infant's emotional and developmental needs are not met. When an infant does not receive intentional and nurturing early care, she is more likely to have behavior problems, difficulty expressing emotions appropriately, and difficulty forming and maintaining healthy relationships.

11   For more details about how to address attachment deficits in orphaned and vul-nerable children's lives, visit the psychosocial care section of ThinkOrphan.com.

12   Visit ThinkOrphan.com for a discussion of the trajectory of problematic behav-iors and psychological symptoms that many children who have incurred loss and attachment deficits experience in their lives.

CHAPTER 10
Cultivating Home-Grown Leaders (National Leadership)

1   Jay and Jonnes—for those who know them, their names are hard to separate. Jay Dangers and Jonnes Bakimi are an American-Ugandan team, brothers in Christ, and more than best friends—brothers. From the world's perspective, they are a very unlikely choice for the leaders of an ever-growing ministry with children. Trained in building construction (Jay), and design and biochemistry (Jonnes), they are not "qualified" for the task God chose to give them. But their submission to His plans and willingness for God to use their weaknesses to reveal His strength have brought hope to thousands of Ugandan children and touched the lives of thousands of people across the world. American and Ugandan, quiet and outspo-ken, child of missionary parents (Jay) and raised as an orphan due to divorced

parents (Jonnes), these men could not be more different in background, culture, and upbringing. But, their love of the Lord Jesus Christ, their commitment to the Word of God, allowing it to define, confront, and determine every aspect of their lives, their "color-blind" view to cultural and racial differences, their commitment to their wives (Vicki and Gertrude) and families, and their commitment to humility and repentance together have caused their brotherhood and partnership to deepen over the years and to affect more and more lives with the gospel.

2   The cultural forces and beliefs affecting leadership in Africa have both similarities and differences to the understanding and practice of leadership in all other parts of the world.

3   Many Africans believe (and it is taught in Ugandan school curriculum) that the white man has money now because he stole it from the Africans during colonialism. Therefore, to *eat the mzungu* (to take from what the *mzungu*—white man—has) is not stealing but simply taking back what rightfully belongs to the Africans. It was also normal and expected for the people working under the king to "skim off the top" of what was collected for the king.

4   See chapter 5 on community integration.

5   For example, one ministry with all Western leaders allows single men and women to stay together in the same house. The community around them assumes the men and women sleep together though unmarried. That the women wear jeans or slacks instead of skirts adds to that perception because trousers are associated with "loose" women. Ministries that push for Western-style dress can lead their children to be stigmatized in the local community.

6   See Luke 22:24–27; John 13:1–17.

7   See Matt. 18:1–6.

8   Some of these include J. Oswald Sanders' *Spiritual Leadership* and Stephen Arterburn and Fred Stoeker's *Every Man's Battle*.

9   See the chapter 12 of this book for more on the spiritual formation journey.

10   Robert D. Lupton, *Toxic Charity: How Churches and Charities Hurt Those They Help (And How to Reverse It)*, (New York: HarperOne, 2012), 191.

11   Not his real name.

12   Mark came to New Hope where Ugandans ministered to him before he left the country, which was significant for him. Jonnes in particular was able to care for him and pastor him as a true brother in the Lord.

13   I use this term throughout because from the Ugandan perspective all Europeans and Americans are white. We recognize that this is not an accurate understanding or view both historically and currently. Ugandans even refer to black Americans as white.

14   Of course, this moves beyond Uganda as each country has generalizations about Americans and other nationalities around the world.

15   In the American-Honduran relationship at Providence World Ministries, they

say that they are not seeking "American excellence" or "Honduran excellence," but "gospel excellence."

16   It is crucial to understand that our goal is to maintain as much as we can of Ugandan life and culture within leadership and the practices of the ministry, so that our children are able to fully integrate with the community of which we are a part and to thrive in that context. This takes time and strategic partnership, training, and death to self on the part of Westerners serving at the various ministry sites of New Hope Uganda.

17   In the end, genuine peer *friendships* are more than working relationships. In peer *friendships*, we are free to show up at each other's houses unannounced. We are free to cry together, laugh together, and share personal prayer requests together. We know each other's personal histories and each other's families (if possible). We celebrate birthdays and holidays together. We can be *real* with each other, mutually sharing our struggles.

18   Because of differences between foreigners and nationals in culture, education, and perspective, there are some jobs that *generally* work better to have one nationality fill as opposed to another, but we at New Hope do not have any hard and fast lines. Foreigners typically fill the more supportive or technical roles (while working under and alongside of Ugandans), while locals tend to fill the more relational roles. The parents for the families we have created for the fatherless children God has entrusted to us have been almost exclusively Ugandan, though there has been significant involvement with the parents by foreigners. The teachers in our primary, secondary, and vocational school are Ugandan, while a couple of our accounts personnel are foreign—but their boss is a Ugandan.

CHAPTER 11
Wanted: Entrepreneurial Minds (Self-Sustainability)

1   Formerly employed by World Relief as the managing director of Urwego, Peter Greer also served as a microfinance advisor in Cambodia and with CARE Zimbabwe implementing fraud protection measures. He has an MPP from Harvard's Kennedy School, a BS from Messiah College, and an honorary doctorate from Erskine College. Peter coauthored a faith-based book on microfinance, *The Poor Will Be Glad* (Grand Rapids, MI: Zondervan, 2009), a children's book on adoption, *Mommy's Heart Went POP!* (Boise, ID: Russell Media, 2012), as well as *The Spiritual Danger of Doing Good* (Bloomington, MN: Bethany House, 2013) and *Mission Drift* (Bloomington, MN: Bethany House, 2014). He blogs at www.peterkgreer.com, and lives in Lancaster, Pennsylvania, with his wife, Laurel, and their three children.

2   Sylvia is not a real person, though she is based on real stories of real children that I know personally. She characterizes many children who grow up in situations like the ones portrayed, as does Stephen in the story to follow.

3   The current usage of the word *self-sustainability* looks toward the long-term ability of a country, business, person, etc. to continue its course of functioning or living, factoring in external variables including the environment's ability to

sustain such a course and the negative impact of their practices on the environment and the quality of the sustainability that is possible.

4   http://dictionary.reference.com/browse/self-sufficiency.

5   New Hope Uganda and La Providencia have created carefully monitored sponsorship programs that seek to mitigate against the "sponsorship mentality" by, among other things, encouraging appropriate relationships between the sponsors and children. For more about La Providencia's Extended Family Adoption program, see https://providenceworld.com/app/invest/extended_family_adoption/.

6   For more examples and details about implementation of best practices and excellence in self-sustainability/self-sufficiency principles in orphan care communities, engage the conversation on the Self-Sustainability page at ThinkOrphan.com.

7   It is crucial to note that the leadership, both national and foreign, seeking self-sustainability in ministry needs to have a firm understanding of the principles laid out in chapter 10 of this book (Cultivating Home-Grown Leaders), so that they can effectively demonstrate servant leadership in all areas pertaining to self-sustainability.

8   See Gen. 2:15.

9   See John 5:17.

10   "If anyone is not willing to work, let him not eat. For we hear that some among you walk in idleness, not busy at work, but busybodies" (2 Thess. 3:10–11).

11   It must be said that the goal is never work for the sake of work or profit. Work is about something much greater than itself and there is no place in this context for child labor or the misuse of children in the venture of self-sustainability. Like a family working together for the care and provision of their family, so should children work alongside of parents who are careful to protect them from overexertion or undue strain.

12   We are now moving into a piggery project that will work in conjunction with the chickens, using the chicken poop as a feed for the pigs.

13   This foundational point is interwoven with the other points and must be an outflow of all of them working together.

14   One aspect of New Hope Uganda's Investment Year program, which is discussed in chapter 12 (It Starts in the Heart), is to provide the children with these opportunities, and we (Keith) have seen many children who thought they wanted to pursue an area decide against it after gaining experience in that field. Visit http://newhopeuganda.org/programs/investment-year-iy/ for more information on Investment Year.

15   For more information about Lifesong Farms, see ThinkOrphan.com or visit http://www.lifesongfororphans.org/orphan-care/sustainable-business/zambia/.

16   Investment Year is described in detail in chapter 12 (It Starts in the Heart).

17   See ThinkOrphan.com for more details on other coffee operations around the world that support excellence-driven orphan care.

18   For more information, see http://www.pearlministries.org/ornaments4orphans/.

CHAPTER 12
It Starts in the Heart (Spiritual Formation)

1   Dan Cruver is the president/founder of Together for Adoption, through which he provides thoughtful leadership on the theology of adoption. Before cofounding and directing Together for Adoption, Dan was a college professor of Bible and theology. He has also served as a pastor of family ministries. Dan founded Together for Adoption to equip churches and educate Christians theologically about orphan care and horizontal adoption. Dan regularly writes and speaks about the gospel and its implications for solutions to the global orphan crisis. He is the editor and primary author of *Reclaiming Adoption: Missional Living Through the Rediscovery of Abba Father*, wrote the foreword to *Heirs with Christ: The Puritans on Adoption*, by Dr. Joel Beeke, and is a contributor to *The Gospel Coalition Blog*.

2   Pastor Johnny Carr, author of *Orphan Justice*, currently serves as vice president of strategic partnerships for Help One Now. Prior to his current position, Johnny worked for Bethany Christian Services as its first National Director of Church Partnerships and served as a full-time minister for fourteen years for several different churches. While Johnny was the pastor of ministry and leadership development at Hillcrest Baptist Church in Pensacola, Florida. He led the church in establishing its first orphan care and adoption ministry. Johnny is married to Beth and has five children: Heather, Jared, James, Xiaoli, and Jerrell. James and Xiaoli were both adopted from China and are deaf. The Carrs also adopted Jerrell, a deaf and medically complex child, through the foster system. Johnny's goal is to inspire the church to truly understand and obey James 1:27, which calls believers to care for orphans.

3   Second Peter 2:7–8 describes Lot as righteous, a righteousness that can only be based on faith. His faith would have rested on his belief in God's promises to Abraham, which were ultimately the hope of the promise of the gospel.

4   See Appendix C for a full description of the orphan heart.

5   For more on theology by Dan Cruver and Johnny Carr, see their article, "Why Theology Must Matter When Orphans Need Our Help Now," which can be found in its entirety on ThinkOrphan.com.

6   Quoted from Spurgeon's sermon, "How to Read the Bible," http://www.spurgeon.org/sermons/1503.htm.

7   John Piper, *God Is the Gospel: Meditations on God's Love as the Gift of Himself* (Wheaton: Crossway Books, 2008).

8   See Matt. 1:20–23; 28:18; Acts 1:9–11; 2 Cor. 15:3–5.

9   David Platt, *Follow Me*, (Carol Stream, IL: Tyndale House Publishers, 2013), 19–20.

10   See Matt. 15:18–20.

11   The cross reveals that Jesus died for sin. Jesus took on sin. Jesus became sin for us (2 Cor. 5:21). In this, God reveals His own love for us (Rom. 5:8). Jesus died to set us free from sin and heal us from the wounds of sin. The cross also reveals the power of the Savior to overcome our ongoing struggle with sin in our hearts. While sin has been dealt with, forgiven, and its power over us has been broken, there is an ongoing battle. Orphans will continue to gravitate toward responses that flow out of their wounds and defense mechanisms. We must lead them to move beyond the action to what is in the heart. We can lead them in prayer to allow Jesus into those heart places. Cultivating an understanding of lifestyle repentance is crucial.

12   See 2 Cor. 15:54–57.

13   This fear comes from the time of Adam, when sin brought death, which reigns over all men (Rom. 5). But Jesus, the second Adam, the perfect man, took our sin and the curse of death upon Himself. Yet death could not hold him! He rose again, conquering death and proclaiming life and victory over the grave (2 Cor. 15).

14   See Heb. 2:15; Rev. 1:18.

15   See Heb. 2:14–15.

16   Before Jesus went to the cross, He said, "Now will the ruler of this world [i.e., Satan] be cast out" (John 12:31). (parenthesis mine) The book of Colossians says that at the cross Jesus "disarmed the rulers and authorities" (2:15). The book of Hebrews says that Jesus took on flesh "that through death he might destroy the one who has the power of death, that is, the devil" (2:14).

17   See Eph. 6:16; note also that in v. 15 the gospel is referred to as "the gospel of peace." It is interesting to find the word "peace" in a warfare passage, but that is just what the gospel has brought for Christians battling Satan.

18   See Ps. 144:12.

19   There are many more than five aspects of spiritual formation, but for the sake of space we have shared these five with you and put more ideas and discussion on spiritual formation on our website, ThinkOrphan.com.

20   For a more thorough discussion on worldview and biblical worldview in a Ugandan context, see ThinkOrphan.com.

21   Some questions that are helpful for understanding and uncovering worldview are: What are the positive and negative values that our cultures promote? How do these values control our actions and pursuits? What areas of our lives are controlled by fear? Why? What does our culture say you "must have" in order to be happy or gain status or popularity among people? How does our culture view and treat others from different cultures and backgrounds?

22   It is helpful to come up with questions that help to uncover worldview. In Uganda, asking someone what they think about the owl, what it means if twins are born, or what they say about another tribe or people group, will uncover quite a lot about their worldview.

23   The following are some helpful ways to establish the authority of Scripture in the minds of children: (1) Examine key passages on the authority of the Bible as God's Word; (2) Explore archaeological evidence that validates Old Testament stories and New Testament history; (3) Look at how the Word of God came to be, the role it played in the early church, and the confidence it gave to the early Christians who were willing to give their lives for the gospel and truths of the Bible; (4) Share stories about how the Word of God has impacted your own heart and life.

24   God is the central character in each story. We must see and teach the unchanging character of God revealed through the Old Testament stories or we will miss the central purpose of each story as the Bible unfolds. The story of Cain and Abel is actually a story about God's response to faith and His justice in judging sin.

25   The sinful human heart is revealed in each story. While we like to identify with the "good" characters, we must learn to see ourselves in the life of each character. For example, in the story of Cain and Abel, we like to identify with Abel. We tell children, "Do not be like Cain who disobeyed. Be like Abel and obey God." In this, we miss the point of the story and fail to understand where Jesus pointed us when He said that being angry with your brother in your heart is like murder. We must lead children to cry out: "I am Cain. I get angry at my brother. I have killed him in my heart. I need a Savior."

26   God's gracious provision for man's sin is seen over and over again throughout the Old Testament. Each of these promises and provisions point to the One who would come and take away sin, while fulfilling all of the promises of God made along the way. (Abel was righteous by faith, not by obedience [see Heb. 11:4]. Jesus was the greater sacrifice whose blood speaks a better word than Abel's blood [see Heb. 12:24]. While Abel's blood condemned Cain, Jesus' blood provides forgiveness to the sinner.)

27   The response of faith is key to rightly applying each story. Instead of simply telling children to "obey" or "be like so and so," we want to lead children (and ourselves) to live lives of *repentance and faith* that lead to Christ-centered obedience. (If I am to overcome my "Cain heart," I cannot master my own sin. I need Jesus, the greater sacrifice for sin, to take my sin, forgive and cleanse my heart, and fill me with love for my brother.)

28   For more on how New Hope Uganda read the Bible through in a year, the schedule used, discussion questions created, and the resulting impact, see ThinkOrphan.com.

29   Afterward, the church put together *highlight* points of the "big story" of the Bible. Children, parents, and staff dressed up as biblical characters and read small parts moving through the story line. After presenting at the church, the groups presented the story of the Bible and shared the gospel around the community. What was most surprising, though, was that the overwhelming majority of children asked to continue the reading the following year. Once saturated in the Scriptures as a part of daily life, the children did not want to see it come to an end.

30   For more on *Abba* and *Daddy* as a title for God, see http://orphanheart.blogspot
.com/2009/05/calling-god-daddy-part-2.html.

31   Graeme Goldsworthy, *Gospel and Kingdom: A Christian Interpretation of the Old
Testament*, (Paternoster, 2012), 53.

32   This reworking of Goldsworthy's quote is by Johnny Carr, who adds in the article, "Why Theology Must Matter When Orphans Need Our Help Now," which
can be found in its entirety on ThinkOrphan.com: "We believe we can frame the
Story of Redemption in this way because in Hosea 11:1 we read, 'When Israel
was a child, I loved him, and out of Egypt I called my son.' Hosea was referring
to God's calling of the people of Israel out of Egyptian bondage at the Exodus.
In the New Testament, Matt. 2:13–15 informs us that God's calling-out action
at the Exodus was ultimately fulfilled in Jesus who in John 14 made it clear that
He both reveals and brings us to the Father."

33   The stories in chapter 4 of this book (Family Matters) highlight the importance
of leading physical and spiritual orphans into relationship with the heavenly
Father. This chapter also highlights the connection that God has made in making His Fatherhood known and experienced through redeemed earthly fathers.
Without earthly family on display or as a place of care and safety, this part of
spiritual formation will be most difficult.

34   Additional ways to lead children on this journey to intimacy with their Father
are as follows:

     ✳ Read Rom. 8:12–17 and Gal. 4:1–7. What would it mean to call God
Daddy? Try it in prayer. Discuss what it means to have God as Father
and Jesus as our big brother (Heb. 2:11–12).

     ✳ Read an account of Jesus' baptism in the Gospels. Discuss the words
that the Father spoke over the Son: "You are my beloved [well-loved]
Son; with you I am well pleased" (Mark 1:11). We are also His well-
loved sons and daughters, and because of Jesus the Father is well
pleased with us. This is not earned or performance based, but lavished
grace and love (Eph. 1:7–8; 2:8–9). What does this mean for us?

     ✳ Spend time reading through and discussing Eph. 1:3–6. Discuss what it
means that we were predestined before the foundation of the world for
adoption into God's family. How do you feel to have been on the heart
and mind of God from before creation? Discuss the truth that declares:
You are not an accident! What does that mean?

     ✳ Read the story of Abraham and Lot focusing on identity, provision,
protection, and security. What would it look like to live dependent on
God for these things?

     ✳ Listen to the song "He Knows My Name" by Tommy Walker or read or
sing the lyrics together. "I have a Maker; He formed my heart. Before
even time began, My life was in His hands; I have a Father; He calls
me His own. He'll never leave me, no matter where I go. He knows my
name; He knows my every thought. He sees each tear that falls, and He
hears me when I call."

35   A friend of mine has the children ask Jesus to reveal the Father to their hearts. When they are scared or not ready, she just tells them to cling to Jesus—who *is* the exact representation of their Father (whether or not they're ready to "meet" the Father) and who will gently draw them into the Father's love one step at a time.

36   Some resources that help facilitate this process are *Rejoicing in God's Good Design: A Study for Youth on Biblical Manhood and Womanhood* found at childrendesiringgod.org; *Manhood Restored: How the Gospel Makes Men Whole* by Eric Mason; *The Dude's Guide to Manhood: Finding True Manliness in a World of Counterfeits* by Darrin Patrick; *Recovering Biblical Manhood and Womanhood* by Wayne Grudem; and *Five Aspects of Woman: A Biblical Theology of Femininity* by Barbara Mouser.

37   This is going to be difficult or impossible in ministries where the number of children far exceeds the number of parents, caregivers, and staff available.

38   Thanks Tim Peterson for this simple and gloriously profound statement.

39   See chapter 10 of this book (Cultivating Home-Grown Leaders).

40   See Matt. 28:18–20; Jesus adds, "baptizing them in the name of the Father and of the Son and of the Holy Spirit."

41   The children also receive deeper training in what it means to establish and live according to a biblical worldview. The children are given life skills—not just academics—like how to study God's Word for themselves, do a job interview, write a resume, manage their personal finances, use computers, and drive a vehicle, among other things. They are equipped on an intentional level as to how to live in the "real world," how to make right choices, and how to be part of the solutions to the problems in their cultures and society.

42   See 2 Cor. 3:18; 4:6–7; Rom. 8:29.

43   See John 7:45; 1 Cor. 2:13; 1 Thess. 4:9; Heb. 8:10.

44   See Ex. 22:22–24; Ps. 68:5–6; Gal. 4:1–4.

45   See Eph. 4:13–14.

CHAPTER 13
Where Do We Go From Here?

1   See ThinkOrphan.com for more information on how you and your friends can participate in ThinkOrphan: an Immersive Experience, which is a six-day intensive study on excellence in orphan care.

2   A great starting point to find opportunities for excellence-driven action is visiting the websites of our contributing authors' organizations, which include Providence World Ministries, New Hope Uganda, World Orphans, Lifesong for Orphans, Asia's Hope, Cherish Uganda, and HOPE International. *Orphan Justice*, by contributing author Johnny Carr, provides further details about ways that individuals can be actively involved in loving orphans with excellence. Johnny provides suggestions at the end of each chapter in his book for ways,

big and small, that everyone can love orphaned children, locally and globally. After examining these resources, I hope that you prayerfully seek discernment and wisdom as to how you can be an advocate for orphans in your own backyard and around the world.

3   For more information about Safe Families for Children, visit its website at http://www.safe-families.org.

4   Again, a great starting point for churches to find opportunities for excellence-driven action is visiting the websites of our contributing authors' organizations, which include Providence World Ministries, New Hope Uganda, World Orphans, Lifesong for Orphans, Asia's Hope, Cherish Uganda, and Hope International.

APPENDIX A
Christian Alliance for Orphans' White Paper

1   Used with permission from Christian Alliance for Orphans and Jedd Medefind.

2   UNICEF, UNAIDS, and WHO. Children and AIDS: Fifth Stocktaking Report. 2010.

3   Note that, as explained in the section "Missing from the Numbers," the estimated number of double orphans—17.8 million—does not include any count of the large population of orphans that live on the streets or in orphanages. Thus, while less than 12 percent of the 153 million children accounted for in current orphan estimates are "double orphans," the percentage of orphans that are double orphan would likely be notably higher if all of the world's orphans were included in global estimates.

4   UNICEF, UNAIDS, and WHO. Children and AIDS: Fifth Stocktaking Report. 2010.

5   Current global orphan statistics are projections based upon data drawn from "household surveys." Thus, they do not include children that are not currently residing in a household.

6   UNICEF estimates that more than 2 million children are in institutional care around the world, but this is an outdated figure based on a limited country scan, and UNICEF frequently acknowledges it is an underestimate. *UNICEF. Progress for children: a report card on child protection. 2009.* Two other credible reports put the figure at 8+ million.

7   Many estimates have been made regarding the number of street children in the world, and the figure 100 million is frequently quoted. However, no hard data is available to make such projections with confidence. We can be certain, however, that the number is very large.

8   Much could be said and debated about the dilemma of seeking to care wisely for "social orphans." In some such cases, a modest amount of outside support could allow these children to return to their families of origin. In others, home-based

foster care presents a positive alternative to residential settings when local or international adoption is not possible. There may be times when legal termination of a parental relationship should be considered, thus enabling children to be adopted rather than grow up with little or no experience of family. When none of these options are available or have proven ineffective for individual children, residential care may be the most practicable care option until additional family-based care options are developed.

9   Studies consistently reveal that consistent parental attention and nurture is vital to the healthy emotional, physical and social development of children. For one overview of studies documenting the negative impacts of institutional care upon children, see Better Care Network. John Williamson and Aaron Greenberg. Families, Not Orphanages. 2010.

10   It is important to affirm that our driving objective should always be to find the care setting that best meets the unique needs of each child. For example, there are cases when the needs of a child (such as intense therapeutic intervention or protection from self-harm or harm to others) may extend beyond what could be provided in a family setting. In cases such as these, while family remains the hope, the importance of quality therapeutic residential settings should not be diminished.

11   While enabling children living in orphanages or on the streets to return to their families of origin should be a definitive priority, it is important to affirm that not all parents are willing or able to provide adequate care, and that abuse, forced labor and other dangers may sometimes await children within their home of birth. Re-integration of families must not be pursued haphazardly, and requires great care and planning. At present, while some general community support exists for struggling families,

12   Roughly 135 million of the 153 million orphans accounted for in current estimates are single orphans and have a surviving parent. While in some cases the surviving widow or widower is unwilling or unable to care for their children, often even modest outside support can help the family to remain intact, or to reunify if it has been separated.

13   Extensive financial giving by Christians every year is invested in disaster relief, community and economic development, and a wide range of other initiatives that help preserve and strengthen struggling families. While not technically focused on "orphan care," these investments should certainly be understood as a vital part of the Christian mandate to care for orphans—both in helping care for current orphans and preventing the creation of new orphans.

14   Christians should take special note of the fact that the Bible regularly pairs orphans and widows. The Bible also consistently uses the term "the fatherless" as a synonym for "orphan." This is because in biblical times the large majority of orphans had lost their father but not their mother. This is the case today as well. An estimated 101 million of the 153 million children classified as orphans—more than six in ten—have a surviving mother. Another 34.5 million have lost their mother but have a surviving father. Whether they've lost father or mother, these single orphans and their surviving families are often highly

vulnerable. As a people who embrace the central role of family in caring for children, Christians should place special priority on preserving and aiding these vulnerable one-parent families to the fullest extent possible.

15 For example, in Bangladesh, Bolivia, and Pakistan, more than half of children living in institutions have a living parent. This number is believed to be 80 percent or more in Afghanistan, Belarus, Bhutan, Kyrgyzstan, Nepal, Sri Lanka, and Tajikistan. *Better Care Network. Global Facts About Orphanages. UNICEF. 2009.*

16 Studies suggest that most orphaned children continue to live in families—typically with a surviving parent or sibling, or members of their extended family. Helping these families to thrive and ensuring that children are well cared for is a vital facet of caring for orphans.

17 This group includes double orphans that have no kin willing to adopt them, as well as single orphans and non-orphans whose living parent or parents are unwilling or unable to provide adequate care, even with outside support.

18 Isa. 1:17, Deut. 10:18

19 James 1:27

20 Ps. 68:6

APPENDIX B
Glossary of Key Terms

1 http://glossary.adoption.com/adoption.html, visited on 10/24/13.

2 See, e.g., Eph. 1:5; Gal. 4:5-7; Rom. 8:14-19.

3 Brian Fikkert and Steven Corbett, *When Helping Hurts: How to Alleviate Poverty Without Hurting the Poor . . . and Yourself* (Chicago: Moody Publishers, 2009), 104–5.

4 http://glossary.adoption.com/foster-care.html, visited on 10/24/13.

5 Stephan Baumann,"Justice 2.0," *Relevant*, May/June 2012, 46.

6 See Appendix A for a more detailed analysis of these statistics.

7 UNICEF website, http://www.unicef.org/media/media_45279.html, visited on 10/24/13.

8 See Appendix A.

9 Fikkert & Corbett, *When Helping Hurts*, p. 104.

10 Ibid.

11 Ibid., 105.

ACKNOWLEDGMENTS

PHILIP DARKE

First and foremost, I want to thank God for putting the idea of this book in my head a few years ago and giving me every bit of wisdom, discernment, boldness, courage, and perseverance to see the project through to completion. It has been, is, and always will be His project— He has shown Himself evident over and over again through the process. I can't wait to share with the world the story of how the collaborative process resulting in this book came together. Without God, it definitely would have been impossible.

I also want to thank my beautiful bride and best friend, Becca, and my five incredible kids, Malia, Drew, Savannah, Kirsten, and Justin, for putting up with the late nights, countless phone calls, and everything else that went into this book. No words can even begin to express how grateful I am that God has blessed my life with you. I love you so much!

Mom and Dad, thanks for being real-life examples of marital and parental commitment, for loving me as much as any two parents can love a child, and for being my biggest fans from my first day on this earth. And Ryan (a.k.a "Brother"), thanks for being my best friend since birth and a constant source of encouragement.

To Judy and Paul Beltis, thanks for your encouragement by showing your belief in me and this project in so many tangible ways. I wish with all my being that Paul could still be with us today to celebrate the finished product with us.

To my Providence team, thanks for your tireless efforts to love our children at La Providencia and beyond with utmost excellence.

To Keith and the rest of my incredible co-authors, I'm full of joy that God has brought us together over the past couple years in some crazy ways. I look forward to working with all of you in pursuit of orphan excellence for many more years to come.

To Matt and Hilary, Kirk, Brenda, Maria, and the rest of the Chick-fil-A Folsom family, thank you for keeping "my table" reserved and letting it be my office over the past several months.

To Dougal and Cathy, Jedd, Gary S., Chuck and Char, Josh, Gary C., Dave and Trish, Dante and Karen, Michael and Marita, Michael and Susan, Dan and Terri, Ed, Scott, Victor and Eileen, Sarah, and so many other people (as Becca has said, you know who you are and you'll reap more rewards in heaven since I neglected to thank you here), thanks for encouraging me with words and actions over the past few years to start this project and keep putting words on paper to get this book finished.

To Wolfgang Amadeus Mozart, for writing incredible music hundreds of years ago that served as my soundtrack for much of the writing and editing of this book.

And thanks to Gary Haugen and John Piper, for writing books that got me started on this great adventure.

Keith McFarland

It has been on my heart for a number of years to write a book that would challenge many of the current practices going on in orphan care and in orphan care communities. When Phil Darke sent me his idea for this book, I remember thinking, *Oh good, someone else is going to write my book.* Then Phil came to Uganda for a visit and stayed with my family. I had no idea that would be the beginning of a working relationship together as collaborators on this project, as well as the beginning of a sweet friendship. Thank you, Phil, for allowing me to invest heavily and be a part of this project. It has been a privilege to be a part of it.

Thank you, Laura Beth, for pushing me forward throughout this whole process, for holding down the fort while I was "under the hood," and for being my best friend, love of my life (not to mention amazing mother and co-laborer), and best critic of my writing.

Thank you, Uncle Jay and Uncle Jonnes, for imparting so much and investing in us as a family over the years. You have truly modeled fatherhood and family. We would not be the family we are today without you both.

Thank you, David Sunday, for taking me under your wing and leading me through the rich journey of the discovery of God's glory in the works of John Piper and Jonathan Edwards which have been so central to our lives and ministry in Uganda.

Thank you, Sam Smith (www.storywarren.com) and Susanne DeJong, for your friendship, encouragement, editing help, and great comments.

Thanks to my New Hope family for feedback and suggestions throughout the writing—especially Jennie Dangers, Tim Peterson, and Chris Vogt.

Thank you, Paul Kusuubira, for showing me the orphan heart and for opening my eyes to better understand the heart of God the Father.

Thanks to the children in Kasana who have helped me to understand and know the Father of the fatherless.

And most of all, thank you precious *Abba* Father, for opening my eyes to behold your glory in the face of your Son, and for granting to me the privilege of adoption and sonship as a part of your glorious global bride.

ABOUT THE AUTHORS/EDITORS

PHILIP DARKE serves as President and CEO of Providence World (providenceworld.com), which exists to inspire and equip others to love orphans, widows, and at-risk communities as God loves them. He received a JD from Vanderbilt University Law School and a BA in rhetoric and communications from UC Davis. Before his time with Providence, Phil worked as an attorney for law firms in Sacramento, CA, and Atlanta, GA, and as a clerk for a federal judge in Honolulu, HI. He serves as a board member for All Things Possible Ministries and Summit Christian School and loves spending time with his wife, Becca, and their five children.

KEITH MCFARLAND, native West Virginian, and his wife, Laura Beth, moved to Uganda in 2004 to work with New Hope Uganda. He currently serves as the head of the New Hope Institute of Childcare and Family and the New Hope Pastoral Training Institute. He graduated from Moody Bible Institute in Chicago with a BA in Bible and theology, and then from Wheaton College with an MA in Christian history and theology. Keith enjoys reading and playing sports, but most of all he loves raising his four sons and one daughter on their journey to manhood and womanhood.